PEER MEDIATION IN SCHOOLS

STUDENTS RESOLVING CONFLICT

Richard Cohen
School Mediation Associates

GoodYearBooks

An Imprint of ScottForesman
A Division of HarperCollins*Publishers*

For the educators who implement peer mediation programs,

the mediators who offer their help, and

the students in conflict who make peace.

And for Rachel.

GoodYearBooks are available for most basic curriculum subjects plus many enrichment areas. For more GoodYearBooks, contact your local bookseller or educational dealer. For a complete catalog with information about other GoodYearBooks, please write:

GoodYearBooks
ScottForesman
1900 East Lake Avenue
Glenview, IL 60025

All photos by ScottForesman.
Book design by Barbara Rohm.
Copyright © 1995 Richard Cohen.
All Rights Reserved.
Printed in the United States of America.

ISBN 0-673-36096-2

3 4 5 6 7 8 9 - PT - 03 02 01 00 99 98 97

Preface

The way that we manage conflict is critical to our collective future. Anyone who knows recent history knows how horribly even the most "civilized" peoples can treat each other when in conflict. And now, people from diverse cultural, ethnic, racial, and religious backgrounds—people with differing beliefs and values—interact more frequently and concerning issues of greater consequence. The end of the Cold War has uncovered vicious hatreds. Population growth causes environmental degradation and increasing competition for limited resources. These and other factors will lead to conflicts so complex and of such far-reaching significance that they are beyond our imagining.

Our children will inherit these challenges. There is no guarantee that when they confront them—and when they confront each other—they will be able to do so in a way that benefits all concerned. One way to increase the odds, however, is to teach them conflict resolution skills.

In the early 1980s, I joined a handful of others who began to teach students to mediate the interpersonal conflicts of their peers. Arguably the most effective programmatic approach to teaching conflict resolution skills to students, peer mediation puts the responsibility for resolving conflicts in the hands of the students themselves. After intensive training, student mediators meet with peers in conflict and help them work together to create satisfactory resolutions to their disputes. As we will see, many benefits are attributed to peer mediation programs, including a reduction in interpersonal violence, an improved school climate, a dramatic decrease in the number of students suspended, a 90 percent rate of agreement for mediation sessions, and an increase in student self-esteem and responsibility (Lam 1989).

My initial work involved creating exercises and programs to teach the potentially complex mediation process to young people. It quickly became clear, however, that developing a methodology to teach students to mediate was only part of the task. An equal challenge lay in convincing educators of the efficacy of this idea, and especially in creating school-based peer mediation programs that thrived. I wrote this book to help you accomplish these goals.

HOW TO USE THIS BOOK

Students Resolving Conflict: Peer Mediation in Schools will assist individuals at every level of experience and exposure to peer mediation. Its purpose is to serve as

- *A comprehensive introduction to conflict resolution and peer mediation*
- *A complete technical assistance manual for those involved in the process of implementing a peer mediation program*
- *A reference work for those who currently operate peer mediation programs*

After discussing the pressures that contribute to the problem of student conflict, the body of the book is divided into three parts.

Part One: The Fundamentals of Conflict, Conflict Resolution, and Peer Mediation makes up the theoretical portion of the book. Chapter 1 introduces basic conflict resolution theory and processes. Chapter 2 discusses conflict in the school setting and the limitations of the traditional approach to managing student conflicts. Together these chapters lay the foundation necessary for understanding peer mediation, which is presented in Chapter 3.

Part Two: Implementing a Peer Mediation Program consists of detailed chapters on all aspects of the design, implementation, and operation of a student mediation program. Chapter 4 discusses how to secure initial support. Chapter 5 covers every aspect of program design, from selecting a coordinator to determining program policies on confidentiality and voluntariness. Chapter 6 comprises a complete guide to training, with an additional section on program outreach for after the training is complete. Chapter 7 discusses everything you need to know about actually mediating cases. And finally, Chapter 8 concerns maintaining a healthy program.

Part Three: Tools includes a number of important sections. Chapter 9 presents complete transcripts of two peer mediation sessions, one from a high school and one from a middle school. In Chapter 10, a set of twelve conflict resolution lessons and materials will enable classroom teachers to begin working with their students. Sample peer mediation forms appears in Chapter 11, followed by a series of appendices including, among other things, a guide to the legal issues raised by peer mediation and suggestions for organizing conferences for peer mediators.

If you are new to peer mediation and have never observed a peer mediation session, I suggest that you read the mediation transcripts early on. This will give you an understanding of the mediation process that will enable you to get the most out of this book. If you are using this book to implement a peer mediation program in your school, read the entire book before you begin the process. Although the chapters in Part Two are laid out in rough chronological order, much of the work takes place simultaneously and you will benefit from having an overview at the start. The Implementation Readiness Survey at the back of Chapters 4, 5, and 6 will be of special interest to you as well.

For readers who live and work outside of the United States, remember that the work described here was formulated in the U.S. educational system and cultural climate. Although educators around the world have adopted the peer mediation concept, the transferability of these ideas varies from country to country. Make sure you adapt the approach described in this book to the unique circumstances in which your students live and learn.

Please be advised that *Students Resolving Conflict* is not designed to teach you how to mediate or how to train students to mediate. No book alone can accomplish this task. The best way to learn to mediate is to participate in a qualified training program that includes extensive supervised practice. This book should be used to supplement such a mediation training program.

Peer mediation has been used primarily with students nine years old and older. The way peer mediation services are delivered in an elementary school differs markedly from a middle or high school, however. Although the theory and the general information presented here will be useful to educators at all levels, this book focuses on the implementation process typical in middle and high schools.

A couple of notes on the writing format are necessary. I have used the term *peer mediation* to refer to what is variously called peer mediation, conflict mediation, school mediation, and conflict managing. And, when describing mediation sessions, I often refer to only two parties even though mediation sessions can involve more. This is both because it is easier to read and because most peer mediation sessions do involve just two parties.

Finally, I encourage you to consider yourself a pioneer in this work. There are no "ten easy steps" to follow when implementing a peer mediation program. The variables are too complex: every school has different resources, needs, personalities, and educational philosophies. I have attempted to offer the collective wisdom of the people who have developed this field during its first decade. But in the end, you will have to make much of this up as you go. Be creative, take calculated risks, share what you learn with others, and most importantly, enjoy yourself.

Good Luck.
Richard Cohen

Acknowledgments

When a jazz musician incorporates another artist's melodic line into a solo, it is considered a compliment and a tribute. This book, a solo of sorts, is full of such tributes. It would be impossible to acknowledge everyone who has influenced my work over the years, but I would like to thank those who have made the most significant contributions.

I am indebted to the many educators with whom I have had the privilege of working—educators who not only care deeply for their students, but who have the skill, the sensitivity, and the courage to reach them. These teachers, administrators, counselors, and especially peer mediation coordinators have been my best teachers. There are too many of you to name individually—and I am afraid I would forget someone—but you know who you are.

Thank you to everyone who has worked with School Mediation Associates, offering their ideas, their enthusiasm, and their good company, especially: Greg Williams, Nancy Grant, Janie Cardinele, Gabrielle Rossmer, Andrea Grundfest, Emily Jonas, and more recently, Carole Christensen, Dina Beach Lynch, Francine Rondina, John Elfrank, Celeste Hettinger, and Elizabeth Gilbert.

Many colleagues both within and outside of the mediation field have shared their wisdom and helped me along the way: Albie Davis, Bill Kreidler, Larry Deiringer, Ann Gibson, Annie Cheatem, Joan Sokoloff, Josh Jacks, Gregory Sobel, Annette Townley, Don Gropman, The Ghost Ranch Gathering, Nic Fine, Fiona Macbeth, my friends at Gernika-Gogoratuz, and the Golubkis. Thank you.

My appreciation to all those who offered insightful comment on drafts of this book: Sarah Keeney, Tom Trenchard, Nancy Grant, Ivan Roy, John Conbere, Pat Barnes, Denice Messina, Connie Mahoney, Holly Marden, Carole Christensen, Dina Beach Lynch, Francine Rondina, and Rachel Nemeth Cohen.

Thanks to Julie Lam for helping write the chapter on evaluation and to Richard McNulty for doing the work that is the basis of Appendix A on legal considerations.

Thank you to student mediators at the following schools for their perceptive thoughts about peer mediation, observations that are featured in the margins of this book: Bowling Green Junior High School (Bowling Green, Kentucky), Thomas A. Edison Middle School (Brighton, Massachusetts), The Fletcher School (Cambridge, Massachusetts), Blue Hills Regional Technical School (Canton, Massachusetts), Beck Middle School (Cherry Hill, New Jersey), Gardner Junior High School (Gardner, Massachusetts), Marblehead High School (Marblehead, Massachusetts), Southeastern Regional Vocational Technical High School (South Easton, Massachusetts), Powder Mill Middle School (Southwick, Massachusetts), D'Ippolito Middle School, Landis Middle School, and Vineland South High School (Vineland, New Jersey), and Gibbons Middle School (Westboro, Massachusetts). Thanks also to Ray Pastorino for letting me quote the students from Mt. Diablo High School (Concord, California) whom he had quoted in his study *The Mediation Process—Why It Works: A Model Developed by Students*.

A heartfelt thank you to Carol, Terry, Marty, Len, Trudy, and my friends who helped me through the long and often difficult process of writing this book.

Most importantly, for supporting me completely during the many months in which I spent more time with my computer than with her, my deepest thanks to Rachel.

Contents

Chapter 3
Peer Mediation

PART II
IMPLEMENTING A PEER MEDIATION PROGRAM

Chapter 4
Securing Initial Support

Chapter 5
Program Design and Planning

Chapter 6
Training and Outreach

Chapter 7
Mediating Cases

Chapter 8
Mediator Meetings and Program Maintenance

PART III
TOOLS

Chapter 9
Peer Mediation Session Transcripts

Chapter 10
Twelve Conflict Resolution Lessons

Chapter 11
Program Forms

Appendices

PEER MEDIATION IN SCHOOLS

STUDENTS
RESOLVING
CONFLICT

Introduction

A large group of seventh-grade students walks toward the lunchroom. When the crowd lurches to a stop, a boy named Rueben accidentally steps on the sneakers of another boy, Jamaal. Angered, Jamaal begins to yell and threaten Rueben.

During a ninth-grade history class, a girl named Anne belligerently accuses another girl, Peg, of spreading rumors behind her back. Peg responds tauntingly, "Do you want to make something of it?" Seconds later the two are wrestling on the floor.

Matt and a couple of his eleventh-grade friends surround another boy named Quang Lee in a high-school hallway. Matt threatens Quang Lee, telling him to stop dating Matt's sister or he will "take him down."

STUDENTS AND CONFLICT

Students have always become involved in conflicts. But today, young people disagree with each other more often and over issues of less real consequence than in the past. Students are quick to resort to violence to get what they want. Physical, and sometimes fatal fights can start at the toss of a remark, a sideways glance, or an inadvertent bump. Ask students in any major American city whether they know someone who has been shot, and a startling number will raise their hands.

The impact that student conflict has upon the educational process—from time on task to academic achievement to staff morale—is undeniable. Consequently, interest has grown in teaching students effective and nonviolent methods of resolving conflicts. Educators are beginning to understand that conflict resolution skills are essential to their students' success both in school and beyond.

This book presents one effective method of teaching students conflict resolution skills: school-based peer mediation. Before exploring peer mediation, however, it is important to understand the larger context within which the problem of student conflict occurs. A quick look at the issue of interpersonal violence will illustrate this. Many educators attribute their initial interest in conflict resolution and mediation to concerns about the violence they observe among their students. Interpersonal violence—hitting, kicking, yelling, threatening, teasing, shooting—is very tangible and disturbing, and it inspires compassionate people to take action.

But interpersonal violence is only the most visible form of violence. Violence occurs *within* individuals, as when self-esteem is low and they criticize and withhold themselves; and violence occurs *outside* of discrete interpersonal interactions altogether. The latter, so-called structural violence, is built into political, economic, and social systems. For example, when an educational system spends far more money per pupil in schools whose students are predominantly white than in schools whose students are predominantly non-white, those students experience structural violence.

Although not as palpable as interpersonal violence, violence within individuals and within systems has equally disastrous effects upon its victims. These forms of violence can

Being a mediator has made me more aware of violence and conflict, not just in school, but in general and how it could be resolved with mediation or talking rather than violence.

Middle school mediator

be present in cultures, institutions, and individuals that appear stable and untroubled. And most important to our inquiry, *intrapersonal and structural violence are almost always contributing factors in interpersonal conflict.*

Interpersonal violence is also the slave of cause and effect. In middle school, Joe feels badly about himself, so he hits Bill. Bill is justifiably angered, so he hits Joe back. Each violent action is in part born of some previous violence. Even at its most haphazard—when someone opens fire with a gun in a restaurant full of strangers—there is often some significant level of violence that was previously inflicted upon the perpetrator and that in part led to his or her actions. Violence rarely occurs spontaneously.

Conflict, as we will see, is a normal part of life. The excitement and the opportunity for self-definition that conflicts provide make them an especially vital part of the lives of young people. But today, many decidedly unhealthy pressures exaggerate the place of conflict in children's lives. To address the problem of student conflict effectively, we must acknowledge the web of pressures that make young people more conflict-prone.

Consider this brief survey:

At Home

- More than one-half of marriages end in divorce, and two-thirds of all American children live with a single parent at some time before the age of eighteen (Persell 1991, 283–98).
- Fully 42 percent of fathers fail to see their children in the wake of divorce, and one quarter of all school-aged children grow up with little or no contact with their fathers (Hewlitt 1991, 12, 88).[1]
- Children today spend ten to twelve hours less time with their parents each week than children in 1960 (Hewlitt 1991, 15; Fuchs 1988, 111).

Economics

- Male wages fell 20 percent between 1973 and 1990, and more than half of all Americans have fallen behind inflation and experienced a decline in their standard of living since the early 1980s. (West 1992, 24–26; Hewlitt 1991, 74; Newman 1988, 21).
- The annual income of 36 million Americans (one in seven citizens) falls below the threshold the federal government uses to define poverty. Many more hover just above that threshold (Edelman 1987, ix).[2]
- Twenty percent of all American children—and 50 percent of African American children—now live in poverty. The United States is the only industrialized country where the number of poor children has increased significantly in recent years (Hewlitt 1991, 37).[3]

---

[1] This is especially relevant to our inquiry because recent research indicates that fathers play an important role in helping children—particularly boys—learn to manage aggression and develop empathy. Both of these are fundamental for effective conflict resolution.

[2] This when it is increasingly acknowledged that the poverty level—the amount of money the federal government estimates is necessary to provide for basic human needs such as food, clothing, shelter, and medical care—is grossly underestimated. One researcher estimates that for a family of four in 1992, the figure should have been $22,000 rather than the federal poverty level of $14,000.

[3] This is based on 1989 data, with the poverty threshold at $9,890 for a family of three and $12,675 for a family of four. See also Kotlowitz 1991, 35 and Hewlitt 1991, 12.

Violence

- More than 20,000 Americans die in homicides every year, far more than in any other industrialized nation (Prothrow-Stith 1991, xvii).
- Every fourth home in the United States contains a handgun (Center to Prevent Handgun Violence).
- Firearm murders of youngsters more than doubled between 1984 and 1990 (FBI, Centers for Disease Control).

The Media

- Americans eight to fifteen years old spend approximately four hours watching television daily (Sarason 1990, 111).
- Those same children will have witnessed 200,000 acts of violence on TV by the time they are sixteen (Toufaxis 1989, 55).
- By portraying violence as a "glamorous, effective, and entertaining method of resolving disputes," the media normalizes and implicitly advocates its use (Prothrow-Stith 1991, 46).

Race

- Almost two-thirds of all African American children still attend predominantly segregated schools (West 1993, 4).
- African American males born in 1989 face a 1-in-27 chance of being murdered (Prothrow-Stith 1991, 16).
- The infant mortality rate for African American children ranks twenty-eighth worst among all countries (*New England Journal of Medicine*).

Taken together, these social forces place untold stress upon young people. They increase the likelihood that students will become involved in conflicts, and they increase the chances that when they do, they will handle them inappropriately. Two additional factors that negatively influence the problem of student conflict deserve special attention. One is school itself. The other is the psychology of adolescence.

CONFLICT AT SCHOOL

A school in Florida has a mascot named "Sam." Sam is a Native American in traditional costume, and his cartoon image adorns the school's stationery and stares down from a prominent wall in the front corridor. Sam stands in a boxer's stance, fists raised to protect his head and lines around his body to give the impression of movement. Whether he is about to attack or defend himself is uncertain.

One thing *is* certain, however: Sam is not about to resolve the dispute he appears to be engaged in collaboratively. The lessons that Sam implicitly teaches the students who file beneath him daily are troubling. One of these concerns racial stereotyping and Native-American culture. But more to our point, Sam models the exact approach to conflict

I think the media-tion program has changed our school because there have not been as many fights that I can see. Having a mediation program helps the kids talk things out with each other and helps everyone think that our school cares about us.

Middle school mediator

resolution that the school—which had a serious problem with fighting—was attempting to discourage. Oddly enough, the logo for this school's peer mediation program became a picture of Sam with a contravening red slash across the middle.

When reviewing the factors that contribute to problems associated with student violence and conflict, we should not overlook the practices of schools themselves. Some of these practices, both structural and pedagogical, frustrate students and indirectly undermine efforts to promote respect and collaborative conflict resolution within schools. For an example, we need look no further than the educational practice known as "tracking." Tracking refers to grouping students into classes according to their ability. Supposed "high achievers"—determined most often by IQ scores, previous achievement, and teacher opinions—attend class with other high achievers, middle achievers with other middle achievers, and so on. Up until very recently, almost all secondary schools in the United States tracked their students.

Over half a century of research on tracking, however, demonstrates that its impact is, on balance, more negative than positive (Slavin 1990 and Oakes 1985). Although there are some advantages for teachers, students on average do not have a higher level of academic achievement in tracked classes, nor do "slower" students receive the individual and appropriate instruction that the practice promises. The lower-tracked students lose out in other ways as well. They tend to have less-qualified teachers and receive fewer resources than their peers in higher tracks. They get caught more easily in a negative spiral of low expectations leading to low performance leading to low self-confidence leading to even lower expectations and leading ultimately to dropping out altogether.[4] Most disturbing of all, the bottom tracks are disproportionately composed of children of color and those from lower socioeconomic backgrounds, resulting in internally segregated schools (Putka 1990, B1).

Tracking is only one educational practice that exhibits the kind of structural violence discussed earlier. Unengaging curricula, competitive rather than cooperative teaching methods, and inappropriate and inconsistently applied disciplinary policies can all leave students feeling bored, frustrated, and powerless. And a frustrated student is much more likely to hit someone with whom he or she disagrees than an engaged and self-confident one.

Schools are not the reason that students are more violent today. And on their own, schools will never be able to compensate for all of the social forces described above, nor should they be expected to. But just as schools can be a part of the solution if they institute necessary reforms, they can be part of the problem if they do not.

---

[4] School practices that limit student performance are especially significant given that "school performance is by far the most significant single predictor of delinquency and future criminality—more accurate than race or economic level or social class, more accurate than any of the sociological variables commonly considered to have an effect on the rate of delinquency" (Falcon Baker, *Saving Our Kids*, 62). In his book, Falcon Baker cites four independent research studies that show that delinquent behavior *decreases* when students drop out of school. It peaks just prior to dropping out.

ADOLESCENT PSYCHOLOGY AND PEER PRESSURE

Adolescence, the time between childhood and adulthood, marks a period in human development during which every aspect of life changes. Bodies are transformed, independent identities are formed, and personal world views are created. Young people self-consciously define themselves, wrestling with polar forces like freedom vs. responsibility, self vs. other, childlike dependence vs. adult autonomy. The quest for self, perhaps the key task of adolescence, is challenging for even the most well-adjusted child.

To accomplish their self-creation, adolescents require and demand increasing control over their lives. Imbued with an inflated sense of self-importance, they want to make their own decisions and resent those who make decisions for them. Parents are the primary target of this resentment. Young people begin to see themselves as separate from their parents during adolescence, and often reject parental values with fanfare.

They replace these values, however, with those of their peers. The peer group becomes the arbiter of good taste and right living during adolescence, helping young people decide what to think, wear, believe, buy, and aspire to. The social world of friends, classmates, boyfriends, and girlfriends dominates daily life, and "peer pressure" becomes a force of great power to all but the most self-assured. Despite their aspirations to independence, many adolescents merely replace the need for parental approval with a need for peer approval.

Adolescents have a nascent sense of their own identity on the one hand and a tremendous concern with what their peers think of them on the other. In this context, interpersonal conflicts take on unusual importance. A great deal is always at stake. Every argument "results in a small accretion of what he or she will become"; every conflict is a proving ground (Rubin and Rubin 1989, 16).

If a student's self-concept is already damaged—suffering the effects of racism, poor family life, lack of academic successes, and the like—then interpersonal conflicts can become life or death matters. This is true regardless of how inconsequential the issues are. Someone stepping on your sneakers is a threat to your reputation, which is a threat to your identity, which, in the fiery logic of adolescence, is a threat to your very existence. When "reputation" is one of the few things a young person has, and the arena of interpersonal conflict is one of very few that they feel they can competently control, students dive in headfirst.

Other psychological characteristics of adolescence make conflict more intense and violence more likely. Adolescents have a feeling of immortality and invincibility. (Throughout history, wars have been fought primarily by adolescents and young adults.) They are impulsive rather than considered, preferring not to delay gratification. And with passions untempered by experience, adolescents can easily lose the distinction between how the world really is and how they want it to be. The psychology of adolescence clearly serves to intensify interpersonal conflict among students.

Mediation works because people need to talk no matter how strong they think they are.

High school mediator

THE INCREASE IN STUDENT CONFLICT AS A SYMPTOM OF A LARGER DISEASE

Ask veteran teachers about their students today, and many will tell you that they get into conflicts more often over less serious issues, and that they use more violence than students of a generation ago. They might add that students are "not like they used to be" in other ways: they have a shorter attention span; they do not show respect for adults; they are more self-centered; they don't apply themselves in school; they are materialistic. In private, some teachers despair over the collective character of today's young people, citing deficiencies that have led to the need for all sorts of programs, peer mediation among them.

To turn a phrase from John Goodlad: Troubled kids are more the symptom of an unhealthy society than the cause of the reverse (Goodlad 1990). Children are born into a world not of their own making, and as this discussion has shown, today's world is not an ideal place for growing up. Like an oppressed minority living in a society that does not take their interests seriously, many children's needs for love, for guidance, and for basic material comfort are not being met. The burden is heaviest upon the nonwhite and the poor, but it cuts across all socioeconomic and racial barriers.

If young people have become more violent, then unfortunately, this is our legacy to them. One student mediator, commenting on the violence among her peers, put it plainly: "The problem is with the adults. The kids didn't start this . . . the adults don't have their acts together worse than we do." Adult society's responsibility for young people's problems is a fundamental lesson that must inform all conflict resolution work.

A second lesson follows from this. The increase in conflict and in violent behavior in young people is symptomatic of broad-based problems in American society. We confuse the symptom with the disease if we focus all our attention on dealing with interpersonal conflict and are not cognizant that the frequency and severity of such conflicts are affected by cultural stresses. As long as young people are perennially the victims of racism and discrimination, as long as they are bored by school, as long as they are barraged by violent images and role models, and as long as they are raised by parents who lack the time, the skills, and the resources to raise them properly, then innovative educational programs like peer mediation will mean little. We must heal the larger disease before we can expect any lasting diminution of the symptoms.

In confronting these issues, we would be well advised to remember the warning that "for any problem, there is a simple, direct answer that is wrong." Our solutions need to be as complex and comprehensive as the problems we face: a tapestry of approaches that target all Americans, young and old, rich and poor, black and white, in school and out. Although it is far beyond the scope of this book to recommend such a program, it needs to include everything from economic restructuring to parenting classes, family law reform to racial justice.

Understanding the extent of the disease does not mean we should ignore the symptoms, however. Peer mediation is a practical and effective program. As we will see, the program reaches students "where they are at" and helps them transform potentially destructive situations into opportunities for learning and personal growth. When implemented sensibly, peer mediation can have a positive impact upon every aspect of school life, from time on task to drop-out rates. And in the end, we have no choice. American students are in conflict, *now*, and we need to help them resolve these conflicts so they can focus on creating a better future for themselves and for us all.

Despite the grim picture painted here, there are a number of reasons for hope. Once we decide to solve the problems that children face, we find that in many cases, the ideas and technologies to do so already exist. It is a matter of making the welfare of young people a priority, and then paying as much attention to the means of change as to ends we hope to accomplish.

The main reason for hope, however, is young people themselves. When offered a positive approach to pulling themselves out of the mess that adults have created, young people will amaze us with their resiliency and good sense. Those involved in peer mediation know this well—it happens in almost every mediation session.

From being a mediator I learned that if people are willing to talk and work things out, there is an answer to every problem. If we were willing to talk more often, the world would be a lot better.

Middle school mediator

Part I: The Fundamentals of Conflict, Conflict Resolution, and Peer Mediation

CHAPTER 1

Conflict and Conflict Resolution

UNDERSTANDING CONFLICT

The thing I like about mediation is that the students would be angry at first, but when they talk it over, they seemed to be happier about their choices and can learn to face them.

Middle school mediator

When were you last involved in a conflict with anyone in your life: a friend, a spouse or partner, a co-worker, a student, a teacher, a neighbor; perhaps a conflict within yourself? If you are like most people, your answer is probably "this morning" or "the other day."

Conflict is a normal and unavoidable part of living, the legitimate outcome of interactions between even the most well-meaning individuals. From our first moments of life to our last, human beings are continually involved in conflicts. We are the baby crying for food, the toddler arguing over a ball, the teenager demanding a midnight curfew. Later, we conflict over a spectrum of issues too large to detail: jobs, parenting, money, religion, values, politics, careers, responsibilities, ad infinitum. We conflict over mundane inanities (closing the toothpaste) as well as the most pressing issues of the times (international disputes, AIDS, race relations). No aspect of life is resistant to becoming the focus of human conflict.

Conflict is not only a normal part of living, it is also a necessary part. It is through the friction of forces in opposition that things change. Fields as diverse as political science, biology, physics, and religion all view conflict as a source of potentially positive change and growth. Democracy, intimacy, electricity, fertility, gravity—all are at least in part born of conflict.

Conflict plays an especially significant role in human psychological development. The conflicts that we face in our lives shape our characters, our cultures, and our world. Conflicts can make us stronger and wiser. They can teach us better ways of solving problems, bring us closer to the people we care about, show us new sides of ourselves, and enlighten us regarding our place in the world. One of the fundamental goals of all conflict resolution work is to help people harness this positive potential of conflict.

But conflicts are not always positive. Ask any group of North Americans to free-associate with the word "conflict," and their ideas are decidedly negative: fighting, sadness, death, violence, pain, divorce, anger, gangs. On an emotional level, people can feel unloved, angry, and depressed as a result of conflicts. People go to war or are forced to live under the inhuman conditions attendant to war as a result of conflict. Certainly, then, conflict can have destructive as well as constructive consequences.

Most broadly defined, *conflict* is a struggle between two or more opposing forces. As such, it is not confined to the realm of human behavior. Animals, land masses, even ideas can be said to be in conflict. Human conflicts operate on one of three levels. They can be *intrapersonal*, as when one is deciding whether to accept a job offer or not; *interpersonal*, as when one argues with his or her partner regarding how to spend money; and *intergroup*, as when neighborhoods, races, and nations dispute. This book is concerned primarily with interpersonal conflict.

No two interpersonal conflicts are identical. Every interpersonal conflict throughout history has been characterized by the unique attributes of the place, the people, and the issues involved. But interpersonal conflicts, in fact all human conflicts, are defined by similar characteristics. Once you can recognize and understand these parameters, you become a more effective facilitator of conflict resolution. The following section will describe these parameters.

First, though, it is necessary to define a number of terms that will appear in this discussion. The word *conflict* will be used to describe an interpersonal dispute in its totality. The entire series of events that is associated with a dispute—from the first time there is tension between people to the time when those tensions are resolved—will be referred to as the *conflict*. The word *party* refers to any person or group of people directly involved in a conflict. And *issues* are those subjects over which the parties disagree. Anything that one party wants to change about their relationship with the other party is an issue.

SIX PARAMETERS OF INTERPERSONAL CONFLICT

To illustrate the parameters of interpersonal conflict, let's look at a typical student dispute, one that might very well end up in peer mediation.

Roxanne and Amy are fifteen years old. Although they grew up in the same neighborhood and have known each other for most of their lives, they have never been friends. Roxanne and Amy currently attend Central High School together where they happen to be in the same English class.

About two months ago, Amy's boyfriend Sidney suddenly broke up with her. She was very hurt by this because she cared deeply for Sidney, and she still has difficulty accepting that Sidney is not "hers." Two weeks after their breakup, Amy discovered that Sidney was dating Roxanne. She immediately assumed that Roxanne had had an influence upon Sidney's decision to break up with her. When Amy discussed this with her friends, they supported her theory. The "discovery" has increased Amy's pain about Sidney, and she has quickly grown to despise Roxanne.

For her part, Roxanne had no interest in Sidney until he approached her at a party six weeks ago. She had no plan to steal Sidney away from Amy; in fact, she never gave either of them a thought until Sidney asked her out. Sidney has since told her some nasty things about Amy, however, and as a result Roxanne tries to have nothing to do with her.

Amy once spoke with her older brother Joe, who knows Sidney, about this situation. Joe told her that Sidney had been planning on breaking up with her for some time. He said that it had nothing to do with Roxanne. Amy believed this for a little while, but not for long.

Although they hardly ever see each other, a tangible level of tension has grown between the two girls. Their relationship has also taken on a life of its own through the rumor mill at school. Each girl hears from her friends that the other wants to fight her. Amy sometimes thinks that she sees Roxanne giving her dirty looks. Roxanne knows that Amy has been spreading a rumor around school that she is an alcoholic. They have never confronted each other with these allegations.

The only time Roxanne and Amy are certain to see each other during the school day is in the English class that they share. Even there, however, they have managed to keep each other at arm's length. One time the teacher assigned them to work together, and when Amy refused, Roxanne was able to convince him to give them different partners.

Today in English class, Amy made a presentation in front of the room. When she looked out, she saw Roxanne laughing, presumably at her. Amy found this extremely distracting, and as a result she did a poor job on the presentation. She felt embarrassed and angry. At the end of class, she went up to Roxanne and confronted her:

> **Amy:** Is something wrong?
> **Roxanne:** No, is something wrong with you?
> **Amy:** What's wrong is that you are a bitch.
> **Roxanne:** What did you say?

In an instant Roxanne jumped up and the two girls threatened and pushed each other until they were separated by the teacher.

Now let's return to our parameters.

History

A climactic moment in a conflict is best understood as the outgrowth of the series of events that precede it. Interpersonal conflicts always have *histories:* past behaviors, experiences, conversations, and perceptions that, taken together, define them. Like the plot of a novel, conflicts have a beginning, a middle, and inevitably, an end. Their "storyline" can span years or only days or hours, but conflicts rarely happen in an instant.

The confrontation between Roxanne and Amy is best understood by referring to their history. A diagram of this history looks like this:

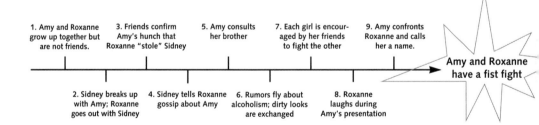

Typically, interpersonal conflicts come to the attention of outsiders only after they have been going on for some time. The English teacher here, for example, watched as a brief and relatively meaningless conversation between two of his students culminated in a fight. One must review the history to understand why the two girls ended up in a physical confrontation.

Past events not directly related to the relationship of the parties should be considered part of the history of a conflict as well. Perhaps Amy failed a test this morning and was in a particularly bad mood. Perhaps Roxanne's father taught her never to back down from a fight. The private and the shared histories of the parties often propel their conflict forward.

Escalation/Intensity

Interpersonal conflicts are rarely isolated events. They are usually composed of a series of actions taken by the parties involved. Like a conversation or a tennis match, one party takes action, the other responds with an action of his or her own, the first party receives that second action and responds accordingly, and so on. Every action by one party helps determine the reaction of the other.

As a result, the level of tension or intensity in a conflict is not static. Tensions between parties *escalate* or *de-escalate* during the course of a conflict, sometimes during the course of a single interaction. When a conflict is escalating, each action taken, each word uttered, serves to increase the parties' distress. Conversely, when conflicts de-escalate, distress between and within the parties decreases. The chart below illustrates some of the contrasting characteristics of escalating vs. de-escalating conflicts.

When Conflicts Are Escalating:

- *Direct communication is difficult and ineffective*
- *Parties talk more about the other's deficiencies*
- *Painful emotions become more intense*
- *Trust is reduced*
- *Extraneous people become involved*

When Conflicts Are De-escalating:

- *Direct communication is fluid and effective*
- *Parties talk more about their own needs*
- *Positive emotions become more intense*
- *Trust is gradually regained*
- *Only people who are part of the conflict (and possibly a mediator) are involved*

One key aspect of escalation is that parties' actions often mirror each other. If one party concedes on one issue (and de-escalates the conflict), the other will be more inclined to concede on another. But if one party acts in such a way as to escalate the conflict, it increases the likelihood that the other will do the same. If Roxanne spreads rumors about Amy, Amy will probably spread rumors about Roxanne. To achieve victory, Amy might even escalate the conflict by having her friends spread rumors about Roxanne as well. This spiral of cause and effect puts parties on a path of escalation that is difficult to alter and that can result in grave consequences.

Peer mediation gives our peers a confidential way of letting out their true feelings. Anger is used to cover up many other emotions. It's a way to speak and be heard. And it's a chance to stop the violence before it escalates.

High school mediator

Amy and Roxanne's conflict, like many student conflicts, was on just such an escalating trajectory. The issue that initiated the conflict was Amy's distress because Roxanne allegedly "stole" her ex-boyfriend Sidney. But these boyfriend difficulties were only the first in a series of events that increased the intensity of their conflict.

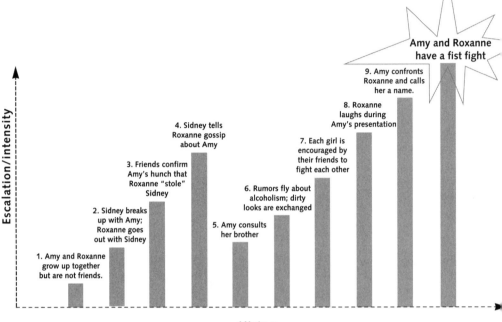

Conflicts often escalate to a point where the original issues in dispute are forgotten, obscured, or minimized in comparison to the parties' concerns over subsequent actions. Amy might in the end be more angry that Roxanne ruined her presentation than because she dated Sidney. Roxanne might similarly be more angry that Amy threatened her in front of the class than because Amy had spread rumors about her. The escalation process adds discrete, extraneous issues to a conflict that can overshadow what were once the primary issues in dispute.[5]

Psychological Need

The third characteristic of interpersonal conflict concerns the separate, inner life of each party. Specifically, it refers to the degree to which a conflict becomes entangled with parties' attempts to meet their personal, psychological needs. This complex, *internal* dimension influences the dynamics of an interpersonal conflict as much as events that occur externally between the parties. To understand this, we must review some simple psychology.

All of us—regardless of age, sex, religion, or cultural background—share basic psychological needs that we strive to fulfill. These include the need to feel safe and secure, to be loved, to be in control of one's life, to belong, and to achieve. Meeting these needs is as essential to psychological health as air, water, and food are to physical health.

[5] This dynamic can be clearly discerned in large-group conflicts which, because of their complexity, have a tremendous potential for escalation. In many wars, the legacy of killings and atrocities motivates the parties as much as the original issues in dispute.

Noted psychologist Abraham Maslow called human beings the "wanting" animal because we are constantly striving to satisfy our needs. Whenever one need is satisfied, another one always takes its place. Striving to meet evermore sophisticated needs, Maslow asserted, is the essence of human development. He formulated the hierarchy of needs diagrammed here.

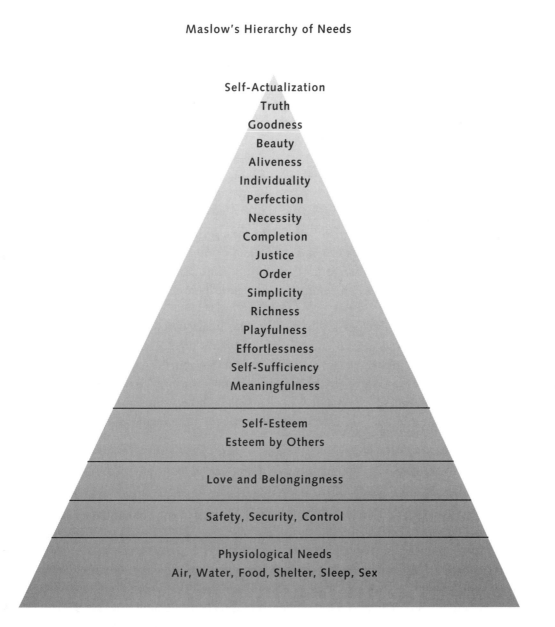

Maslow's Hierarchy of Needs

Self-Actualization
Truth
Goodness
Beauty
Aliveness
Individuality
Perfection
Necessity
Completion
Justice
Order
Simplicity
Richness
Playfulness
Effortlessness
Self-Sufficiency
Meaningfulness

Self-Esteem
Esteem by Others

Love and Belongingness

Safety, Security, Control

Physiological Needs
Air, Water, Food, Shelter, Sleep, Sex

From *Motivation and Personality* by Abraham H. Maslow (Harper & Row, 1954)

I think peer media-

tion works because

everyone, deep down

inside, really wants

a safe school. It's

just the pressure.

High school mediator

A desire to meet basic psychological needs often motivates people's behavior during interpersonal conflicts.[6] In our story, Amy felt sad and angry because Sidney broke up with her. Her needs for love, for security, and for control over her life were not being met. In her distress, she convinced herself that she could regain some of the love and esteem she had recently lost by striking out at Roxanne. For Roxanne, spreading rumors about Amy was motivated by psychological needs of her own. Perhaps she thought her peers would like her and invite her into their group—meeting her needs for belonging and security—if she teased Amy. Or perhaps she wanted to assuage her unconscious feelings of guilt about causing Amy so much pain.

This third parameter—psychological needs—helps explain why self-esteem is such a powerful asset for effective conflict resolution. People with self-esteem feel fundamentally "okay." They accept their psychological needs as normal and assume that these needs will be satisfied. Such people are better able to tolerate periods when one need goes unmet and are less likely to feel psychologically threatened by the actions of others. Being called a "jerk," although troubling, does not threaten their self-concept. They assume that confrontations are as much the other person's problem as their own. People with high self-esteem tend to meet their needs in as direct and prosocial a manner as possible.

Individuals with low self-esteem, however, have lived for extended periods of time unable to meet their basic psychological needs. Consequently, they have learned that meeting these needs is an uncertain process. Like a starving person protecting a small cache of food, they are easily threatened by actions of others that appear to take away the little they have. When called a "jerk," they need to eliminate this threat. People with low self-esteem are likely to use indirect methods to meet their needs, because direct ones have not worked well in the past.

What role did self-esteem play in our example? Perhaps Amy has low self-esteem, and Sidney's leaving unconsciously confirmed that she is unlovable. To prove this wrong, she redirected her legitimate anger at Sidney toward Roxanne, devising a scenario in which Roxanne is responsible for the breakup. If Amy felt better about herself, she might not have been as upset at Sidney nor as likely to take out her anger at him on somebody els In addition, Roxanne's laughter during her presentation might not have upset Amy as much as it did.

Triggers of Conflict

Taken together, the dynamics of history, escalation, and psychological need lead to another important characteristic: the *trigger of conflict*. A trigger of conflict is an incident that focuses and externalizes a conflict. As we have seen, a dispute can have complex, intrapersonal origins, and parties often share a history of tension and misunderstanding that spans weeks or even years. Triggers of conflict release the accumulated tension *within* parties, resulting in a visible and often dramatic expression of conflict *between* them.

In the school setting, almost anything can serve as the trigger of an interpersonal conflict: a remark, a bump in the halls, a rumor, even lack of contact altogether. In our example, Roxanne's laughter during Amy's presentation was the trigger of their conflict.

---

[6] This is one reason why many student conflicts can be resolved quite easily in mediation. Young people are usually not fighting over rumors or stepping on sneakers or name-calling. They are trying to meet their basic human needs for recognition or control. Once they understand that an interpersonal conflict is not meeting these needs, they are usually quick to resolve it.

This incident led both girls to release the full force of the emotional tension they had held inside.

Often the trigger incident does not concern the key issues in dispute. Presumably, the fact that Roxanne laughed during Amy's presentation was not of primary importance to either party and could be easily resolved if they were of a mind to do so. At other times, the trigger of the conflict and the source of the conflict are one and the same. If one student teases another about his or her ethnic background and a fight ensues, the trigger incident and the key issue in dispute are identical.[7]

Perception

A contributing factor in many interpersonal conflicts is a discrepancy between reality and what the parties perceive to be real. This occurs because the manner in which we perceive and attribute meaning to the world is a complex and highly subjective process. If one student passes another in the hallway with a scowl, the latter is left to conjecture: Is she threatening me intentionally? Is she threatening someone behind me? Perhaps she failed a test? Or maybe she just has indigestion? It is difficult to know for certain without asking the scowling student directly. But because of the extraordinary volume of perceptions we register every day, it is impossible to confirm the meaning of everything we perceive. Usually we can only infer the intentions of others.

Complicating this process further is the fact that human beings are not neutral recipients of information. Everything that an individual perceives is filtered through the lens of his or her beliefs, past experiences, values, ideas, and prejudices. Parties in conflict regularly witness the same behavior and attribute a different meaning to it. Like the parable of the six blind men who, each touching a different part of an elephant, decide the animal looks like a snake (tail), a tree (leg), a pancake (ear), and so on, perception is essentially a subjective process. A pat on the back can be perceived as a gesture of friendship or domination; a nickname might be understood as a term of endearment or ridicule.

Such differences in perception are fertile ground for interpersonal conflict. As an example, suppose Marlene, misinterpreting her neighbor Angel's shyness as aloofness, does not invite him to her block party. Angel is hurt by this, and the following week when he sees Marlene struggling to lift a heavy package into her apartment, he does not offer his help. This only confirms Marlene's initial misinterpretation of Angel's character, and she vows to have nothing to do with him. With each action and response, a real conflict grows based upon a foundation of simple misunderstanding. And strangely enough, each action engenders a reaction that seems to confirm the original misperception.

At least two differences in perception contributed to our sample conflict between Amy and Roxanne. Amy's assumption that because Roxanne started dating Sidney soon after they broke up, Roxanne "stole" Sidney from her. And Amy thought Roxanne was laughing at *her* during the oral presentation, when in fact, she was laughing at a cartoon in her textbook.

---

[7] The trigger of conflict characteristic applies to large-group conflicts too. The verdict in the Rodney King beating trial, for instance, was a trigger for the riots that followed in Los Angeles in 1992. Those riots were obviously fueled by tensions long unresolved and needs long unmet, not solely by outrage at the verdict.

The Role of Non-Parties

Last week my

friends got into an

argument. I didn't

want to get involved.

So when my friends

asked me questions

about what they

should do, I told

them some things

that we discussed in

mediation training.

Not only did this

give them something

to talk about, but it

eventually solved

their fight.

Middle school mediator

A final parameter of interpersonal conflict is the role played by people who are not a party to them. Those we will call *non-parties* can escalate or de-escalate the conflicts of others, even if those conflicts do not affect them directly.

It is first important to understand that people find few things as compelling as the conflicts of others. Conflicts are unpredictable and intensely emotional, and when they escalate into physical violence, conflicts exhibit extraordinary human drama. Students surround their peers and cheer when a fight occurs. The hallways buzz with talk about the fight for days afterwards. Conflicts elicit an almost primitive fascination.

But conflicts are compelling for reasons beyond sheer spectacle. *Conflicts can meet the psychological needs of those who are not directly involved in them.* Identifying with a party in conflict provides non-parties with a sense of meaning. They feel like they belong to something, that they too are fighting for something. Non-parties can also hope to earn the esteem of others by identifying with a party whom they feel is "right."

Unfortunately, the influence of non-parties more often than not escalates conflict. This is especially true in schools. A primary motivation for students' behavior in conflict is to win the approval of their peers. But non-parties escalate conflicts in other ways as well. They spread rumors that increase misunderstanding and tension between parties. They encourage their friends to fight with statements such as, "Are you going to let him get away with that?" or "You should beat her down." They even join in the fray themselves—perhaps to defend a friend, perhaps to meet their own psychological needs—with the net effect of escalating the conflict and creating secondary interpersonal tensions. Most large-group conflicts begin in this manner.

Non-parties can de-escalate interpersonal conflicts too. By talking to parties in private, they can defuse emotions and help formulate constructive solutions. By expressing their disapproval of violent approaches to conflict resolution, they discourage other students from fighting to look good. Non-parties can also act as informal or formal mediators. The more that non-parties model and advocate effective and nonviolent approaches to conflict resolution, the greater the likelihood that they will de-escalate conflicts.

We cannot know for certain the role that non-parties played in the conflict between Roxanne and Amy. But by bad-mouthing Amy, Sidney implicitly encouraged Roxanne to fight her. And by enthusiastically passing along and perhaps even embellishing rumors about their relationship, the friends of both girls helped to escalate the conflict.

A familiarity with the characteristics of interpersonal conflicts will help you understand and resolve all conflicts more effectively. But what does it mean to "resolve" a conflict? And how should you go about achieving resolution?

APPROACHING CONFLICT RESOLUTION

To resolve any conflict or contest effectively, one needs to understand the rules of the game: how to play, what one risks by playing, and what one stands to gain. In organized conflicts such as the game of basketball, detailed regulations address every conceivable concern. This information is available for study prior to a game, and all players tacitly agree to follow these rules.

But the jump from sports to even the most mundane interpersonal conflicts is a leap of enormous complexity. Rules aren't posted—they are spontaneously created during the conflict. Can parties involve friends, bring up the past, criticize each other, walk out, use violence? Parties in conflict must be prepared for the rules to change at any moment.

And what does winning mean in relation to interpersonal conflicts? Winning is defined as "achieving victory over others as if in a competition; achieving by effort." Simply stated, winning means getting what one wants. In basketball, the team that has the most points at the end of the game wins. But in interpersonal conflicts, each party has its own definition of winning. These definitions may overlap (both want to be treated with respect), or they may not (Party A wants to remain friends, Party B doesn't; Party A wants his or her money back, Party B wants a public apology). Sometimes parties aren't even sure what they want—what defines winning—at all.

With the rules in flux, and with the definition of winning uncertain, how does one go about "winning" an interpersonal conflict?

The Limits of Competition

Most people approach winning interpersonal conflicts as they would a basketball game. The model that games theoreticians use to describe contests such as basketball is called a *zero sum game*. In a zero sum game, there is only one winner. Every time one side gains, the other side experiences an equal and opposite loss. Because winning in a zero sum game is defined in relation to the opponent, *getting more than the opponent is the primary concern*. It is more important than either the quantity or the quality of the winnings. In basketball, the team that has the most points at the end of the game wins, regardless of whether it played poorly or well, or whether the score was 82 to 80 or 127 to 80.

A chart of the possible outcomes of a zero sum game looks like this:

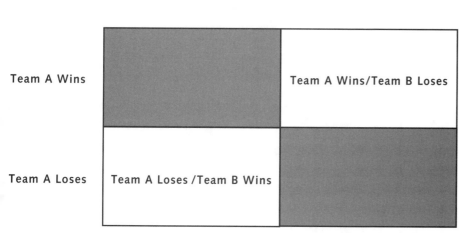

	Team B Wins	Team B Loses
Team A Wins		Team A Wins/Team B Loses
Team A Loses	Team A Loses /Team B Wins	

Either A wins and B loses, or B wins and A loses, which, depending upon the perspective, is either a win-lose or a lose-win outcome. While this model works well for basketball, it is completely inadequate to describe the workings of most interpersonal conflicts because interpersonal conflicts are not zero sum games. In addition to the outcomes of win-lose and lose-win, two other outcomes are possible: win-win and lose-

lose. To illustrate this, let's look at another sample conflict:

Manya and Susan are two friends who have not seen each other for many months. They meet at 1:00 to spend the afternoon together. Manya, who has been sick at home for over a week, wants to spend time outside, ideally in the park. Susan is hungry, however, and wants to go to a restaurant for lunch. They need to resolve this conflict.

Of course, the two outcomes noted above, win-lose and lose-win, are possible.

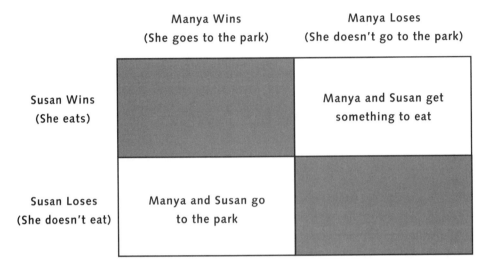

But there are other possible outcomes as well. So-called lose-lose outcomes do not satisfy either party. Rather than going to the park or to lunch—what each truly wants to do—Susan and Manya will "compromise" and go to see a movie instead. Or, during their attempts to resolve this situation, the two friends might become so angry with each other that they decide they can't even spend time together. Now neither of them wins; they both lose. Deciding itself is too difficult.

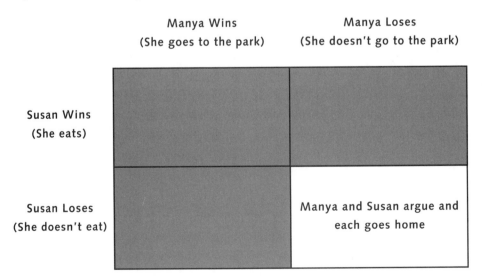

But most significantly, there are also win–win solutions. Manya and Susan might agree to purchase some food at the supermarket and then have a picnic in the park. Or they might decide to eat in a restaurant across town and stroll through the park to get there. In each case, both would get enough of what they want to consider themselves winners.

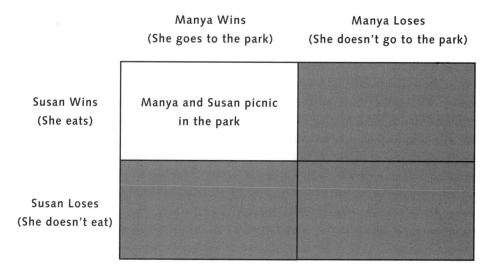

	Manya Wins (She goes to the park)	Manya Loses (She doesn't go to the park)
Susan Wins (She eats)	Manya and Susan picnic in the park	
Susan Loses (She doesn't eat)		

What lessons can be drawn from this about how to win interpersonal conflicts? For the zero sum game illustrated first, the most suitable approach to conflict resolution is *competition*. When competing, one person strives to get what he or she wants without concern for the needs of the opponent. In fact, preventing an adversary from achieving his or her goals usually helps the first person to succeed. Because the choice is between doing whatever one can to win, or losing, zero sum games have to be played to win.

Since interpersonal conflicts are not zero sum games, even the simple conflict illustrated here has a wider range of outcomes than a seemingly complicated game like basketball. It requires an altogether different approach to conflict resolution.

Collaborative Conflict Resolution

The possibility of the win–win outcome, as well as other factors, necessitates an alternative to competitive conflict resolution. It requires *collaborative conflict resolution*.

When parties collaborate to resolve conflicts, they work together to find a solution that satisfies *both* of their needs. Parties might not get everything they want, but they get enough of what they need to feel satisfied. Unlike competition, collaboration requires a respect for the needs of the other party, communication skills, patience, and creativity. And sometimes, collaborative solutions leave parties even better off than if they had competed and won. Consider this example:

> *Mr. Dreyson, the high-school drama teacher, had scheduled a 10:00 A.M. dress rehearsal for his cast. When he arrived at the auditorium five minutes early, he found the seats filled with hundreds of eighth-grade students who were visiting the high school. Ms. Lau, the middle-school counselor, was talking to the students from the*

stage. Mr. Dreyson politely interrupted and asked Ms. Lau to step to the side so that they could discuss this problem.

If each educator went ahead with their activities as planned, they would distract each other to such a degree that their plans would be ruined (lose-lose). At first, both attempted to convince the other to reschedule his or her activity and leave the auditorium (win-lose), but neither succeeded with this approach. Finally, they devised a solution that, to their surprise, left them better off than before the problem arose (win-win):

a. *The high-school actors would try on their costumes behind the curtain for the first fifteen minutes while Ms. Lau finished her talk.*

b. *The eighth-grade students would then watch the drama students rehearse two songs.*

c. *Finally, the middle-school students would give Mr. Dreyson and his actors their opinions of the two songs they performed. One of the numbers had to be cut in order to shorten the play.*

Mr. Dreyson and his students got an audience, while Ms. Lau and her students got an exciting taste of high school life.

On balance—and contrary to popular wisdom—parties usually do better for themselves when they collaborate to resolve conflicts than when they compete. Here are some of the reasons why:

- **One party will echo the other's tactics.** As was discussed in regard to escalation, the manner in which parties approach a conflict is determined in reaction to one another. Taking a competitive approach to a conflict will probably convince an opponent (if he or she was not already so inclined) to do the same. There is little choice: Why collaborate when the other party will take advantage? And so the opponent will "echo" the competitive behavior, and try to beat the first party back (Axelrod 1984, 121).

  The problem is, when both parties compete, often neither gets what it wants. Manya and Susan both go home, frustrated and unable to agree whether to go to the park or to the restaurant; Mr. Dreyson and Ms. Lau, continuing with their programs in spite of each other, get little accomplished. When parties collaborate rather than compete, however, if one party echoes the other's behavior, it will be of a positive and collaborative nature. This increases the likelihood of achieving a win–win resolution.

- **Winning is not the only thing; the winner must collect what has been won.** When one team wins a basketball game, it does not depend upon the losing team to certify or provide it with the win. But in interpersonal conflicts, the "winner" is often still dependent upon the loser: *the loser must take actions or refrain from taking actions for the winner to achieve his or her goals.*

  When people feel like losers, however, they usually will not go out of their way to help the person responsible for their loss. Perhaps they won't do what they claimed they would. Perhaps they will do it, but they will not do it well. Manya may go to the restaurant with Susan, but she may be miserable company. Ms. Lau may agree to end her presentation, but she may do it slowly and in such a way that it is a nuisance to Mr. Dreyson.

When parties collaborate, the actions or resources one expects from the other will be more forthcoming, for they will be delivered by someone who is equally satisfied. Better that parties collaborate and receive all of what they need, than compete, win everything, and collect very little.

■ **One party benefits from the other's wisdom.** There is truth to the adage that two heads are better than one. One party might have access to information or resources that would enable both to craft a resolution superior to any that one could create alone. Susan might know of a restaurant that has outdoor dining in a courtyard even more beautiful than the park. Mr. Dreyson might be aware of other activities in school that Ms. Lau's students would enjoy seeing. Approaching conflicts in a competitive manner limits each party to just one head—his or her own. Solutions will be more sound when parties create them collaboratively.

■ **What about the relationship?** Whether the other party is a partner, child, teacher, student, colleague, or grocer, we have ongoing relationships with most of the people with whom we conflict. Sometimes our futures can become entwined with people we least expect to meet again. The driver of the reckless car turns out to be a new neighbor. The long-lost boyfriend or girlfriend becomes a daughter's soccer coach. The former co-worker becomes the new boss.

Competing with people usually deteriorates the quality of the relationship in other areas. Manya and Susan's friendship may collapse completely. Ms. Lau and Mr. Dreyson's lack of trust may hamper their efforts on the union negotiating committee. People with whom one competes to resolve interpersonal conflicts will trust that person less, for they have firsthand experience of the competitor's lack of concern for their interests. And they will not seek to collaborate with him or her in the future.

Collaborative conflict resolution, on the other hand, maintains healthy relationships. People will trust and seek out someone who collaborates because they know that he or she will work together with them to maximize joint gains. In an ongoing relationship in which long-term interests outweigh short-term ones, the future should "cast a shadow back" upon you, influencing the way that you handle conflicts in the present (Axelrod 1984, 12).

■ **Parties will not have to "watch their backs."** Competition can fix parties on a destructive course that is difficult to change even though it leads to mutual disappointment. This is because losers assume that they will need to compete even harder the next time. Manya suddenly realizes that she has "forgotten" her wallet, forcing Susan to pay for her dinner. Or Ms. Lau begins to spread rumors that Mr. Dreyson is difficult to work with. Even lying and violence have an undeniable utility when parties approach conflicts competitively. If it is a question of using dirty tricks or losing, using dirty tricks can seem like the best alternative.

When parties collaborate, they will not waste time and energy dealing with unnecessary interpersonal tensions. Neither will they have to "watch their backs" to protect themselves from the attacks of others. Collaboration leads to a more trouble-free future.

Mediation has changed our school slightly because people are starting to get into it. So many people have chosen peer mediation instead of fighting it out and I think it has saved a lot of friendships.

Middle school mediator

I tell my friends and family (brothers and sisters) that mediation works and I try to talk to them when they are mad or upset so that I can try to get them to talk things out instead of fighting. I tell them that fighting isn't the answer and that talking helps a lot more than ignoring a problem.

Middle school mediator

Clearly, collaborative conflict resolution should be the first resort for interpersonal conflicts. But here are two important cautions. First, *the collaborative approach is sometimes inappropriate and/or ineffective.* Collaborating or competing are not the only ways to approach interpersonal conflicts. Kenneth Thomas and Ralph Kilmann (1974) developed a popular classification system of "conflict modes" that defines three additional alternatives: avoiding, accommodating, and compromising. When the potential losses associated with confronting a conflict directly outweigh the possible benefits of resolving it, *avoiding* might be the most appropriate response. *Accommodating,* or giving in, is most effective when the issues in dispute are not very important to a party. And *compromising*—splitting the difference—works well when time is limited and parties want to put a matter to rest quickly. Remember that the terms *collaboration* and *compromise* describe very different approaches in this system. In collaboration, parties work together to see if they both can get what they want. Compromise, however, means giving something up. Whereas collaborative solutions always leave parties feeling like winners, compromise solutions are sometimes lose-lose outcomes in disguise.

Even *competing* can be the resolution method most suited to a conflict. Perhaps one party is certain both of superiority over the other and of the fact that they will never come into contact again. Perhaps there seems no room for compromise. Under these circumstances, employing a competitive approach to conflict resolution might make sense. In addition, sometimes one party is unable to reach a satisfactory resolution despite the best efforts to collaborate with another party. In these instances, parties must resort to one of the other approaches.

The second caution is that collaboration is difficult to practice. Effective collaborative conflict resolution requires a range of subtle communication skills. Participants need to be able to listen well, to express their needs and feelings without making each other defensive, and to create and then evaluate alternative solutions. Often these skills must be applied under pressure. And, although conflict resolution training can help people develop these skills, they are nevertheless difficult to apply.

In addition, from a short-term perspective, competing is always the safest approach, the one most likely to protect a party's interests. If one party competes, the other is prepared for his or her aggression. And if an opponent chooses another conflict resolution approach, then competing will gain the maximum advantage. Those who understand the potential benefits of collaboration face a dilemma: if they collaborate, the other party may simply take advantage of them by competing.

The difficulty of engendering collaboration is the subject of Robert Axelrod's wonderful book *The Evolution of Cooperation* (Basic Books, 1984). Axelrod invited top games theoreticians to submit strategies for winning a simulated conflict, and then he used computers to test each strategy against the others. He discovered one strategy that was better than all the rest for promoting cooperation and increasing the winnings of *all* parties. His "tit-for tat" strategy recommends the following:

- Do not envy the other party's success. You do not have to do better than the other party to do well for yourself.
- Do not be the first to compete. If you compete, the other party will probably follow suit and this can easily lead to a destructive spiral in which you both lose.

- Immediately reciprocate the competitive or collaborative approach of the other party. Send a consistent and clear message. You would much prefer to collaborate than compete, but you will compete if you must.
- Do not try to be clever and outsmart the other party. This usually leads to negative consequences in the long run.

For the large percentage of interpersonal conflicts, collaborative conflict resolution produces the best results. It creates trust, builds relationships, and maximizes benefits to all concerned. Competitive conflict resolution, on the other hand, accounts for an enormous drain of time, energy, and resources at every level on which it is practiced. Collaboration involves no small risk, and it requires skill and courage to practice. But in the final analysis, it is usually the best way to resolve interpersonal conflicts.

CONFLICT RESOLUTION PROCESSES: NEGOTIATION, MEDIATION, ARBITRATION

So far we have discussed six important characteristics of interpersonal conflicts and the advantages of collaborating rather than competing to resolve them. Now we will consider the processes that people use to resolve their conflicts.

The majority of interpersonal conflicts are resolved utilizing one of three conflict resolution processes: negotiation, mediation, or arbitration. *Negotiation* is a process in which parties attempt to resolve a conflict by discussing it directly themselves. It is the most informal of the three processes, and it takes place spontaneously whenever people talk out their differences. The strength of the negotiating process is that all power rests in the hands of the parties themselves. They control both the process and the outcome.

In *mediation*, a third party enters the process to help the parties negotiate. Mediators try to help parties create win-win resolutions by listening to their needs and assisting them to communicate with each other. Although the mediator takes charge of the process, the parties still control the substance of what is discussed as well as the outcome of the discussion. Participation in mediation is usually voluntary, and the mediator cannot force the parties to do anything they do not want to do. The strength of mediation is that parties receive assistance in facilitating their negotiations while still maintaining control of the outcome.

In *arbitration*, the third party not only controls the process, he or she also controls the outcome. Arbitrators—sometimes known as "judges without robes"—decide what parties must do to resolve their conflict, and they usually have the power to force parties to comply with their decision. In making their determination, arbitrators are often influenced by institutional and personal concerns as well as the concerns of the parties themselves. Parents regularly arbitrate between their children. Educators often assume that they are mediating with their students when in fact they are arbitrating. Whenever the third party determines the outcome instead of the parties in conflict doing so (or uses his or her power to advocate for a certain outcome), he or she is *arbitrating* rather than mediating. Arbitration is effective when parties can't resolve a conflict on their own or with the help of a mediator, and it is useful to enforce institutional rules and norms. Arbitration can also take much less time than either negotiation or mediation.

These three processes—negotiation, mediation, and arbitration—build upon each other. Negotiation is a part of both mediation and arbitration, and many arbitrators try to serve as a mediator first. Proceeding from negotiation to mediation to arbitration, however, the process becomes increasingly formal and disempowering to the parties. Whereas parties are in complete control of both the process and the outcome when they negotiate, they control very little when they sit before an arbitrator.

The progression to arbitration

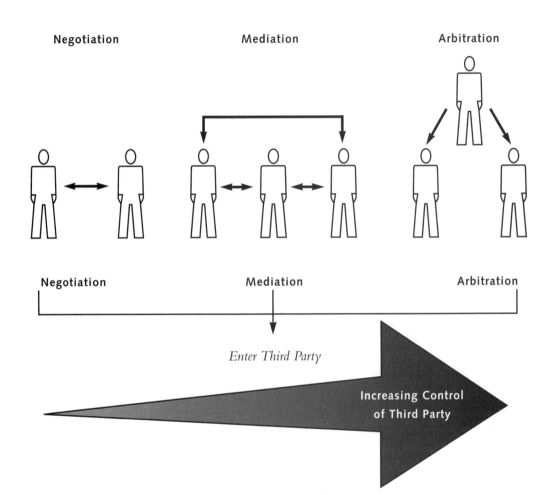

The operative word here is *process*. Negotiation, mediation, and arbitration are all means to an end, the end being the resolution of conflict. Just as one can take a bus, a car, or a bicycle to reach the same destination, each of these processes can result in a similar substantive outcome. One party may return stolen property to the other by a specific date as a result of informal negotiations, a mediated agreement, or the decision of an arbitrator.

But the means do have a potential impact upon the ends. Negotiation requires the least amount of outside intervention, it can build relationships, and it provides parties with the greatest opportunity to develop their conflict resolution skills. As such, it is an ideal first resort. But often parties cannot resolve a conflict on their own; they need help. How do mediation and arbitration compare for resolving interpersonal conflicts?

MEDIATION AND ARBITRATION: A COMPARISON

The Differences Between Mediation and Arbitration

Mediation and arbitration are profoundly different in many important ways:

- **Distribution of Power.** Mediation attempts to give parties the opportunity, the support, and the power to control their own destiny. Mediators only intervene as much as is necessary to help parties create a satisfactory solution to their dispute. In arbitration, the arbitrator retains power over both the process and the outcome. Arbitrators use their power to require parties to comply with their decisions.

- **Control of Outcome.** In mediation, parties create their own resolution. They are also free to end the process if they feel it is not working to their advantage. In contrast, arbitrators, not the parties, decide the outcome based upon what they think is fair (and when necessary, regardless of the parties' wishes).

- **Impartiality.** Impartiality is fundamental to mediation and mediators assiduously guard against taking sides. Arbitrators, although ideally neutral as well, often have obligations to the system in which they work and even relationships with the parties that explicitly influence their decisions. This is especially true of informal arbitration by parents and educators.

- **Third-Party Judgments.** Mediators do not offer their opinions regarding the substance of the conflict and politely defer from doing so when asked directly. Within reason, all that matters in a mediation session are the judgments of the parties themselves. In contrast, the arbitrator's primary function is to formulate a sound judgment about the parties' situation.

- **Disciplinary Function.** Mediation is completely nonpunitive. Although agreements sometimes include contingencies for what will happen if one party fails to live up to his or her commitment, ideally no consequences result from a session that are not created by the parties themselves. Arbitration *can* be punitive; arbitrators recommend and usually have the power to force parties to accept punishment for their actions.

- **Temporal Orientation.** Mediation helps parties create a satisfactory arrangement for the future. Actions and events from the parties' past are discussed, but only to the extent necessary to move them toward thinking and planning for the future. In arbitration, parties are often punished for their past actions, and the questions of "who started it" can be pivotal to an arbitrator's decision.

- **Winners and Losers.** Mediation is designed to help parties reach a resolution without compromising what is important to them: everyone must "win." It is better not to reach an agreement than to reach one with which the parties are dissatisfied. After arbitration concludes, parties often feel like winners or losers because the arbitrator controls the outcome. It is not uncommon for both parties to be unhappy with the decision of an arbitrator.

- **Voluntariness.** Mediation is a voluntary process. Parties usually choose to participate, and they agree to resolve their dispute only if they are satisfied with the terms. Arbitration is often involuntary. Parties can be required to participate and to abide by whatever outcome is prescribed.

I like being a mediator because it's a challenge. It's like a mystery sometimes when we don't hear the whole story, we have to let the disputants open up and calm down. Sometimes there are some tears, but that's great because they get to see the other's feelings.

High school mediator

- **Definition of Dispute.** Mediators work with the dispute as defined by the parties, not according to their own agenda or that of the institution in which they mediate. Mediators may encourage parties to raise underlying issues, but it is the parties' prerogative to do so. Arbitrators define the dispute in accordance with their own judgment and the rules or norms they are expected to uphold. Arbitrators create their own agenda even if it de-emphasizes or even ignores the issues that are most important to the parties.

- **Scope.** In mediation, any relevant issue raised by the parties is a legitimate topic for discussion. Mediators know that hidden issues or those that appear tangential can be integral to resolving a dispute effectively. Arbitration discourages parties from discussing issues not directly related to the critical areas in dispute because this distracts the arbitrator from the issues at hand.

- **Confidentiality.** Mediators guarantee a significant degree of confidentiality to the parties. Parties are informed of any exceptions in advance of their participation in the process. In arbitration, the extent to which information discussed during the session remains confidential is usually unclear. Sometimes the arbitrator does not even raise the issue of confidentiality.

Mediation's Advantages

Mediation has a clear advantage over arbitration for resolving most interpersonal conflicts because mediation is fundamentally concerned with facilitating collaborative, rather than competitive, conflict resolution. To illustrate mediation's strengths, let's look at another simple school conflict:

> *Louis and Rafael, two sixth graders, have been arguing for a number of months. Louis calls Rafael fat, and this upsets Rafael very much. The boys have not been able to resolve this themselves. Rafael asks the administrator in charge of discipline for help.*

- **Mediation recognizes that ultimately, conflicts can only be resolved if the parties themselves choose to do so.** Third parties like mediators and arbitrators can never truly resolve a conflict; that power rests in the hands and hearts of the parties alone. If Louis and Rafael went before a school disciplinarian or arbitrator, the latter would in all likelihood use his or her influence to make Louis stop his offensive behavior. Louis might be threatened with punitive consequences or punished outright to discourage him from continuing his behavior. As a result, he might discontinue teasing Rafael.

But though Louis's behavior might stop, he and Rafael would likely still harbor feelings of anger and resentment toward one another. Such feelings can never be erased by order of an outside authority. An internal, emotional reorientation is required, one that can only be accomplished by the parties themselves. Mediation, by encouraging parties to make their own choices, is more capable of engendering this kind of reorientation than arbitration.

- **Mediation recognizes that parties must feel comfortable if they are to work out their differences.** For mediation to be effective, the parties must trust the mediator and the process. The mediator's first priority, therefore, is to help the parties feel safe. This is accomplished by carefully explaining the process, encouraging parties to speak, listening without judging, showing compassion for the parties' situation, and guaranteeing confidentiality. Parties respond by revealing information and making choices that would be unlikely in arbitration. Rafael can show how Louis's comments hurt him without losing face. Louis can admit his mistake without fearing that the mediator will use it against him. Mediation makes it safe to change.

- **Mediation recognizes the importance of fostering trust and respect between the parties.** With its emphasis on face-to-face negotiations, mediation dissolves barriers between parties in a way that arbitration can't. As parties listen and eventually speak directly to one another, the experiences and feelings of each party come alive. Louis, for instance, can experience firsthand the pain that his slurs have caused Rafael. Although they disagree and perhaps even dislike each other at the start, the mediation process transforms the adversary into a human being not so different from oneself. And by voluntarily participating in the process, parties give each other an implicit respect.

- **Mediation recognizes the importance of an open exchange of information between the parties.** In mediation, parties not only get to know each other better, they get to know their conflict better as well. Before mediation, parties see the dispute from their own perspectives and know only part of the "story." Mediation helps them combine their stories to create a shared version of events. Misperceptions and contradictory information can be clarified. Rafael hears that Louis's stepfather is overweight and that is why it bothers him. Louis understands that Rafael was not trying to get him "in trouble" by going to the disciplinarian; he just wants the teasing to stop. Once parties agree upon what the problem is, they take a giant step toward being able to agree upon how to resolve it.

- **Mediation recognizes that parties are the best judge of what will resolve the conflict.** Mediators encourage the people who know most about the problem, the parties themselves, to come up with the resolution. Though an arbitrator's decision may be consistent with community standards of fairness, if it isn't what the parties need to resolve their dispute, the conflict will persist. Mediation acknowledges that parties are the "experts" on their dispute.

- **Mediation recognizes that parties are more likely to implement agreements that they have created.** Just as only the parties can end the conflict, only they can implement the resolution. If parties have done a large part of the work to create an agreement, they are more likely to uphold its terms. Parties are less invested in following through on contracts that have been created for them by an arbitrator. Even the fear of an arbitrator's punishment does not equal the motivation to implement a resolution that results from having created it oneself.

When I mediate, I remember that I have to be neutral. I just look and see two human beings who have a lot of courage for coming to mediation.

High school mediator

Agreement and Reconciliation

One final advantage that mediation has over arbitration—and one of its unique strengths as a method of resolving interpersonal conflicts—is that mediation facilitates two distinct levels of resolution. We can call these levels *agreement* and *reconciliation*. *Agreement* refers to the terms and conditions that parties create to settle a conflict. Agreements concern the substantive issues in dispute; Joe, for instance, agrees to give Sam ten dollars on Friday before homeroom. A large percentage of all mediation sessions—almost 90 percent of school mediation sessions—result in the creation of agreements that are acceptable to the parties. These agreements might not include everything they had initially desired, but they provide the parties with enough of what they need to enable them to end their conflict.

The second level of resolution, *reconciliation*, refers to a more intangible aspect of the process. Instead of the substantive issues in dispute, reconciliation is concerned with the relationship of the parties. When parties reconcile, they come to appreciate each other's feelings, ideas, and interpretation of events, realizing that "we were all trying to do our best." Reconciliation is ultimately about forgiveness.[8]

The structure of mediation—with parties listening and speaking directly to one another and mediators clarifying perceptions and feelings—facilitates reconciliation. Arbitration, focused as it is upon the arbitrator's decision rather than the parties' resolution, is limited in its ability to bring about reconciliation. The following example will illustrate this clearly:

Seth and Devon have been friends for about two years. They became friends when they were featured in a school talent show together. They both like to rap. Although they spend time together in school—joking, talking to girls, practicing their raps—they don't really see each other outside of school.

Last week Devon's rap group was putting on a show at a teen center and he asked Seth if he could borrow his coat to wear on stage. Seth knew that Devon had always liked the coat, and so he gave it to him on the condition that he take good care of it.

The concert went very well. At one point Devon, in his excitement, wrestled the coat off and threw it backstage. When the show was over, however, the jacket was not where he had thrown it. He searched everywhere in the teen center, but the coat was nowhere to be found.

The two boys have been unable to work out a resolution to this problem, and Seth has been angry with Devon ever since. The coat cost $145. Devon does not have that kind of money. Not knowing what else to do, Devon asked to come to mediation.

If this conflict were to be resolved through mediation, Devon and Seth's agreement might read something like this:

1. Seth and Devon agree that this problem is resolved.
2. Devon agrees to pay Seth $40 today and then $15 each week for seven weeks until he has reached the $145 Seth needs to buy a new jacket. He will make the payments every Monday morning in math class.
3. Both Devon and Seth would like to be friends in the future.

---

[8] Although this distinction between agreement and reconciliation may appear beyond the conceptual grasp of students, young people do understand it. Reconciliation means that parties don't just agree, but they "make up." Students see and feel the difference between agreement and reconciliation quite clearly in a mediation session.

Reconciliation, on the other hand, would likely involve Seth understanding how Devon could have become so caught up in his performance that he didn't watch the coat. It might involve Devon acknowledging how sorry he was for the trouble he had caused Seth and thanking him for his willingness to lend the coat in the first place. It might even involve both friends acknowledging that their friendship was important to them. In the end, either implicitly or explicitly, the two would forgive each other.

Reconciliation and agreement do not always follow one from the other, and both, neither, or only one of them may result from a mediation session. Although satisfied with the terms of an agreement, Seth might still be very angry at Devon and unwilling to forgive him for being "stupid" and losing the coat (agreement without reconciliation). Or Devon and Seth might forgive each other but be unable to fashion the terms of an agreement that are acceptable to both of them (reconciliation without agreement).

The ability to facilitate reconciliation is a central strength of mediation. When parties reconcile, they are able to devote 100 percent of their energy to resolving the substantive issues in dispute. Reconciliation increases the likelihood both that agreements will be reached and that those that are reached will be effective. Reconciliation also has value apart from its effect upon the creation of agreements. When parties reconcile, they have the experience of conflicting with *and* caring about a person simultaneously. This is a new and valuable experience for many parties, and one they may carry with them and apply to future disputes.

Clearly, mediation has distinct advantages over arbitration for the resolution of interpersonal conflicts. This is not to say that mediation should be used every time people in conflict seek assistance. Arbitration is quick and efficient in the short term, and it effectively demonstrates authority. Whenever parties break rules and must receive appropriate consequences, arbitration is a logical process to determine these consequences. And parties sometimes are unable to reach an agreement through mediation. On balance, however, mediation is far more effective for resolving interpersonal conflicts than arbitration, and it should be used as a first resort whenever possible.

FINAL WORDS

In this chapter we have covered the fundamentals of conflict and conflict resolution:

- Conflicts are normal, human experiences with a potential for positive impact upon those involved in them.
- All interpersonal conflicts, regardless of the parties and the issues, share similar dynamics.
- When resolving conflicts, one party doesn't have to lose for the other to win. Often, both can win.
- A collaborative approach to conflict resolution, used wisely, is more beneficial for all concerned than a competitive approach.
- The most common processes for resolving interpersonal conflicts are negotiation, mediation, and arbitration.
- When parties need help resolving an interpersonal conflict, mediation is usually preferable to arbitration.

CHAPTER 2

Conflict Resolution at School

THE TRADITIONAL APPROACH TO MANAGING STUDENT CONFLICT

onflict is a normal part of life in general, but it is an especially normal part of school life. Every person within a school community becomes involved in conflicts, and students especially conflict over a wide range of issues. Many of these issues—name-calling, boyfriend or girlfriend difficulties, gossip, borrowing things and not returning them—do not appear of great consequence to adults. Other student conflicts are more serious and may involve physical violence, racism, gangs, or sexual harassment. Educators discover these conflicts throughout the school day and anywhere students interact. They can begin outside of school and lead to problems within the building, or they can start at school and reach a climax in the community.

When considering interpersonal conflict in the school setting, a fundamental point must be stressed at the outset: *Student conflict is essentially extracurricular.* Conflicts divert administrators', teachers', and students' attention from the *academic* mission of school. Even when schools implement programs to teach students conflict resolution skills, the time students spend using those skills to resolve actual conflicts is time away from language arts, math, and science.

The fact that students' interpersonal conflicts are common distractions in schools argues for educators to develop a comprehensive system for managing them. Ideally, a school-based conflict resolution system would

- Create a school climate that encourages caring, honesty, cooperation, and appreciation of diversity so that students are less likely to become involved in conflicts
- Teach conflict resolution skills to students so that they are better able to resolve conflicts on their own
- Offer conflict resolution services to students who need help
- Motivate students to utilize these conflict resolution services
- Intervene in conflicts that require outside assistance as early as possible to prevent them from escalating
- Employ effective conflict resolution processes
- Make efficient use of the school's monetary, time, and human resources

This ideal system can be visualized in the shape of a pyramid. At the bottom of the pyramid are potential conflicts that never occur because of a positive school climate, engaging curriculum, effective classroom management, and democratic school structure. The largest percentage of interpersonal conflicts that do occur would be settled by students themselves using self-control and negotiation skills. Those conflicts that students cannot resolve on their own would go to mediation with student or adult mediators. And finally, the smallest percentage would be arbitrated by an adult.

From *Students Resolving Conflict: Peer Mediation in Schools*, published by GoodYearBooks. Copyright © 1995 Richard Cohen.

The ideal system of conflict resolution

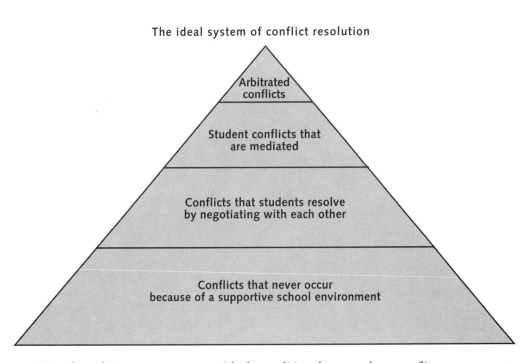

Arbitrated
conflicts

Student conflicts that
are mediated

Conflicts that students resolve
by negotiating with each other

Conflicts that never occur
because of a supportive school environment

How does this system compare with the traditional approach to conflict management in American schools? Let's take a look.

SHORTCOMINGS OF THE TRADITIONAL APPROACH

Schools vary tremendously in their ability to create a climate that minimizes the incidence of student conflict. Some schools—even those that serve a supposedly "difficult" student population—do a wonderful job with this. Others do not. With few exceptions, however, schools give students little explicit guidance regarding how to resolve their interpersonal conflicts. When students initially come into conflict, they are usually on their own (unless an adult happens to observe them).

Students' peers are the first non-parties to become aware of a conflict, but their influence tends to escalate it. The first adult to become aware of a student conflict is usually the classroom teacher. The teacher is the front line of most schools' approach to managing student conflict. Traditional wisdom states that if teachers are competent, most of the interpersonal conflicts that occur among their charges will not escalate in their classrooms. There is some truth to this. Teachers have a variety of tools that they can use to manage student conflicts. Some are employed preventively, before conflicts arise or before students become seriously invested in them. Others are used after a conflict has occurred. These tools include

- **Creating a positive classroom climate.** Teachers work with their students to create an atmosphere in which students respect the teacher, respect each other, and collaborate in their work. Such "climate setting" is an integral part of most teachers' practices.
- **Suppressing, defusing, or ignoring conflict.** When conflicts appear likely to arise, teachers employ techniques to discourage their development. Familiar strategies

include asking students to be quiet, moving students' seats, finding and highlighting the positive in students' negative behavior, giving students "time out" or other consequences, ignoring the conflict altogether, assigning students in conflict to do a project together, using humor, quickly engaging students in something else, and so on.

■ **Asking students to resolve conflicts themselves.** When students become involved in a conflict, teachers encourage them to try and resolve it on their own.

■ **Mediating conflict.** This option, wonderful in theory, is very difficult in practice. The biggest challenge is time. Most postelementary educators meet with five to seven classes a day for approximately forty-five minutes. Each class has between twenty-five and thirty-five students. These teachers cannot spend class time mediating an interpersonal conflict without detracting from the majority of their students.

■ **Arbitrating conflict.** This is a more common teacher intervention, although time constraints also limit its use. Arbitration's effectiveness ultimately rests upon the teacher's power over the students and the students' respect for the teacher. When arbitrating, teachers can ensure that the outcome is fair, and if any rules are broken, they can apply the appropriate sanctions.

A generation ago, these options may have been more effective in managing student conflicts. But the techniques teachers have relied most heavily upon—diffusing, arbitrating, even creating a positive classroom climate—have never been very effective with conflicts that have a strong emotional component. As the frequency and severity of such student conflict has increased, many teachers find themselves turning to the option that had always been a last resort: referring students outside the classroom to the administrator in charge of discipline. Similar to the classroom teacher's, the disciplinarian's first responsibility is to create a school environment that decreases the incidence of interpersonal conflict. But once angry students are sitting in their office, disciplinarians almost exclusively employ one conflict resolution process: arbitration.

How does this approach measure up? For a variety of reasons, the traditional approach to student conflict management falls far short of the ideal outlined at the start of this chapter.

■ It does not teach conflict resolution skills to increase students' ability to resolve their own conflicts.

■ It does not proactively offer students collaborative conflict resolution services once they become involved in a conflict.

■ It does not intervene in conflicts as early as possible. Students usually do not receive attention until their conflict has escalated and they have broken a school rule.

■ It minimizes the use of negotiation and mediation, the processes that are best suited for interpersonal conflict resolution. Instead, in the classroom and especially in the office, arbitration is used almost exclusively.

■ It does not utilize human resources efficiently. Too many minor conflicts are handled by senior administrators who have other important responsibilities. There is no educational reason why an assistant principal, the school's second in command, should spend a good portion of his or her day listening to students discuss why one teased the other. A virtually unlimited number of students can do this just as well—and develop essential skills in the process.

SCHOOL DISCIPLINE VS. CONFLICT RESOLUTION

Key to understanding why the traditional approach to student conflict is lacking is this: *Most schools simply do not employ a systematic approach to managing student conflict.* Rather, they have a disciplinary system that by default is used for conflict management. Unfortunately, the latter is not well suited for the former.

The rationale of the typical school disciplinary system can be summarized as follows:

> *For schools to accomplish their educational mission, students must behave in a manner that is conducive to learning. To ensure that they do so, students are subject to the strictures placed upon them by a disciplinary code. The code prohibits everything from physical violence, destroying school property, and drug use, to teasing, talking out of turn, and passing notes in class. Negative consequences are assigned to offenses in order to discourage students from engaging in them. When violations do occur, offending students are brought before a disciplinarian where they receive punishment. The entire school community is informed of this code.*

How effective such disciplinary codes are at ensuring that students behave appropriately is uncertain. But they are clearly ineffective at helping students reconcile interpersonal differences. The recent increase in student conflict has made this clear. There are a number of reasons for this.

- **Disciplinary systems do not distinguish between disciplinary offenses and interpersonal conflict.** Most interpersonal conflicts between students are just that, *between students.* They do not involve the violation of a school rule. Two students in conflict over a boyfriend, for instance, might never take action that constitutes a disciplinary offense. As a result, their conflict, like the majority of student interpersonal conflicts, does not come to the attention of the system. In effect, students must wait for their conflict to escalate, leading one of them to break a school rule, before the system pays attention. The potential for students to refer themselves or their peers for conflict resolution assistance is also lost.

  Even when conflicts come to the attention of the system, the focus is primarily on the disciplinary offense and not on the interpersonal dimension of a conflict. It is quite common for two students who fight to be suspended for their behavior, but never encouraged by the school to resolve the issues that led to the behavior in the first place. Such students serve their three-day suspensions and then return to classes without discussing their conflict in any depth.

- **The disciplinary system relies almost exclusively upon sanctions and negative reinforcement.** The power of school discipline lies in its ability to mandate punishment for students who break the rules. Short of expulsion, suspension and detention represent the ultimate sanctions in the disciplinary arsenal. Theoretically, this "negative feedback" steers young people away from destructive behaviors and toward proper conduct. Unfortunately, however, sanctions are often ineffective and even harmful to students involved in interpersonal conflicts.

I definitely think peer mediation has changed our school. When we did not have it students were always fighting and they had no other options and now that they do, many are coming to mediate their problem instead of fighting.

Middle school mediator

- Rather than resolve the issues in an interpersonal conflict, sanctions can escalate a conflict. Both students, angered because each was suspended on account of the other, retaliate with even greater force when they return to school.
- The degree to which sanctions deter the violation of the school rules is unclear. Many students are suspended more than once for the same offense. Suspension alone does not help young people understand, take responsibility for, or control their actions.
- Sanctions like suspension undermine the basic educational mission of the school by removing those students from school who can least afford to miss it. And by giving them the message that they do not belong in school, suspension can contribute to students' desire to drop out altogether.[9]
- Suspensions and other sanctions are often applied inequitably. Some research has shown that children of color receive these punishments more frequently than Caucasian children who commit the same offenses.
- The effectiveness of suspension and detention has been diminished by changes in the contemporary family. Whereas in the past, being suspended from school would be met with disapproval and even additional punishment at home, today this is less likely. Some students enjoy the time away from school, where they can watch TV and spend time with friends who have already dropped out. "In-house" suspension, in which students are suspended from classes but are required to spend the school day doing schoolwork in a supervised room, was designed in part to prevent this.

Of course, disciplinary consequences serve an essential function within schools. Some students must be suspended or even expelled because of their behavior. Punishment can frighten students into doing the right thing or not repeating antisocial behavior. And teachers and students are sometimes able to put their relationship on a more productive footing after they have had a break from one another.

But disciplinary sanctions have a limited usefulness. Schools need methods that not only deter inappropriate behavior, but that motivate students to "do the right thing." Though sanctions may enforce compliance and conformity, they do not inspire prosocial behavior.

Most relevant to our inquiry, however, *applying sanctions does little to help students resolve interpersonal conflicts.* In the end, school disciplinary systems are simply not designed for this purpose. Educators who seek to integrate collaborative conflict resolution into their schools must create approaches that work separately from the disciplinary system.

INTEGRATING COLLABORATIVE CONFLICT RESOLUTION INTO SCHOOLS

To design an effective conflict management system within a school, two basic considerations must be borne in mind. The first is that schools are complex institutions. If possible, all aspects of a school's structure and day-to-day operation should be informed by collab-

---

[9] For an excellent study of the effects of "student exclusion practices," see *The Way Out: Student Exclusion Practices in Boston Middle Schools* (Boston: Massachusetts Advocacy Center, November, 1986).

orative conflict resolution principles. The second is that conflict resolution efforts are most successful in schools in which, for lack of a better expression, people feel cared for. Only when teachers and students feel valued, when they are engaged in the educational process, when their opinions are solicited and appreciated, will conflict resolution efforts have more than a limited impact.

Educators have integrated collaborative conflict resolution into their schools in four primary ways.

Four primary ways educators have integrated collaborative conflict resolution

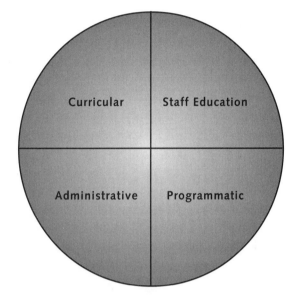

- **Curricular.** The goal of the curricular approach is to integrate conflict resolution into the academic program of the school. Schools accomplish this in a number of ways. One is to teach the skills directly in conflict resolution classes or in classes that can incorporate conflict resolution units (health, civics, advising). Students learn basic conflict theory and engage in exercises to practice the skills and relate them to their own lives. (Conflict resolution skills, like all skills, require practice to master.) The other is to weave conflict resolution into the curriculum of core subjects like history, English, and even math. Students might analyze and dramatize the conflicts in a novel or in history using the principles of collaborative conflict resolution. The strength of curricular efforts is that they provide a basic introduction to conflict resolution to all students in a school. Obstacles include ensuring effective delivery of the curriculum, providing opportunities for students to practice their skills on real-life conflicts, and finding room in already crowded curricula to insert this material.

- **Staff Education.** It is difficult to expect students to resolve conflicts collaboratively if teachers and administrators do not. A second approach, then, focuses on staff education. (Until recently, most teacher training did not include information on conflict resolution.) Through in-service presentations or more extensive courses, teachers learn how to model collaborative conflict resolution, teach it directly to students, and use

Being a mediator has helped me become a more understanding person, and has helped me appreciate my life because I have seen the problems others have to face every day. I am a better listener, and I have a more peaceful lifestyle now that I know how to handle my problems.

Middle school mediator

techniques such as class meetings, class contracts, and cooperative learning to support it. The results include improved classroom management, better application of cooperative learning principles, and more satisfying teacher-student relationships. The strength of the staff education approach is that it reaches the human foundation of the school, the teachers. If school-based educators are conflict resolution advocates, any effort has a much greater chance of success. Limitations are that it is difficult to deliver enough training to make a lasting impact on teacher practice, some teachers are not interested in conflict resolution, and on its own, staff education may never reach students directly.

- **Administrative.** A third way to integrate conflict resolution principles into a school is through its administrative structure. Examples of this approach include providing opportunities for administrators, students, and teachers to administer the school collaboratively; modifying the disciplinary policy to include peer mediation; encouraging adults to mediate disputes with their students and with each other; and training union and school system negotiators in conflict resolution principles and techniques. Each of these ideas has it own strengths and limitations, but they all reinforce the practical lessons at the heart of collaborative conflict resolution.

- **Programmatic.** The final approach to bringing conflict resolution skills into the educational setting—and the one that is the focus of this book—is through conflict resolution programs like peer mediation. Students in these programs are first trained in conflict resolution and mediation skills, and then given the opportunity to practice and develop their skills by helping their peers resolve conflicts. Disadvantages of the programmatic approach include that programs can be difficult to implement and that although many students use the services of the peer mediators, only a small percentage receive intensive training. The strengths of the programmatic approach include that it teaches conflict resolution skills directly to students, that it addresses a pressing institutional need for conflict resolution services, and that it enables students to apply their conflict resolution skills where they matter most—in real conflicts. This last point gives programmatic approaches a unique advantage. By using real student conflict, arguably the best resource for learning about conflict resolution, as its vehicle for teaching conflict resolution skills, peer mediation turns an institutional liability into an educational tool. As a result, increasing numbers of school systems have implemented peer mediation programs as the centerpiece of their student conflict management efforts.

When integrating collaborative conflict resolution into schools, the ideal is to design an effort that effects change on all of these levels: teacher training, curricular modifications, school administration, and programs like peer mediation. Because work on any one of these levels reinforces work on the others, together they make a more profound impact upon students than any one of them can alone. Ideally, students should find collaborative conflict resolution processes modeled for them at every turn.

FINAL WORDS

In this chapter, we have explored how schools resolve student conflicts. The most important lessons are:

- Even when teaching conflict resolution skills is part of the curriculum, actual student conflict is essentially extracurricular.
- Schools should ideally have a comprehensive system for managing student conflicts.
- For a variety of reasons, the traditional school approach to student conflict is not ideal.
- School discipline is not the same as conflict resolution, and on its own, the disciplinary system is not adequate to resolve student interpersonal conflict.
- Collaborative conflict resolution can and should be integrated into schools through the curriculum, through staff education, and through administrative practices as well as through effective programs like peer mediation.

CHAPTER 3
Peer Mediation

A BRIEF HISTORY OF SCHOOL-BASED PEER MEDIATION

Being a mediator has changed my life because now I realize that working it out on your own is better than getting other people involved. That'll just make things worse. Any time I get into an argument, I find it easy to talk it out and listen to how the other person feels.

Middle school mediator

Peer mediation has its roots outside the field of education. In the 1970s, the administration of President Jimmy Carter encouraged the creation of the first Neighborhood Justice Centers. The goal of these centers, soon to be known as "community mediation programs," was to provide an alternative to the courts where citizens could meet to resolve their disputes. Those who pioneered community mediation asserted that mediation was a more effective process for resolving a wide range of conflicts than adjudication, especially if the parties had an ongoing relationship.

In the typical community mediation program, a cross-section of neighborhood volunteers were trained to mediate the disputes that arose in their community. The disputes they mediated included those between neighbors, family members, landlords and tenants, consumers and merchants, friends, and small businesses. Although some disputes were referred directly by local residents, many programs were affiliated with local courthouses and social service agencies which could provide a steady flow of cases.

The notion of individual and community empowerment was fundamental to the community mediation movement, growing as it did in response to the social and political upheaval of the late 1960s. Leaders in this field wanted to give the skills and the power to resolve disputes back to the citizens who were involved in them. By helping people transform their interpersonal relationships, they hoped to build stronger communities and more satisfying lives.

The success of the early mediation programs was impressive. In the large majority of mediation sessions, parties were able to create agreements that effectively resolved their disputes. Parties reported high levels of satisfaction with the process, and often their relationships were preserved if not improved as a result of their participation in mediation. In addition, community mediators found the work extremely fulfilling. When research began to show that parties carried out mediated agreements more frequently than an order of the court, even skeptics began to take notice. The community mediation concept spread around the country.

In the early 1980s, a number of community mediation programs attempted to replicate their success within schools by teaching students to mediate the conflicts of *their* peers. This move into the schools was based upon four assumptions:

1. That conflict is a normal part of living that can be used as an opportunity for student learning and personal growth.
2. That since conflict is unavoidable, learning conflict resolution skills is as "educational" and as essential to the long-term success of young people as learning geometry or history.
3. That in most instances, students can resolve their conflicts with the assistance of other students as effectively as they can with the assistance of adults.

4. That encouraging disputing students to resolve the causes of present conflict collaboratively is usually a more effective method of preventing future conflict (and developing student responsibility) than administering punishment for past actions.

Efforts to integrate mediation into schools were not without their difficulties. But student mediators—known variously as conflict managers, peer mediators, fuss busters, conflict mediators and so on—proved to be as effective as their adult counterparts. And in the decade that followed, a range of forces converged to create ideal conditions for the growth of peer mediation:

- Schools were experiencing numerous problems and were being criticized from all quarters. One of the most unsettling problems was that despite educators' best efforts, student conflict and violence were increasing. As a result, schools were uncharacteristically willing to look outside the educational establishment for assistance.
- Numerous cultural forces placed increasing pressure upon children and led to a deterioration in their social skills. Students were simply less disciplined. Although many educators bemoaned that dealing with students' social and developmental needs came at the expense of academics, there appeared to be no other choice. Peer mediation seemed to be one effective way to redress students' social deficiencies within the school.
- An interest developed among educators in peer education programs generally. Teachers began to see value in training young people to help each other do a variety of things: counseling, tutoring, "mentoring," helping younger peers transition to upper grades, and so on.
- Peer mediation involved relatively little risk for the schools that implemented it. Every other tool educators used for handling student conflict—suspension, detention, parent conferences, and so on—remained in place. Peer mediation could even be used *in addition* to these traditional disciplinary actions.
- Peer mediation is a concrete process that enables students to make a measurable contribution to the quality of school life. As such, peer mediation provided a practical way to apply the skills that many educators, especially "peace educators," had been encouraging schools to teach for years with more limited success.[10]
- Peer mediation is a visible and media-friendly process. This meant that funding sources could see their dollars at work, news media could feature peer mediators in human interest stories, and educators could show the program off at conferences and school committee meetings.
- The growth of community mediation and developments in the legal, psychological, and educational professions led to an increased understanding of mediation among the general public. This made educators, parents, and school committee members more receptive to peer mediation.

---

[10] Because it focuses more on means than on ends, peer mediation is not as politically charged as peace education work. This may have facilitated its acceptance, especially during a decade as conservative as the 1980s in the United States.

In 1984, a small group of community mediators and educators came together to form the National Association for Mediation in Education.[11] At that time only a handful of peer mediation programs existed. Today, a decade later, there are many thousands located in schools in every state in the United States. Large school systems like those in New York City, San Francisco, and Broward County, Florida, have implemented student mediation programs in many of their schools. And interest in peer mediation is not limited to the United States. Educators in Europe, Central and South America, Africa, and Asia are adapting peer mediation to their own needs and cultures.

Whereas initially most of the people involved in peer mediation were community mediators, soon law-related educators, peace educators, and others integrated peer mediation into their own efforts. Even teacher training programs have begun to include courses in conflict resolution and mediation as part of their core curricula. As of this writing, there is every indication that the growth of this idea will continue unabated until every school with the need will have some form of peer mediation program.

THE STRENGTHS OF STUDENTS AS MEDIATORS

Peer mediation works because we are on the same level as them. The kids won't be ashamed to come to someone his or her own age. We are better equipped to understand teenage problems.

Middle school mediator

Peer mediation programs do not only emphasize the efficacy of the mediation process for resolving interpersonal conflicts. They are designed so that students themselves do the mediating. In part this is a recognition of the unavoidable constraints that adults face when mediating the conflicts of young people. (Students often experience adults as "trying to get us to do something," making it more difficult for educators to create the environment that is essential if mediation is to be effective.) But more significantly, students bring unique strengths to this work:

- **Students understand their peers.** Despite the best of intentions, a gulf of understanding will always separate generations. Young people know from experience what it is like to be a student, in these times, under these circumstances. They know the pressures, the attitude, and the language of youth; they know what their peers think is important and why. This gives them a natural advantage as mediators.

- **Students make the process age-appropriate.** The work of Robert Selman has shown that young people's approach to problem solving changes as they develop. Egocentric and impulsive at first, they ideally progress through a series of stages until they can collaborate to resolve conflicts. Using peer mediators ensures that disputes are framed in a developmentally appropriate way. (Adults often talk over students' heads.) In addition, the essentially collaborative nature of the mediation process guides students toward ever higher stages of development.

- **Students empower their peers because they have no power over them.** When students mediate, they command respect solely by the way they conduct themselves in the session. They have no power over their peers. Consequently, students feel more in

---

[11] The National Association for Mediation in Education (NAME) is a clearinghouse for information on mediation and conflict resolution in schools. It publishes a newsletter as well as an annotated bibliography of conflict resolution/mediation materials, and it organizes a bi-annual conference. NAME can be contacted in care of Mediation Project, 205 Hampshire House, Box 33635, University of Massachusetts, Amherst, MA 01003-3635. Phone: 413-545-2462

control of their disputes. And with no authority figure to resist, they are forced to confront themselves and each other.

- **Students command the respect of their peers.** Young people look to their peers to fulfill many of their basic needs. In some ways, a student's peers command more respect even than adults. When student mediators conduct the session with maturity and poise, this positive peer pressure makes parties take the process seriously.
- **Students normalize the conflict resolution process.** Students are accustomed to meeting with disciplinarians or other adults when they are in conflict. This attaches a stigma to conflict resolution. In peer mediation, however, parties sit and talk with other students. It is not unlike regular life. Peer mediators normalize conflict resolution and implicitly communicate that it is okay to talk out problems.

Young people are uniquely suited to mediate their own conflicts, and this accounts in part for peer mediation's effectiveness. Let's now look at how peer mediation programs work.

THE PEER MEDIATION PROGRAM

Peer mediation programs employ a design similar to the community programs that inspired them. After winning support for the program within a school, a diverse group of students is selected to participate in intensive training in mediation and conflict resolution. Training programs run anywhere from twelve to twenty-five hours and teach students the general and specific skills they will use as mediators. Most training programs include age-appropriate lessons on

- Conflict Resolution Theory
- Conflict Resolution Styles
- Negotiation and Problem Solving
- The Mediation Process
- Communication and Active Listening
- Expressing Needs and Feelings
- Giving and Receiving Constructive Criticism
- Winning Trust
- Maintaining Control
- Staying Calm Under Pressure
- Neutrality
- Teamwork
- Note Taking
- Transmitting Information
- Building Agreements
- Critical Thinking
- Writing Agreements
- Confidentiality
- Understanding Bias and Prejudice

I use mediation skills when people start making fun of me and I feel like hitting them but then I stop to think and I know that hitting them is not going to solve the problem.

Middle school mediator

Mediation is a wonderful program and has many great things about it. For example, it resolves conflicts, of any nature, through the disputants' own ideas and words. The peers set a comfortable atmosphere for the disputants and help them to agree to a resolution they can live by. You get an overwhelming feeling when you help a person who needs it.

Middle school mediator

Mediation training is fast-paced and appeals to students of all levels and academic abilities. Teaching methods include lectures, demonstrations, written exercises, games, small- and large-group exercises, and most importantly, role-plays of actual mediation sessions. Students and teachers are often trained together, learning from each other and using their personal experiences with conflict as a reference. At the conclusion of the training, the participants have an understanding of mediation skills and theory that enables them to mediate real disputes.

School administrators who operate mediation programs regard them as an important asset to their disciplinary system. Staff and students decide which types of disputes are appropriate for mediation—usually all disputes except those involving weapons, drugs, or serious physical violence—and in some cases recommend mediation in addition to traditional disciplinary action. Participation in peer mediation is almost always voluntary. Referrals are accepted from any member of the school community by an adult mediation coordinator. This coordinator oversees all aspects of the program, including explaining the mediation process to disputing parties, scheduling mediation sessions, supervising mediators, and following up on mediation cases.

Peer mediation sessions usually take less than one class period, and approximately 90 percent of these sessions result in agreements that are acceptable to all concerned. Those few sessions that do not produce acceptable resolutions are referred back through the usual disciplinary channels. It is important to note that peer mediation programs do not serve only troubled students. The majority of parties in peer mediation sessions are average, relatively well-adjusted students.

THE PEER MEDIATION PROCESS

Although there are variations among mediation programs, most peer mediation sessions in middle and high schools follow a process similar to the one outlined here.

- **Intake.** An adult coordinator meets with students in conflict, answers their questions about peer mediation, and asks if they would like to try the process. If they would, the coordinator selects appropriate student mediators and schedules a session to occur as soon as possible.
- **Joint Session.** A pair of trained student mediators meets with the parties together, beginning the formal mediation process. The joint session includes the following steps:

  1. Setting the Stage: Student mediators describe the process, set the ground rules, answer questions, and confirm the parties' willingness to participate.
  2. Hearing the Story: Each party is given an opportunity to describe the situation without interruption. The mediators listen with concern and summarize each party's presentation.
  3. Defining the Problem: Mediators ask questions of the parties to uncover feelings, clarify differing perceptions, and help the parties understand the situation more fully. Parties can ask each other questions as well.
  4. Generating Alternative Solutions: Mediators ask each party *what they want* in order to resolve the conflict. The parties then brainstorm possible solutions and with the

mediators' assistance, negotiate a settlement to their dispute. This moves the process to the agreement writing phase or to . . . .

- **Optional Private Sessions and Caucuses.** Sometimes peer mediators meet with each party separately while the other waits outside with the coordinator. This is called a *private session*. Private sessions enable mediators to explore issues in depth, and they allow parties to modify positions and share private information while saving face. *Caucuses* refer to discussions between student mediators without either party present.
- **Agreement Writing and Closing.** If the parties have been able to create an agreement to resolve their conflict, the mediators write down the terms, ask parties to sign it, and give each a copy. Student mediators close the session by thanking the parties and offering their services in the future. Parties complete a written evaluation of the process before leaving. Sometimes parties are referred to other school programs, but most often they return to class.
- **Follow-up.** Adult coordinators and/or student mediators check in with parties to make sure that the agreement is working and to offer assistance. This follow-up can take place anywhere from one day to one month after the mediation session.

Mediation helped me see that there is a way to solve my problems without violence. It also prepares me for the future to trust, respect, understand, and listen with an unbiased opinion.

High school mediator

THE BENEFITS OF PEER MEDIATION

Educators who have implemented peer mediation programs attribute many benefits to them. Hundreds of educators, separated by many miles and vastly different circumstances, report similar experiences. Although it is essential to be cautious because most of these claims are unsubstantiated and based on anecdotal evidence, it is likely that peer mediation programs have some degree of positive impact on all of the areas listed below.[12]

- **Peer mediation resolves student conflicts.** The most fundamental benefit of peer mediation is that it effectively resolves student conflicts. Approximately 90 percent of all mediation sessions result in an agreement that satisfies not only the parties, but teachers, administrators, and parents as well. And when students choose to end a conflict in mediation, it is resolved for good. This is because mediators encourage their peers to discuss all issues in dispute, not only the precipitating incidents. Even in cases where written agreements do not result, parties often learn enough about the situation to defuse their conflict.
- **Peer mediation teaches students essential life-skills.**

  The emerging global economy requires workers . . . who can analyze new situations, come up with creative solutions, and take responsibility for decisions relating to the performance of their jobs (Fiske 1991, 21).

  Just as reading and writing are essential skills for leading a productive life, so too are conflict resolution skills. Young people need to be able to communicate effectively, appreciate the consequences of their actions, generate and evaluate alternative solutions

---

[12] A handful of research studies have been conducted on peer mediation, but much of the research has been flawed by a lack of uncontaminated comparison groups, small samples, or unreported sample sizes. Because of the growth of this idea, five years from now the quality and the quantity of research on peer mediation should be much improved.

Being a mediator

makes me feel ecstatic

because I leave the

mediation room

knowing I've helped

resolve a problem

and relieved another

person's mind.

Middle school mediator

to problems, and coexist with people with whom they disagree. Peer mediation teaches these fundamental skills and attitudes to both mediators and parties.

- **Peer mediation builds students' conflict resolution skills through real-life practice.** All skills require practice to master, and peer mediation enables students to develop their conflict resolution skills where it matters most: on real-life conflicts. This makes the skills come alive with a power and relevancy sometimes missing from school. Mediating real conflicts at school also encourages the transfer of these skills to life outside of school. Being a mediator helps students approach conflict in their own lives and in their communities with new perspective and skill. Comments like "My husband and I can't argue without Glenda coming in to help us resolve it," or "What have you done to my son? He listens to me now!" are not uncommon from parents of mediators.

- **Peer mediation motivates students to resolve their conflicts collaboratively.** Peer mediation motivates students to talk things out rather than fight things out. Programs accomplish this in a number of ways. Outreach efforts convey that mediation is the *students'* process. They are in control, the proceedings are confidential, and there is much to gain and little to lose. Students learn from friends who are mediators or who have been parties that mediation works. Disciplinarians and teachers guide students toward peer mediation as an alternative to arbitration. Eventually, a significant percentage of mediation sessions are initiated by the students themselves.

- **Peer mediation deepens the educational impact of school.** Peer mediation uses an essentially extracurricular distraction—interpersonal conflict—as a teaching tool. While mediators model prosocial methods of resolving conflicts, student parties practice resolving their differences using criteria of fairness and mutual benefit rather than brute strength and intimidation. Confronting their adversaries in a nonpunitive forum like mediation encourages students to accept responsibility for their actions.

- **Peer mediation empowers students.** Just as teachers don't teach students algebra by solving problems for them, adults don't teach young people to resolve conflicts by doing it for them. Peer mediation teaches students the skills and then encourages them to resolve their own conflicts in a supervised setting. It also gives students a forum for resolving conflicts that might never have come to the attention of adults. And, although mediation enables students to resolve their own conflicts, it does not exonerate them from responsibility for their behavior. The school disciplinary system remains uncompromised.

- **Peer mediation increases self-esteem.** Self-esteem is increasingly regarded as essential to students' success, and peer mediation enhances self-esteem in a variety of ways. Mediators experience their ability to make a profound difference in the lives of others, and their contribution is valued by adults and students alike. Parties participate in a process that enables them to take charge of their lives and leaves them feeling successful rather than diminished. When a mediation session is successful, every person involved feels like they have done an honorable thing.

- **Peer mediation gives students greater insight.** Students gain many important insights from their involvement with peer mediation. Most significantly, students learn that many conflicts cannot be reduced to right vs. wrong, us vs. them, but are instead the result of misperception, misunderstanding, and legitimately differing needs. Peer mediation also helps students appreciate diversity. Students of different races, classes, ages, and religions communicate and work together to resolve important problems in mediation. At the conclusion of one peer mediation training, a tenth-grade girl explained that when she first saw girls of a different race on the training team, she thought to herself, "I am going to beat those girls up." After the training, she understood how "stupid" this was, and how one "should not judge people by the way they look."

Other insights accrue to students who participate in the mediation program. They learn how to give and accept criticism. They appreciate the necessity of taking risks and making mistakes to learn something new. They understand the power of helping people help themselves. Taken together, this explains why experienced student mediators display an uncommon level of maturity and poise.

■ **Peer mediation expects the best from students.** One perceptive middle school student, commenting on the mediation process, put it succinctly: "Mediation asks us to do the best that we can; this doesn't happen a lot in school." Many school structures—hall passes, seating assignments, disciplinary policies, adult-generated curricula—implicitly assume that students are incapable of acting responsibly. In contrast, the mediation process provides a forum where young people can rise to their highest potential. In this setting, students regularly impress educators with their creative thinking, their willingness to forgive, and their propensity to act upon motives other than self-interest. This is as true for parties as it is for mediators. Mediation challenges students to be the best that they can be, and they usually respond to the challenge.

■ **Peer mediation engages all students, even those considered "at-risk."** Peer mediation enables students to learn from and manage a most vital part of their lives. As such, it stands out against a curriculum that sometimes seems abstract and divorced from their real concerns. Even students who have chronic behavior problems come to appreciate mediation. It provides them with a face-saving way to settle their disputes, and many of these same students excel when they are trained as mediators. Becoming a mediator gives "at-risk" students more than important life-skills—it gives them a badly needed way to contribute to their school.

■ **Peer mediation creates more time for learning.** Although difficult to measure, it appears likely that peer mediation programs create more time for education. The decrease in suspension rates that can follow the implementation of a peer mediation program means students spend more time in class. The timely and lasting resolution of conflicts means that students are less distracted when they are there. Disciplinarians need only spend time on conflicts that involve the violation of a school rule or are beyond the capabilities of student mediators.[13] And with students resolving their conflicts in mediation, teachers spend less of their valuable time disciplining students and more of it teaching them.

■ **Peer mediation is preventive.** Peer mediation is not only used after a conflict has erupted into violence, it works in numerous ways to prevent violent conflict. The development of conflict resolution skills in both mediators and the students-at-large enables them to resolve more of their own conflicts. Outreach efforts encourage students to come to mediation soon after conflicts develop and before they escalate. Even after a conflict

[13] One school reported a 50 percent decrease in office referrals after operating a peer mediation program for one year.

Having a mediation program has changed our school because kids aren't getting in trouble with the administration as much and are solving their problems before they develop into bigger problems.

Middle school mediator

has erupted, mediation can prevent it from leading to more or greater conflicts. Most large-group disputes can be prevented if the interpersonal conflicts at their core are resolved in a timely manner. Peer mediation may also be a boon to other prevention efforts. Many of the factors that contribute to problems like substance abuse and teen pregnancy (low self-esteem, lack of decision-making skills, negative peer pressure) seem to be positively affected by peer mediation programs.

■ **Peer mediation improves school climate.** Peer mediation seems to have a positive impact upon "school climate." The program fosters feelings of belonging, ownership, and control over school life. It decreases the tension that results from unresolved and escalating conflicts. It improves communication among students and between students, teachers, administrators, and parents. It preserves old friendships and begins new ones when former adversaries become friends. All of this helps make schools safer and more productive places.

■ **Peer mediation suits both the psychosocial needs of students and the professional needs of educators.** Young people require an ever-increasing degree of autonomy and control over their lives. At the same time, their immaturity and lack of experience can lead them to make mistakes, behave irresponsibly, and hurt one another. Educators must therefore find a balance between autonomy and supervision. Peer mediation accommodates these competing needs by providing a structure within which students are free to make their own choices. As long as they obey the rules of mediation, students control their own destinies. Young people are happy because they are in control; educators are satisfied because their students are supervised—a win-win solution!

■ **Peer mediation offers a "gender-balancing" method of conflict resolution to schools.** Recent research suggests that males and females conduct their lives in reference to a different moral center. Males seem to decide what is morally appropriate in reference to what has been called "fairness"—abstract concepts of rights, rules, or laws. Women appear to use a standard based more upon "caring"—one's relationship with and responsibility to others. Whereas men might explain that stealing is wrong because people have a right to their possessions, women might explain that stealing is wrong because it harms another person.

American schools, mirroring American society, use predominantly rights-oriented conflict resolution processes (for example, administrators arbitrating according to school rules). It is therefore important for schools to use conflict resolution processes that incorporate the female as well as the male "way of knowing." Student populations are usually 50 percent female, and young people, regardless of their sex, develop their moral framework during the years they attend school. With its emphasis upon relationships, and because it allows students to act according to their own needs, peer mediation represents an important addition to the way schools approach conflict management.

Peer mediation has an unequivocally positive impact on the lives of young people. Teaching students skills to resolve their own conflicts not only improves their lives, but improves the schools in which they learn.

FINAL WORDS

This chapter has introduced something of the background, process, and benefits of peer mediation, including these important points:

- School-based peer mediation has its roots in the community mediation movement.
- Numerous social and educational factors have combined to lead to the rapid growth and acceptance of peer mediation.
- Students have unique advantages over adults when mediating the disputes of other young people.
- Peer mediation programs appear to bring numerous benefits to students, teachers, and schools.

Part II: Implementing a Peer Mediation Program

CHAPTER 4

Securing Initial Support

In the initial stage of program implementation, your goal is to answer two basic questions. Bear these questions in mind as you read this chapter:

- Is there enough interpersonal student conflict in your school to justify implementing a peer mediation program?
- Will administrators, teachers, parents, and students support this program?

First, let's step back and explore the process of school change.

SCHOOL CHANGE [14]

Student conflict is not a special event in schools. Conflicts occur every day, and resolving these conflicts can involve every level of the school community, from students to the highest administrators. Because of this, peer mediation cannot be a special "add-on" program in a school—it must be fully integrated into its day-to-day operation. Peer mediation programs only reach their potential if the *institution,* as well as individuals within it, changes.

This is a tall order. Changing any institution is a difficult and time-consuming process. But schools are particularly resistant to change. Three characteristics of schools frustrate even the most experienced institutional change agents. The first is that the purpose of school is amorphous. Although educators agree that schools should promote "learning," learning is a conceptual goal with varied means and with ends that are difficult to measure except in the most limited form. Despite well-crafted mission statements, the purpose of a school is open to as many interpretations as there are people who care about that school.

A second reason why schools are difficult to change is that they are so-called loosely coupled systems. In this type of organization, change in one part of the system does not necessarily lead to changes in other parts. Each worker has a great deal of control over the way the system's "services" are delivered. A school's teachers are the most obvious example of this: teachers control discipline, grades, the tenor of interaction within the classroom, the way curriculum is delivered, and sometimes even the content of the curriculum itself. As one teacher summed it up, "The administration can hand down policies from above, but as soon as teachers shut the classroom door, we do what we want" (Sarason 1990).[15] In this environment, it is challenging to make any systemwide change.

---

[14] The presentation in this section is heavily indebted to the work of Seymour Sarason, especially *The Predictable Failure of Educational Reform: Can We Change Course Before It's Too Late?* (San Francisco: Jossey-Bass, 1990).

[15] Originally quoted in Edward Pauly's study *The Classroom Crucible* (New York: Basic Books, 1991). Although this makes schoolwide change very difficult, it also represents one of the strengths of schools. Students learn differently, and by offering a wide range of teaching approaches, schools ensure that students may find at least a few teachers who meet their needs.

A third obstacle to school change is the fact that schools are patterned after an out-dated industrial model of organization popular in the late nineteenth century. The characteristics of this type of organization—centralized authority, standardization, the reduction of activities to simple and repetitive tasks—do not even make for effective factories, much less effective schools. Although some schools have changed, most are still administered as rigid hierarchies. One consequence of this is that people within schools often feel like they have very little power to affect the things that are important to them. Administrators answer to school boards, teachers answer to administrators, students answer to teachers, and no one feels like they control their own destiny.

These three characteristics of schools—an amorphous purpose, a loosely coupled structure, and a hierarchical method of administration—create seemingly insurmountable obstacles for schoolwide change efforts. They also help to explain why so many efforts fail. Some of the most experienced and skillful educators agree with Seymour Sarason, himself a school change expert with decades of experience, when he writes, "The characteristics, traditions, and organizational dynamics of school systems are more or less lethal obstacles to achieving even modest, narrow goals" (Sarason 1990, p. 12).

It must be stressed that in an institution in which members often feel like they do not have enough power, peer mediation's goal is to *empower*. And empower not just anybody; although everyone in the school gains, peer mediation's most direct beneficiaries are the bottom feeders on the power food chain—the students! This indicates how radical peer mediation can appear. A great deal of structural and attitudinal reorientation must take place in traditional schools if this program is to succeed.

Six Principles of School Change

Six principles of institutional change can guide you through this difficult process.[16] Keeping them in mind as you implement the peer mediation program will increase your chances of success.

1. **Start with the needs of the school.** The first question to ask when considering peer mediation or any other program is: Does my school need this program? This may seem obvious, but surprisingly, people often forget to ask. The case can be made that since conflict is normal, all schools will benefit from peer mediation. But not all schools have a level of conflict among their students that warrants the investment of time and energy needed to make a peer mediation program work. Most do, but some do not. The only way to find out is to explore the needs of your school.

2. **Win the support of school leaders.** Power—the ability to "exercise control over or influence others"—is distributed in most schools in a typical organizational pyramid. Only if initiators of peer mediation programs win the support of those with the most power in the school will their efforts bear fruit. Research has shown that support of the principal in particular is key to any successful change effort. This support cannot be only in the abstract—school leaders must be willing to take the controversial actions necessary to make your efforts succeed. Staff are also more likely to

---

[16] These guidelines are written from the perspective of someone who works within a school, but who is not the administrative leader of it.

become involved in and support programs to which their leaders are committed. Some peer mediation trainers feel that this support is so important that they will not even work with a school unless the principal participates in the training program.

3. **Encourage the participation of all members of the school community.** When asked if his staff was supportive of the peer mediation program, one principal replied, "Yes, the teachers have been informed of my plans." Having the support of school leaders is one thing. Initiating a program through top-down decisions is another. Ultimately, the success of a mediation program results from hundreds of individual decisions made by teachers and students, not from the directives of one or two administrators. The best way to win such broad-based support is to get people involved from the start; to paraphrase Sarason, anyone who will be affected by the program should stand in some relationship to its formulation and implementation (Sarason 1990, p. 24). Though support from the top is essential, if a school is to change, it will be changed by the bulk of people who work and learn in it.

4. **Work with the school as a system.** Educational reform cannot be piecemeal; it has to work with the school as a system. You must ask whether peer mediation fits into the overall mission of your school. Or conversely, what changes must be made in the school—pedagogically, structurally, in curriculum, in administration—to reinforce and deepen the impact of the lessons taught by peer mediation? Peer mediation programs work best in schools that have already or are in the process of "reinventing" themselves—schools where administrators, staff, and students are encouraged to work together; schools where the disciplinary system is fair and consistent, where diversity is appreciated, and where students and teachers feel safe. As an isolated quick-fix within a largely dysfunctional school, peer mediation will have only a limited impact.

5. **Think long term.** Making any change in schools requires consistent effort over an extended period of time, and institutionalizing a peer mediation program is no exception. It takes time for teachers and students to have an opportunity to utilize a program, time to generate and publicize the program's successes, time to develop trust between the program and the individuals it serves. Program initiators set themselves up for failure by promising glowing results for the first year of the program. They need to have the patience and commitment to keep at it while peer mediation slowly gains acceptance. Try to arrange for funding, training, staffing, space, and administrative support for as long into the future as possible.

6. **Understand that school change is an ongoing process.** Any school reform effort is initiated to resolve a perceived problem. Perhaps the drop-out rate is high, or teachers are disaffected, or student conflict is an issue. The solution to one problem, however, invariably leads to the creation of others. This is especially true of peer mediation, a program that is very effective at resolving interpersonal conflicts but that creates as many conflicts as it solves when first implemented. School change must be approached as an ongoing process rather than as the simple task of solving the original problem. Because there is no end point when all problems are solved, processes for evaluation and reevaluation must be built in from the start.

With these fundamentals to guide you, the first step in securing support for a peer mediation program is to present the concept to people within the school. Let's now consider how to do just that.

PRESENTING PEER MEDIATION

Stereotypes of educators abound, but they are as diverse a group of people as any in the United States. One generalization that can be made with some certainty, however, is that educators have a healthy skepticism about "new" ideas. Experienced educators have seen so many educational trends come and go, have been presented with so much advice about how to do their increasingly difficult jobs, that they can become jaded. As each educational fad is replaced by the next, teachers must return to the classroom to face their students on their own.

At first glance, peer mediation seems like yet another crazy idea, one that contradicts some educators' beliefs about the responsibilities of teachers and the capabilities of students. Many educators have long assumed that punishing students who misbehave is the most effective way to prevent them from misbehaving again. Authority *over* students is seen as key. But peer mediation encourages a different approach to changing student behavior, one that gives power back to students rather than wielding it over them. In this light, peer mediation may appear naive and ill-conceived.

Asking educators to support peer mediation may therefore involve asking them to change. And as we have just discussed, change does not come easily. The beliefs and habits of experienced teachers are forged through years of formal education and on-the-job problem solving. To modify their professional practice, teachers may have to "unlearn" as much as they have to learn.

Keep this in mind as you approach the challenging task of securing support for a peer mediation effort. Your goal is more than merely to inform educators about the program; you want to encourage them to *work with you* to make student mediation a success. The following six guidelines will help you present the program most effectively:

1. **Elicit their needs and interests.** School staff members will make peer mediation a success only if they perceive the program to be in their own interests or in the interests of their students. The place to begin is therefore this: You must ask educators what they need. And then you must listen.

    What problems have teachers had with student conflict? What might their goals be if they were to set about resolving those problems? Do they want to teach students conflict resolution life-skills; do they want to reduce fighting and suspension rates; do they want to increase students' sense of ownership of the school? Would instituting a peer mediation program be an appropriate step toward meeting their goals?

    Strive to engage people in resolving the problems that they themselves identify. If during this process you find that peer mediation is not the right program, that is for the best. If, however, you find that peer mediation is appropriate, that is even better. The program will be more effective both because it is consistent with the educators' goals, and because people are more committed to programs that they have helped to create.

    Sometimes individual staff members do not easily perceive the systemic problems connected with student conflict. You can make them aware of such problems by providing data from schoolwide indicators like the number of office referrals, fights, suspensions, and dropouts. Or, analyze a specific student conflict with which the staff is familiar. By dissecting that conflict, you can illuminate larger trends within the

Peer mediation has

relieved a lot of the

pressure the principal

and faculty had to

deal with before the

program began.

High school mediator

school. Discussing how the institution might have reacted differently to the conflict is one way to demonstrate how peer mediation might be of use.

2. **Be an effective messenger: apply mediation skills from the start.** People focus on the messenger as much as on the message. You should therefore model the approach to problem solving that you are asking your colleagues to support. Be honest with them and encourage them to be honest in return. Listen to their concerns, don't back down from the tough questions, and admit when you don't know the answer. Approach the process as an opportunity for collaborative problem solving and try not to be defensive or take criticism personally. Be patient. If you approach educators with the same respect and attention that mediators approach parties, it will go a long way toward convincing them of the merits of the program. *You* are one of your biggest assets in the effort to win support for peer mediation.

3. **Stress the benefits of student mediation.** When building support for peer mediation, it is obviously important to stress the benefits associated with it. (See Chapter 3 for a detailed list of these benefits.) Highlight the educational value of the program, the fact that it resolves conflicts permanently, the fact that it requires very little teacher time once it is operational, and the fact that it builds children's self-esteem. Ideally, the benefits you attribute to peer mediation will help the educators with whom you are working to meet their own goals.

4. **Discuss the program's limitations and difficulties.** Peer mediation is an effective program, but it is not a panacea for the problems faced by educators. It is expressly *because* peer mediation programs are challenging to implement that you require their support. You and the program will be taken more seriously when you are straightforward about the work involved in making peer mediation a success. And by "testing" your audience in this way, you will get a better sense of the level of support that you have.

5. **Go slowly.** It is best not to rush things when building support for a peer mediation program. This is especially important to keep in mind when a school crisis, such as a shooting or a large-group conflict, has generated a great deal of interest in peer mediation. Although such incidents provide an entree for this program, they do not automatically generate the necessary support to make it work. Educators are used to seeing programs come and go, and the level of support required for peer mediation implementation usually takes time to develop. When possible, err on the side of caution and take your time.

6. **Show as well as tell.** One of the best ways to generate interest, support, and understanding of peer mediation is to have people observe a demonstration mediation session. If possible, invite a coordinator and student mediators from another school to help with your presentation. Student mediators "sell" peer mediation better than adults ever can. They answer questions—even questions designed to stump them— with a maturity and insight that is always impressive. Using students also immediately puts to rest one of educators' most basic concerns: Do students really have the ability to mediate conflicts? If you do not have access to student mediators, use a video. With peer mediation, seeing really is believing.

Addressing Ten Common Concerns About Peer Mediation

As you present peer mediation to members of your school community, you will likely hear every conceivable objection to it. Some objections will be theoretical and concern the nature of education, the psychological capability of students, or the appropriate use of personal and political power. Others will have to do with practical, programmatic issues like efficacy, scheduling, and the potential for violence during mediation.

Regardless of their focus, welcome these objections. The program initiator's job is to encourage people to express their concerns about peer mediation forthrightly. Only concerns that are expressed can be effectively addressed, and only after people's fears are calmed is it possible for them to become active supporters of the program.

If handled correctly, even objections that are offered to invalidate this concept will have the opposite effect. Exploring peer mediation's potential limitations simultaneously clarifies the program's strengths. Though not without its faults, it is difficult to deny that peer mediation meets a pressing need in most schools and teaches young people essential skills in the process. Understanding the program's shortcomings only helps people utilize it most appropriately.

Remember that implementing a peer mediation program should be a personal exploration as well. Over the weeks and months that you are working on the program, you may wrestle with these same concerns yourself. Below are ten of the most common objections to peer mediation, presented in the first person, followed by a synopsis of a response.

Objection 1. Peer mediation compromises my ability to punish students for their actions. Peer mediation represents an *addition* to an educator's conflict resolution toolbox. It takes nothing away from what educators already do to address students' inappropriate behavior. Students can still be suspended, given detention, or given any other sanction that has been effective. Educators also have ultimate control over which conflicts go to mediation.

Objection 2. Peer mediation minimizes my responsibility to tell students when their behavior is unacceptable. This concern is related to the first. Educators rightfully feel a responsibility to: a) inform students when their behavior is inappropriate, and b) help them learn prosocial ways of resolving their conflicts. Some fear that peer mediation will prevent them from doing this. Two students who get into a physical confrontation over an alleged rumor, for example, may very well be able to work out the issues in a peer mediation session. But without someone telling them that fighting is wrong, they may behave the same way the next time someone spreads a rumor about them.

The key here is to understand the difference between the disciplinary and the mediation function in a school. It is important for educators to reward and sometimes to punish students for the way that they behave. But however effective this is at discouraging antisocial behavior, it *does not* help students resolve their conflicts. An administrator can inform two students that fighting is unacceptable, but this alone will not reconcile their differences. Schools need to provide ways for students to talk out their conflicts.

One of peer mediation's strengths is that it teaches students prosocial approaches to conflict resolution. The mediation process confronts students with the consequences of their actions in a way that is essentially educational. It enables students to discover for themselves that, in the long run, fighting and violence are almost always ineffective.

Objection 3. Given the state of the world, I would rather teach students to be uncompromising advocates for their rights than to be "compromising" mediators. This concern springs from a fear that training students to be mediators will leave them too "soft": too willing to sacrifice what they deserve to reach agreements and unappreciative of the need to work tirelessly for what they believe is right. Organizers and advocates create

From *Students Resolving Conflict: Peer Mediation in Schools*, published by GoodYearBooks. Copyright © 1995 Richard Cohen.

Ever since I've been

a mediator I've been

in less fights. I've

learned to solve

other problems, not

just fighting. The

program teaches you

how to listen and

understand the other

person and to know

where they are com-

ing from.

Middle school mediator

social change, these educators assert, not mediators.

Of course, it is important to teach students to be advocates for what they believe. Assertiveness is an essential part of interpersonal—and all—problem solving. But this does not minimize the *equally* important need to train students to work collaboratively with others to resolve conflicts. Educators should inform students that not all conflicts are appropriate for mediation. But for the many that are—and to teach students how to work together to resolve those conflicts—peer mediation is a wonderfully effective program.

Objection 4. Because peer mediation takes time away from academics, school is not the appropriate place for teaching students such social skills. Some educators are justifiably frustrated that each year they seem to have less time to work on the academic curriculum with their students. They prefer not to spend school time on seemingly extraneous programs like peer mediation.

It is easy to sympathize with this sentiment. In an ideal world, young people would come to school possessing age-appropriate social skills that would make peer mediation less relevant. But in this less than ideal world, deficiencies in students' social skills, combined with the effects of a host of other social problems, hamper the educator's ability to teach academics no matter how much time is allotted for it. As stated by Selman and Glidden: "Like it or not, teachers, principals, and other educational professionals invest as much energy every day in fostering children's social development as they do in furthering their academic progress" (Selman and Glidden 1987, 18).

Mediating student conflicts does take time. But by resolving conflicts effectively and efficiently, it potentially provides *more* time for academics. Classes will not be disrupted by conflicts; students will be able to focus on their work and not be distracted by interpersonal tensions; fights that do occur will be resolved rather than persist to disrupt the educational process again. Schools can also schedule mediation sessions to minimize interference with academics and train enough mediators so that students do not miss classes regularly.

We can bemoan the fact that educators have to teach students social skills, but there currently appears to be no other choice. Programs like peer mediation are becoming essential to making schools work.

Objection 5. Young people cannot mediate as effectively as adults. Interpersonal conflicts, even those among children, sometimes involve psychological subtleties beyond the capabilities of student mediators. This has led to a concern that peer mediation short-changes students by using other students rather than adults to mediate their conflicts.

Indeed, although young people may not mediate with the sophistication of adults (in fact, many do), they mediate with an age-appropriate level of psychological insight. This is all that is necessary to resolve the large majority of student interpersonal conflicts, conflicts that concern issues like teasing, exclusion from a group, rumors, boyfriend or girlfriend difficulties, and even issues like racism. The coordinator can also ensure that those conflicts that require adult intervention receive it.

In addition, mediation is a "forgiving" process in that the process itself "forgives" the mistakes of mediators. When people in conflict come together with the intention of creating their own solution, and when they are accompanied by trained peers doing their best to help them, things invariably work out. Many program coordinators—in both school-based and community programs—have observed peer mediators making what appear to be ruinous mistakes, only to see the session move forward and result in an agreement satisfactory to all parties.

Objection 6. What if students do not follow the agreements they create in mediation? Educators are often initially concerned that agreements created in mediation will break down, leaving students worse off than before mediation. Mediators are trained, however, that it is better not to come up with an agreement than to let the parties create one that will not work. Because of this, and because the agreements are voluntarily created by the parties themselves, 90 percent of school mediation agreements nationwide hold up over time. If for some reason agreements do break down, the school has all of its other resources available to resolve the situation (including, perhaps, a second mediation session).[17]

Objection 7. Peer mediation is just a fad that will be soon forgotten. Because conflict is an unavoidable part of living, and the amount of conflict in modern lives will only increase, it seems clear that this work will continue. Peer mediation and conflict resolution programs teach practical knowledge and skills that help students manage conflict more effectively. Although the forms educators develop to teach conflict resolution skills may change, such instruction will never disappear completely. Peer mediation, or at least the lessons that are its foundation, is here to stay.

Objection 8. Peer mediation is fine, but I would prefer to teach all of our students to be mediators, not just a select few. Teaching conflict resolution skills to all students within a school is an important objective, and this should ideally be part of the implementation process in any peer mediation program. But the fact remains that students will continue to become involved in interpersonal conflicts, and except in elementary schools, it is difficult to mediate these conflicts during class time. Student conflicts demand an extracurricular response, and peer mediation has proven to be one of the most effective.

Objection 9. What if students misuse the process? The concern here is that students will take advantage of peer mediation in a number of ways. Perhaps they will make up fights to get out of class. Perhaps they will not be truthful in the session. Perhaps they will create agreements just to end the mediation and then fight after the session is over.

Peer mediation is a very difficult process to abuse, however. If student parties are not committed to the process, this quickly becomes clear to the coordinator in the intake interview or to the mediators during the session. Even if students begin with the intention of misusing peer mediation, they often discover that their interests are best served by trying to get what they want *through* the process. As for lying, students have no more reason to lie in mediation than in any disciplinary forum. In fact, because mediation is confidential (except for life-threatening information), young people may be more likely to tell the truth in mediation. Student abuse of peer mediation is a minor problem.

Objection 10. What if a fight breaks out during the session? Some educators are concerned that student parties, alone but for the company of their peers, will become angry and begin fighting with each other during a session. But this has not been a problem, in large part because of the numerous preventive measures that are built into the process: cooling-off periods before sessions are held, rules about violence, choosing mediators who will be respected, and so on. In addition, there is usually an adult either in the

A group of my friends were in a huge fight over one boy. Luckily I was able to hold a mediation at my house with the six girls and boy and we were able to come up with an agreement. I felt so good and responsible for this. They all come to me now for advice and help.

High school mediator

---

[17] It is worth noting here that negative consequences for breaking an agreement, typical of the "contracting" approach to discipline popularized by William Glasser in *Control Theory in the Classroom* (New York: HarperCollins, 1986), are not included in peer mediated agreements. ("If Arthur continues to call Greg names, he will have three days detention.")

room or right outside during the sessions. If anything, students usually become impressively calm, considered, and even respectful of each other during the course of most mediation sessions.

FINDING YOUR AUDIENCE

Once you are ready to present peer mediation, to whom should you present it? Although your goal is to assemble as broad a group of supporters as possible, where to begin will differ in every school and will be determined by a number of factors.

The first factor is you. As the program initiator, you are key to making this initial phase a success. Assess your position, your contacts, and the school culture; then use this information to your best advantage. A teacher might speak to trusted peers, a principal might describe the program at a meeting of department heads, a community mediation coordinator might approach a school committee member. Begin with those to whom you have the most access.

A second factor involves determining who will be most receptive to this idea. Has a counselor expressed interest in conflict resolution in the past? Is there a faculty committee exploring multicultural education that might see peer mediation as a means to further its goals? Perhaps a member of the school committee has shown a special interest in issues of violence in the schools. By starting with those who might be predisposed to the idea of peer mediation, you quickly expand your core group of supporters.

A final factor has to do with the way that decisions are made within the school. If your school has a traditional structure, it usually makes sense to approach your immediate superior (department head, house master, cluster leader, principal, superintendent) first. If your school practices school-based management, then approach the appropriate committee. Remember too that looking at an organizational chart may not reveal who is powerful within the school. Winning over a few well-respected teachers or administrators can influence many others to support your efforts.

Just as important as finding the right people is not overlooking the "wrong" ones. Avoid making enemies within the system at all costs. The disciplinarian who feels threatened by the program, the school committee member whose ego is bruised by not being invited to a meeting, the vocal parent who favors another idea—all can make your life miserable. Peer mediation advocates need to use their skills from the start to promote the program without alienating anyone.

Each constituency within the school has unique concerns. As you work to win the support of each of them, keep in mind the special considerations that follow.

Administrators

The importance of administrative support for the long-term viability of peer mediation programs cannot be overemphasized. Too often, initiators of school mediation programs have minimized the principal's role in implementing this program. Perhaps they know that they do not have the principal's support; perhaps they fear that they will not receive it if they ask. In either case, they start a program without the administration's blessings. "If we can just get this program going," they convince themselves, "we can demonstrate the worth of peer mediation and win the principal's support."

This approach has little chance of long-term success. At the conclusion of the first year, program statistics will lack the undeniable glow necessary to convince skeptical administrators. (Mediation programs that have limited institutional support are consistently underutilized.) Without the assistance of the principal to overcome attitudinal and structural resistance in the system, many pioneering mediation efforts fail after their first year.

Even principals who have "no serious objections" to peer mediation may in the end become impediments to its success. There is a difference between casually supporting this idea in the abstract and taking the controversial actions that will turn it into a reality. Some of the tough decisions that administrators inevitably face when starting a mediation program are

- allowing students and teachers to miss classes to attend the mediation training and, later, to mediate;
- finding and funding class coverage for teachers who participate in mediation training;
- freeing a staff person, whether part time or full time, to coordinate the mediation program;
- locating a private space where mediation sessions can be held. (Space in many schools is at a premium);
- funding training and other programmatic needs;
- educating staff, superintendents, school committee members, and others responsible for the continued financial and philosophic support of the program.

These are difficult decisions for any administrator to make. Given schools' limited resources, even those most committed to mediation are likely to flinch. But it is certain that without the support of key administrators, these decisions will not be made in favor of the mediation program. You can do a number of things to win this support:

- Administrators are ultimately responsible for what goes on in their schools, and student discipline is one of the few areas in which they provide direct services to students. It is therefore vital that administrators understand and feel comfortable with the program. Involving them in the design and implementation of this effort from its earliest stages will mean a great deal to its ultimate success.
- Ask principals and other administrative leaders to support the program with actions as well as words. They should use the mediation process in their own offices in addition to encouraging its use in classrooms and mediation sessions. One principal even participated in a mediation session as a party with a group of students. This delivered a clear message to the school community that peer mediation was an important part of school life.

I used my mediation skills one day out of school when we were on April vacation and I had gotten into a conflict with another kid and within a two-minute period this little voice popped in my head and said why don't you try and talk about it. We talked and it was just a big misunderstanding. It was a lot better talking than fighting with my friend.

Middle school mediator

Administrators in Charge of Discipline[18]

Mediation has changed my school. When I talk to my classmates who have been involved in a disagreement, they often seem excited to attend a mediation session. This is a major variation from the postfight attitudes these students had before the mediation program was enacted.

High school mediator

Administrators in charge of discipline have an unmatched level of control over a school's approach to conflict management. They spend a good portion of their working day, sometimes as much as two-thirds of it, handling student conflict. (One assistant principal in a large middle school estimated she intervened in twenty interpersonal conflicts every day.) By redirecting the conflicts that come to their offices, these individuals can ensure that peer mediation will have a profound impact upon the school. If disciplinarians do not refer students to mediation, many peer mediators will be out of work. A cooperative and trusting relationship between mediation program and school disciplinarian is therefore crucial to your success.

When you present peer mediation to disciplinarians to secure their support, stress the following three things:

1. Peer mediation programs do not compromise disciplinary authority in any way; they are an additional tool for the disciplinarian. Disciplinarians can still administer punishment, and they can use any other approach to discipline that they have found to be effective. Disciplinarians recommend mediation at their discretion, and it can even be used *in addition* to traditional procedures.

2. Some disciplinarians fear that the implementation of a peer mediation program will reduce their personal effectiveness. A student might resolve a conflict through mediation, for example, and then end up in the assistant principal's office a month later for fighting. If the disciplinarian is uninformed about the previous incident, it puts him or her at a disadvantage in handling the situation. To prevent this from occurring, express your desire to work closely with disciplinarians to create a process with which they are comfortable.

3. Make sure that disciplinarians do not experience the peer mediation effort as a personal attack. Schools still need disciplinarians. Many situations—violations of school rules; conflicts involving drugs, weapons, or serious violence; conflicts that cannot be resolved through mediation—require disciplinary attention. Peer mediation is effective in part because the disciplinarian is waiting in the wings if students cannot create their own agreement. A fair and consistent disciplinary policy benefits everyone in the school, including the peer mediators.

Once they feel comfortable with the peer mediation concept, most disciplinarians are happy to refer student conflicts to the program. Doing so saves them time (which they can devote to other important responsibilities) while it teaches students essential skills. Invite disciplinarians to participate in the mediation training to give them firsthand experience of the mediation process and the proficiency of student mediators.

Two final thoughts: Be advised that some disciplinarians enjoy and are quite skilled at helping students resolve conflicts. Behind more than one peer mediation program with a small caseload is a disciplinarian hesitant to relinquish this rewarding part of the job.

---

[18]*Administrator in charge of discipline* is preferable to *disciplinarian*, which has fallen out of favor in schools. For ease of reading, however, the term *disciplinarian* is used here.

Note too that the people who do the most conflict resolution in schools might not be disciplinarians at all. They may be teachers, coaches, or counselors whom students seek out first when they are in conflict. It is important to win the support of these individuals because they can make a significant contribution to the program's success.

Teachers

Peer mediation programs cannot thrive without the blessing of teachers. As Fullan and Hargreaves have written, "Educational change that does not involve and is not supported by the teacher usually ends up as change for the worse, or as no real change at all" (Fullan and Hargreaves 1991, p. 14). Mediation program initiators therefore need to make teachers allies and active contributors to the program's success.

Teachers have three primary concerns about peer mediation:

1. Many teachers are concerned about the impact peer mediation will have upon academics. As it is, too many programs eat into the time students spend in class. You should therefore work closely with teachers to minimize this problem whenever possible. Some ideas include:

- schedule mediations during nonacademic time;
- require that mediators keep up with their schoolwork or they will not be allowed to mediate;
- pull mediators out of classes only if they have the teacher's permission;
- pull mediators out of elective classes and not core curricular classes;
- pull mediators out of only those classes in which they are doing well; and
- do not pull mediators out of any class more than once a month.

In addition, stress the positive impact that peer mediation can have upon academics:

- Conflicts are permanently resolved and so do not continue to distract students during class.
- Students learn essential life-skills, such as listening and note taking, that help them in class and beyond.
- Peer mediation prevents disruptive conflicts from occurring.
- Students' self-esteem is increased, leading to more risk taking and potentially to better academic performance.
- Peer mediation makes some students more invested in school, and this can have a positive effect upon their class work.

After you explain how peer mediation furthers the educational mission of the school, teachers should be willing to support it.

2. Some teachers feel that their school's disciplinary policy is ineffective. Students sent out of class to be disciplined return sooner than these teachers feel is appropriate and behave no better than before they left. These teachers fear that with the implementation of a peer mediation program, students will not even receive the inadequate discipline currently in effect—they will just be asked to talk to each

I learned from peer mediation that I can work together with others and I can concentrate.

Middle school mediator

other. It is important to stress that mediation does not compromise discipline policy, and students who violate school rules will receive consequences as always. Concerns about the way that disciplinary policy is enforced, though potentially valid, are a separate issue from peer mediation. A school's conflict management system is only made more effective with the addition of a peer mediation program.

3. Some teachers fear they will be forced to mediate conflicts with their students. This sentiment reveals a misunderstanding about the mediation process that you can easily clarify. *No one—especially a teacher—is ever forced to participate in mediation against his or her will.* Teachers' tendency to fear that mediation will be used against them, however, leads some program initiators to focus on student-student conflicts when first implementing this program. Whenever possible, work extensively with the teachers before students are ever trained. In this way, they become comfortable with mediation and can teach by example by using the process to resolve their own conflicts. Many programs eventually facilitate teacher-student and even teacher-teacher mediations with great success.

Counselors and Social Workers

At first glance, mediation and counseling appear to be similar processes. Both mediators and counselors help participants resolve their own problems; both processes use verbal communication as a method for achieving this goal; in both, people participate voluntarily and the information disclosed is held in confidence. But mediation and counseling are different in form as well as function. It is important for counselors to understand this difference.

Mediation is a *short-term, interpersonal* process. Mediators help "parties" negotiate the terms of a mutually satisfactory agreement. Although they explore the feelings and personal histories of the parties, they do this only to the extent necessary to resolve the conflict at hand. When that conflict is resolved, or when it becomes clear that the conflict cannot be resolved through mediation, the mediation process is concluded.

Counseling, on the other hand, is a *long-term, intrapersonal* process. Counselors help "clients" understand themselves and improve their ability to meet their needs. They accomplish this using a wide range of techniques: discussion, role-playing, free-association, journal writing, painting, body work, dream analysis, and so on. There is no limitation upon how deeply counselors will explore the feelings and personal histories of their clients; helping clients understand and even re-experience their histories is a central goal of the process. Counselors, unlike mediators, have no clear and consistent indicator of the success of their work, and no product results from its conclusion. Counselors meet with clients for months and sometimes years.

To illustrate the differences between these two processes, suppose that one student, Sandro, bothers his friend Ricky to the point that a near physical fight ensues. In mediation, Ricky and Sandro would both share their versions of events, talk about their history as friends, and consider what they wanted for the future. Sandro might apologize for teasing Ricky, and together they might develop a signal to indicate to each other when they don't want to "fool around." Approximately thirty minutes after mediation began, the boys would sign an agreement, shake hands, and be on their way.

A counselor would handle this situation differently. He or she might arrange to work with Sandro independently with the intention of addressing issues in his personal life that led to his behavior. In their sessions, the counselor would encourage Sandro to open up and honestly discuss his thoughts and feelings. Let's suppose that Sandro's brother, to whom he was very close, recently died. Sandro and the counselor would explore this and other issues over the course of many sessions. Ideally, in the end he would come to accept the loss of his brother and learn to meet his needs in more socially acceptable ways.

Mediators are not insensitive to the intrapersonal dimensions of student problems. To the extent that Sandro's difficulties at home were relevant to his conflict with Ricky, they would discuss them in the session. But if Sandro needed more intensive assistance with his problems, mediators would refer him to a counselor.

When counselors do not understand the goals of mediation, they assume that the process does not go "deep" enough into students' emotional lives to be effective. Mediation is not counseling, and it does not replace counseling. If anything, the two complement each other. Peer mediators can refer students that need help to counselors, and counselors can refer students in conflict to peer mediation.[19]

Parents

Because of their ability to reinforce at home what children learn in school, parents are an important, but often underutilized resource for peer mediation programs. Most of the concerns typical of parents have already been addressed. A few, though, deserve mention:

- Considerable numbers of parents express concern for the safety of their children during mediation sessions. Although there is some risk, there have been no reports of harm befalling mediators or parties after hundreds of thousands of peer mediation sessions nationwide. An adult supervisor is always either in the room or nearby when a session is underway, and potentially dangerous conflicts are not sent to mediation. A related concern is that student parties will be out to "get" the mediator after the session is over. Because peer mediators don't make judgments, however, it would be unusual for parties to feel hostility toward them. Experience has shown that parties sincerely appreciate the assistance of peer mediators, showing them respect, gratitude, and even friendship long after the session is over.
- A second concern of parents regards the program's impact upon academics. As we've seen, one goal of the peer mediation program is to provide *more* time for academics. Interpersonal conflicts are swiftly and effectively resolved using the process, and students learn skills that help them in class. In addition, the program makes every effort to minimize its impact upon academics by mediating during nonacademic time, rotating mediators, and requiring that mediators keep up with their schoolwork.

Once parents understand and feel comfortable with peer mediation, they are among its most devoted supporters. Some programs include parents in training sessions or conduct separate training programs for parents and then employ them as coordinators and/or mediators. A few schools have even begun to offer parent-child and parent-teacher mediation.

Being a mediator has helped me to be more open to other people's problems. When you see a situation from all around, it's easy to see where attitudes develop and where they could lead. When the disputants lay their problem on the table they're saying we trust you. That's a great feeling. Our peers know that any one of us will talk to them even without an appointment.

High school mediator

---

[19] As the mediation field develops, its approach to interpersonal work is being integrated into other helping professions. Counseling is one of them. When counselors meet with two individuals on a short-term basis, their work can be very similar to mediation.

Students

Winning the support of students for a peer mediation effort is not difficult. After viewing a mediation demonstration, 20 to 30 percent will express interest in becoming mediators. Students' initial questions often have to do with logistical matters: Where and when will mediations take place? Why should students try mediation? How will mediators be chosen? Will being a mediator affect their schoolwork? These questions are easily answered.

One of the primary purposes of peer mediation is to encourage students to take responsibility for their lives. You should therefore involve students as partners in planning and implementing this program from the start. (One middle school even utilized a student-run hiring committee to interview potential training sources.) Not only will they learn a great deal, but the program will benefit from their ideas and enthusiasm.

TOOLS FOR NEEDS ASSESSMENT AND SUPPORT BUILDING

You can accomplish a great deal of the initial work of building support for peer mediation through informal, one-to-one discussions. In addition to these discussions, there are a number of tools you can use to introduce peer mediation to groups. Most program initiators use some form of all of them. Three of the most common are explained here.

Questionnaires and Surveys

Program initiators ask staff and students to respond to surveys that can help to

- introduce peer mediation;
- determine whether there is a perceived need for peer mediation;
- provide quick feedback regarding how much support exists for peer mediation;
- provide a focus for discussion during meetings;
- provide information that can help you design the program to meet your school's needs;
- demonstrate to respondents that you are interested in their needs and invite their participation; and
- build support for peer mediation.

These surveys usually focus on student conflict, with questions about the frequency, the severity, the issues, and the impact of student conflict on school life. (See pages 220–221 for an example.) An alternative focus might be on teachers' beliefs about discipline. All surveys should include a brief description of the peer mediation process as well as questions that enable you to gauge potential support for this program. The results of the surveys are tabulated, reported to respondents in meetings, and used to inform the implementation effort.

Meetings and Presentations

Introductory presentations are another essential part of the process of generating support for peer mediation. Effective presentations provide people with an opportunity to consider their needs, witness the mediation process firsthand, voice their concerns about peer mediation, and offer suggestions about the design of the program.

Presentations should be made in accordance with the guidelines outlined earlier. Consider offering them to a variety of groups, including:

> PTA
> School board/school committee
> Teachers (at staff meetings or in-service days)
> Student council/senate
> Administrative staff
> Student assemblies and classes
> Cluster leaders/house masters
> Judicial or "fairness" committees
> Human relations committees
> Teachers' union
> Racial harmony task forces

Although ideally the audience at your presentations should be attending voluntarily, this is not always possible in the school setting. Unless you are a dynamic speaker, presenting peer mediation to a roomful of educators who would rather not be there can be demoralizing. Try to minimize your expectations. If after your presentation, 5 percent of the audience want to become involved with the program, 50 percent think that peer mediation is a good idea, 30 percent aren't sure what they think, and the remainder are sure you are a fool, then the response has been typical! Try to offer short, overview presentations at mandatory meetings and in-depth presentations for those who are sincerely interested in the program. The former at least minimally informs everyone about peer mediation and gets people involved who otherwise might not have heard about the program. The latter allows for the kind of information sharing and dialogue that is critical to building support for your program.

Workshops and Training

A third effective way to win support for peer mediation is to conduct workshops and training sessions. Regardless of whether they are initially interested in the subject or not, educators find conflict resolution and mediation training to be engaging and highly useful. Because information can be presented in great depth, trainees gain an experiential understanding of the efficacy of mediation and often become strong advocates for the program.

Trainings vary in length from two hours to five days. Professional development days are perfect for shorter sessions. Some school systems enable educators to attend longer trainings during the school year and over the summer. Of course, it is important to have qualified trainers conduct these sessions.

Workshops and training programs can be designed for a single constituency (department heads, counselors, parents, and so on), or they can be open to anyone within the school community. The agenda should combine conflict resolution theory, opportunities for personal and professional growth, and mediation skill development. Many schools make preliminary training for staff an integral part of their implementation process.

There are a variety of ways to introduce peer mediation, so do not limit yourself to these. You can create "infomercials" for the school television station, write articles in the school newspaper, produce dramatic works, organize "speak outs" on student violence, and use any other approach that you find effective.

DECIDING WHETHER TO MOVE FORWARD

I use my mediation skills all the time. It has become an everyday problem solver for me.

High school mediator

Eventually, the time comes when you have to decide whether there is enough support for peer mediation to justify moving forward. Unfortunately, with few hard and fast rules, it is easier to determine when you should *not* implement a peer mediation program than when you should. If the principal indicates that he or she will not support the program, or if the amount of student conflict in the school does not warrant training mediators, then it is best to devote your energies to other efforts. But barring such a clear negative indication, deciding whether to move forward can be difficult.

In one sense, how much support is "enough" depends upon your instincts and the depth of your commitment to implementing this program. But there are two key factors to consider, and here we return to where we began this chapter:

1. Your school must have a need for the program, a need expressed in the form of student conflicts that can benefit from peer mediation services. Educators have many objectives for peer mediation programs: reducing the suspension rate, improving school climate, teaching conflict resolution skills, promoting racial tolerance, and so on. But mediation programs are designed in such a way that these goals can only be met if students are mediating cases.

2. You must have been able to assemble a core group of school-based supporters of peer mediation. Institutions change when a critical mass of people within them demands that they change. It is a good sign if educators, parents, and students are willing to take responsibility for making student mediation a reality in your school.

There will always be resistance within schools; developing support for peer mediation is a slow and steady process. It is important to note, however, that once you have enough support to implement peer mediation, the program generates its own support by winning over people who use its services or who interact with others who have. Outreach and support building are explicit parts of the program's work for years after it is implemented.

Even after you have established that both the need *and* a core of support exist for this program, you cannot decide with finality whether peer mediation will be effective in your school at this stage. To do this, you must begin the program design process described in the next chapter.

But first, use the survey that follows to determine your readiness to move forward. If you score poorly, then student mediation will probably not be effective in your school. If you do well, then move on to the next phase—designing your program.

PEER MEDIATION IMPLEMENTATION
READINESS SURVEY

By administering a test to a bride and groom prior to their wedding, researchers can now predict with 90 percent accuracy whether their marriage will end in divorce. The following survey has an analogous purpose (although it cannot make a similar claim regarding its accuracy). By taking this survey, you will be able to predict whether your school and a peer mediation program are "right" for each other. Will you flourish together, or will your union be unsatisfying? Use the results first to determine whether to move forward with this program, and then to strengthen your effort if you decide to do so.

When taking this survey, select the answer that best represents your situation. If there is a discrepancy between a question's intention and its literal meaning, answer questions according to their intention. For example, if you are going to buy a curriculum and do your own training, but you are already an experienced mediation trainer, then indicate that in your answer. Similarly, if your training group is homogeneous, but your student population is the same way, your answer should reflect this fact.

Each section of the survey—Securing Initial Support which follows here, and Program Design and Training following Chapters 5 and 6—is scored separately. When you complete a section, add up your points to determine your rating. If your score is in the "excellent" range, your program should be very successful. If your score places you in the "caution" category, try changing certain aspects of your program design so as to increase your chances of success. Finally, if your score is "poor," consider not implementing a peer mediation program under current circumstances.

Peer Mediation Implementation Readiness Survey

PART A. SECURING INITIAL SUPPORT

1A. Need

We have a great deal of apparent student conflict in our school.	+ 30
We have some apparent student conflict in our school.	+ 10
We have very little apparent student conflict in our school.	-160

2A. Philosophical Match

Programs that empower students are consistent with our school philosophy.	+ 20
Programs that empower students are something new to our school.	+ 10
Programs that empower students are inconsistent with the way our school is run.	– 20

3A. Support of the Principal

Peer mediation is one of our principal's top priorities.	+ 20
The principal is moderately supportive of peer mediation.	+ 10
The principal does not actively support peer mediation.	– 50

4A. Support of the Disciplinarian

Peer mediation is one of our disciplinarian's top priorities.	+ 30
The school disciplinarian is moderately supportive of peer mediation.	+ 10
The school disciplinarian does not actively support peer mediation.	-160

5A. Support of the Staff

The majority of staff members are very supportive of peer mediation.	+ 20
The majority of staff members are moderately supportive of peer mediation.	+ 10
The majority of staff members are not supportive of peer mediation.	-50

6A. Support of the School System

The superintendent of schools/school committee is very supportive of peer mediation.	+ 20
The superintendent of schools/school committee is moderately supportive of peer mediation.	+ 10
The superintendent of schools/school committee does not know we are planning to implement peer mediation.	+ 0
The superintendent of schools/school committee is not supportive of peer mediation.	– 10

7A. Interested Core Group

After introducing peer mediation in the school, many people
    are willing to work to make the program a success.   + 20

After introducing peer mediation in the school, a small core group
    of people are willing to work together to make the program a success.   + 10

After introducing peer mediation in the school, I am still the only one
    willing to work on this project.   – 50

TOTAL:

Scoring

80–160 points: Excellent. You are ready to begin planning your peer mediation program
    in earnest.

0–80 points: Caution. Try to win more support in the school before you move forward.

< 0 points: Poor. You are not ready to move forward with a peer mediation program.

CHAPTER 5

Program Design and Planning

After securing initial support for peer mediation, the next stage of implementation is to design a program that will work in your school. The information that you have already discovered—your school's needs, your objectives for the program, the level of support that exists for peer mediation, and the resources that are available to help meet your goals—will determine the unique character of your mediation program.

Like the process of winning support, the design process continues long after the program is first implemented. Some issues like funding and coordination must be addressed immediately. Others, such as when and where to mediate, can be addressed later in the process. Though you will solve many of your design problems through trial and error, it is ideal to consider all of the issues in advance. This will prepare you for the hard work necessary to implement a peer mediation program.

The first design issue is the one most crucial to a program's success: Who will coordinate the program?

THE PROGRAM COORDINATOR

Although the ultimate goal of peer mediation is to help students resolve their own conflicts, this cannot be accomplished without the support and supervision of adults. The most important adult in this regard is the peer mediation coordinator. Like the coach to the football players, the conductor to the musicians, the mediation coordinator supervises student mediators and oversees all aspects of the program's operation.

The success of any program is intimately linked to the abilities of the person in charge, and this is certainly true about peer mediation programs. The more resources the mediation coordinator has—in terms of skill and commitment, and in terms of institutional support and time—the better off the program will be. While an unskilled coordinator can take a program that has much to its advantage and fail, a talented coordinator will make a program successful in spite of many obstacles.

The coordinator is many things to the mediation effort: the school change agent, guiding the program on the difficult road toward institutionalization; the counselor, listening to people's concerns and assuaging their fears. The coordinator is also the secretary, the meeting planner, the public relations manager, the cheerleader, and just about everything else. Given the central role that coordinators play in the peer mediation process, they really are the unsung heroes of this concept.

Two roles of the coordinator are especially noteworthy. The first is that coordinators must be supreme mediators themselves, embodying the conflict resolution principles that they promote. Implementing a peer mediation program inevitably causes conflict, and the coordinator must resolve these conflicts without alienating potential supporters.

The other interesting role of the coordinator is as mentor and friend to students. Because they have no agenda beyond listening uncritically to young people, peer mediation coordinators have a unique position in their schools. They are often among the few adults in school to whom students look for advice and emotional support. Some coordi-

From *Students Resolving Conflict: Peer Mediation in Schools,* published by GoodYearBooks. Copyright © 1995 Richard Cohen.

nators describe this relationship as one in which they are a "second parent"; others say they function as a trusted and more experienced friend. But no matter what the relationship is called, students regard the mediation coordinator as someone who will listen and accept them as they are.

The Coordinator's Responsibilities

The responsibilities of the coordinator include

- **Program Design**
  Identifying potential sources of financial support
  Creating and overseeing an advisory council
  Overseeing all aspects of program design
  Designing the referral process and related forms
- **Outreach and Publicity**
  Coordinating in-school publicity and education of both staff and students
  Maintaining positive relations with administrators, disciplinarians, and teachers
  Maintaining relations with parents and the community
  Keeping the school and community updated on the program's progress
- **Training**
  Overseeing selection of trainees
  Coordinating all aspects of the training, including locating trainers, arranging for the training site, obtaining parental permission, and providing refreshments
  Training mediators themselves if they are able
- **Casework**
  Coordinating mediator availability
  Taking referrals
  Explaining mediation to parties and encouraging them to try it
  Determining when an intervention other than peer mediation is necessary
  Scheduling mediation sessions
  Locating appropriate mediators for each session
  Mediating cases when necessary
  Supervising mediation sessions
  Helping mediators improve their skills
  Following up on all cases
- **Program Maintenance**
  Keeping records
  Recruiting new mediators
  Facilitating regular meetings with mediators
  Coordinating program evaluation

Coordinators need not do all of this work themselves, but they must ensure that it gets done.

The Qualities of an Effective Coordinator

Coordinators must meet three mandatory criteria:

1. **Coordinators must be based in the school.** Although they may be employed by an outside agency, it is essential that the coordinator has an office at the school and is easily accessible to students, teachers, and administrators.
2. **Coordinators must be able to devote time during the school day exclusively to peer mediation.** Obviously teachers who have responsibilities every period of the day do not make effective coordinators.
3. **Coordinators must not be school disciplinarians.** Because mediation is a nonpunitive procedure with a guarantee of confidentiality, having a disciplinarian in the role of mediation coordinator undermines the process.

In addition, the more of the following qualities that coordinators possess, the better:

- Coordinators should have excellent communication and presentation skills. These skills are essential to win the trust of educators, parents, and students.
- Coordinators should genuinely enjoy working with young people and be able to make them feel comfortable and appreciated. They should command students' respect by giving them respect.
- Coordinators should be competent mediators with an aptitude for conflict resolution work. They need to lead by example.
- Coordinators should have a personal interest in and commitment to peer mediation. The best coordinators have a passion for their work that is unquenchable, and they continually strive to improve their own and their mediators' skills.
- Coordinators should understand the politics of the school in which they work, knowing how to "play the system" to get things accomplished.
- Coordinators should be capable of handling individual and systemic resistance while still advocating for the program. They should not be easily intimidated or quick to become defensive.
- Coordinators should have the respect and confidence of their fellow educators. Peer mediation programs are doomed if they employ a coordinator who has a history of strained relations with his or her peers.

If it appears that the best person for the job of coordinator is dynamic, sensitive, assertive, and politically astute, you are right! Given these requirements, the next question becomes: Who in the school would make the best coordinator? And further, how can it be arranged so that the best individual will be able to do this job? There are no pat answers to these questions. Arranging for an appropriate coordinator is perhaps the fundamental challenge of peer mediation program design. But before we discuss the ways that schools have met this challenge, we need to answer one other question.

How Much Time Does a Coordinator Need?

Peer mediation programs permanently resolve conflicts, and by so doing, they enable teachers, administrators, and students to focus their attention on education. In this regard, they "save" school time. A portion of this time savings, however, is "spent" in the form of the time needed to coordinate the program. How much time must a coordinator devote to peer mediation to be effective?

The caseload of peer mediation programs varies widely. While some mediate four hundred cases a year, others mediate only fifteen. (Middle and upper elementary school mediation programs generally have a much higher caseload than high school programs.) The nationwide average is probably less than five cases per week. Aside from complex cases that involve many parties and require hours of meetings and logistical time, student disputes generally take between twenty and sixty minutes to mediate. Adding an hour of logistical time for each case, casework alone does not warrant a full-time mediation coordinator.

But as is evident from the responsibilities listed above, mediation coordinators must do more than merely schedule and supervise cases. This is especially true during the first months of program operation when trainees need to be selected, the training must be organized, and the program must be publicized. And, in some schools, peer mediation coordinators become more than just coordinators. They become what might be called "conflict intervention specialists." These coordinators conduct class presentations on conflict resolution and communication; they help teachers develop curricular materials or negotiate student contracts; they intervene in large-group tensions; they might even work with students in other schools within their system. A conscientious coordinator finds no shortage of work to be done if given the time to do it.

And so the answer to the question, "How much time do you need to allow for mediation coordination?" is an unqualified "it depends." Most schools can benefit from having a full-time coordinator. A talented, full-time coordinator can deepen the impact that the peer mediation program has upon school life. But full-time coordinators are the exception, and many schools would simply not have enough for a full-time coordinator to do. The overwhelming majority of peer mediation programs function effectively with coordinators who devote ninety minutes to three hours each day to the program.

Who Will Coordinate?

The answer to this question is fundamentally determined by how the program is funded and how the coordinator is compensated. For many years, the only compensation most coordinators received was time during the school day to devote to this program. A welcome trend is for mediation coordinators to be paid for their work, either as full- or part-time employees or in the form of stipends.

Schools use many approaches to coordinate peer mediation programs including:

- The school or school system is able to devote its own money to hire a full-time mediation coordinator.
- An outside agency (public or private) funds one of its own staff to work in a school as a peer mediation coordinator.
- A single individual is hired—either by the school system or an outside agency—to be a part-time peer mediation coordinator in several different schools.
- A school police officer or security person coordinates the program. Some schools even

ask a community police officer to come into school for a few hours every day to coordinate their program.

- A teacher is given a reduced class load or is assigned to coordinate the mediation program in lieu of an administrative duty like cafeteria supervision. These teachers have anywhere from one period to half the day to devote to the program.
- A counselor takes on the responsibility of coordinating the program, integrating it into his or her more flexible schedule.
- A department head, cluster leader, or other nondisciplinary administrator coordinates the program.
- Increasing numbers of schools have full-time, school-based, nonacademic educators who coordinate substance-abuse prevention, counseling, advisor-advisee, student support, drop-out prevention, or desegregation programs. Coordinating peer mediation is often integrated into these educators' job responsibilities.
- Community volunteers, university students, or parents—all trained as mediators— spend time in school each week functioning as program coordinators.
- Student mediators themselves are used to assist an adult in coordinating the program. Students introduce parties to the process, walk them to and from class, follow up on cases, and keep records.

Co-coordinators

Many schools successfully employ more than one person to share responsibility for coordinating their peer mediation program. Although it is still necessary to assign someone to oversee the entire effort, using co-coordinators expands a small program's ability to serve the school. In a common scheme, several teachers devote a number of periods each week to the program. These co-coordinators work on different days, or they are available at different times of the same day.

Using co-coordinators prevents the program from becoming dependent upon one individual. When a solo coordinator changes positions or is transferred to a different school, it can be difficult to find someone else who is capable of or interested in taking on his or her responsibilities. Co-coordination is also a boon in another way: coordinator compensation. Although many dedicated educators have coordinated peer mediation programs and received no financial remuneration, volunteer coordinators eventually "burn out" or move on to other interests. With co-coordinators, schools do not overburden anyone and someone is always capable of running the program.

An obvious caution about co-coordinating: make sure that coordinators work well together. More than one peer mediation program has imploded as a result of tensions between adults. One dispute between co-coordinators resulted in two competing peer mediation programs within a single school!

Selecting the Coordinator

When considering the process of selecting a coordinator, the first thing to discuss is what *not* to do. Schools make three common mistakes:

1. The first person to volunteer is selected to be the coordinator.
2. The person who works the hardest to initiate the program is automatically selected to be the coordinator.
3. Administrators *assign* someone to be the coordinator, not because that person is interested in this program, but because he or she is available.

In each of these cases, the person selected does not necessarily make the best program coordinator. It is always preferable to have an open selection process during which candidates are chosen upon their merits. Although the politics can be tricky, an open selection process results in a higher quality coordinator and a more successful program. This approach is most effective when money is available to compensate the coordinator. When it isn't, programs must select from among whomever is willing or able to take on the job.

Strive to select the coordinator as early as possible in program development. The sooner a coordinator becomes involved in shaping the program, the more committed and capable he or she will be at implementing it. In addition, there are more opportunities for outreach and support building at the beginning of school than at any other time during the academic year. You will want the coordinator to be able to take advantage of these opportunities.

Up until this stage, the work of implementing the peer mediation program has been in the hands of those initiating it. From this point forward, however, the coordinator, and those who are willing to assist and advise him or her, becomes the motivating force behind the mediation program.

ADVISORY COUNCILS

To ease the burden of their work, coordinators often form advisory councils. Advisory councils help out in a variety of ways by

- providing differing perspectives and ensuring that the program addresses the needs of all segments of the school community;
- facilitating acceptance of the program by disseminating information about peer mediation to peers and colleagues;
- providing emotional support to the coordinator during the sometimes frustrating process of program implementation; and
- providing more hands to get the job done.

The approximately ten members of an advisory council should include administrators, disciplinarians, students, teachers, people from sponsoring agencies, parents, and perhaps even community members involved with juvenile justice or human services. It is best to throw your net wide: parents will know of a corporation in the community that might fund the program; teachers will know the best way to win the support of the staff; students will know how to reach their peers. Recruit council members from your core group of mediation supporters as well as by asking key, influential people for their participation.

The work of an advisory council is most intense during the early phases of program implementation, and you will meet perhaps every other week for the first three months. During these initial meetings you might draft a policy on mediation and confidentiality, plan an outreach campaign, investigate sources of training and funding, recruit trainees, or evaluate different ways to schedule mediation sessions.

Later in the life span of the program you will meet less frequently with the council. One meeting per month, supplemented by memoranda and informal conversations, will keep the council updated on program activities. Special meetings can be called to discuss changes in program design and to evaluate the program. After the program has been in operation for a number of years, you might meet with this council only a few times annually.

Be explicit about the commitment that people make when they accept a seat on the council. As an example, inform them that the council will meet twice monthly on the first and third Wednesdays between seven and eight in the morning in the counseling office. After December, the council will meet only on the first Wednesday of the month at the same time and place. In addition, approximately one hour of work outside of meetings will be required of each member for the first three months.

The work that it takes to organize an effective advisory council is well worth the effort. There is no better way to gain ten boosters who are well informed and committed to making peer mediation a success.

DETERMINING THE SIZE AND SCOPE OF YOUR PROGRAM

It is now time to determine the unique size and character of your peer mediation program. Two considerations compete in this regard. On the one hand, you must restrict your scope to ensure that your efforts will be successful. Despite people's enthusiasm for this project, human and financial resources are always limited, and to fail or to fall far short of expectations saps the momentum from a peer mediation effort. It is best to set realistic goals that can be accomplished and then expand the program upon this strong foundation.

On the other hand, the more comprehensive your program is, the more effective it will be. Students should use and observe collaborative conflict resolution skills at every turn: in the curriculum, in the way their teachers interact with them, in peer mediation sessions, and in the disciplinary office. This enables the program to have the most powerful impact upon students and the school.

And so you must balance these considerations, applying your energies in a way that provides the best return. Be sure to consider these important questions:

- Whom will the program serve?
- Will the program have a special focus?
- What supplemental activities will the program engage in to support its work?
- What relationship will peer mediation have to related programs in the school?
- What relationship will peer mediation have to related programs in the community?

The following list notes just some of the ways that schools design peer mediation programs to meet their unique needs and resources:

- Peer mediation programs serve one classroom, one cluster, or one grade level instead of an entire school.
- Students mediate only within their own classrooms (elementary schools).
- A conflict resolution curriculum is taught to all students (as part of health class, English class, and so on), or to new students during orientation week.
- Peer mediators walk to nearby schools to mediate conflicts between younger students.
- Older students train younger students in mediation and conflict resolution skills and serve as their mentors.
- Student mediators focus their services on conflicts that occur at particular locations (the school bus, the cafeteria), or on particular problems (violence, racism, teasing, gangs).
- Peer mediation programs conduct monthly conflict resolution workshops for staff.
- Mediation training is offered as an elective class for which students receive credit.
- Peer mediation programs train a cadre of adult mediators who then offer their services for any appropriate conflict involving students, teachers, support staff, and administrators (student-teacher, teacher-teacher, staff-teacher, custodian-student, teacher-administrator, and so on).
- Peer mediation is given the status of a school club so that time for mediators to meet together is built into the schedule.
- A mediation homeroom is created enabling mediators to meet as a group every day.
- Student mediators conduct workshops for students in "in-house" suspension.
- Student mediators serve at local YMCAs, boys' and girls' clubs, after-school programs, and summer camps.
- Student mediators create dramatic productions, concerts, and television shows about mediation and present them at their own and at other schools.
- Student mediators, after receiving appropriate training, co-conduct workshops for their peers on communication, conflict resolution and mediation, anger management, violence prevention, sexual harassment, racism, substance abuse, AIDS, leadership, and teamwork.
- Peer mediation programs offer mediation services to parents and children, using one adolescent mediator and one adult (community, parent, or educator) mediator.
- Peer mediation programs train parents to use and reinforce collaborative conflict resolution skills at home.
- Peer mediation programs simultaneously train "at-risk" students and their parents in conflict resolution skills.

Two ideas deserve special attention. A few schools now offer parent-child mediation—an application of the mediation process that has proven very beneficial—as part of their program. In these mediation sessions, parents and their adolescent children communicate and create agreements on both school-related issues (truancy, absenteeism, grades, behavior) and typical family concerns (curfew, responsibility, chores, respect, trust).

From *Students Resolving Conflict: Peer Mediation in Schools*, published by GoodYearBooks. Copyright © 1995 Richard Cohen.

I love the mediation program! It has decreased the number of fights and is a great method for working a small conflict or a big conflict out in a good way. The program makes everyone involved a winner!

Middle school mediator

School counselors refer families to this voluntary service based at the school when they become aware of tensions in the home.[20]

A second noteworthy idea is to integrate peer mediation with peer counseling programs. Many schools have some form of peer counseling program that trains students to listen to and support their peers. Though peer mediation and counseling programs have different focuses, similarities between the two include their use of adult coordinators and their emphasis on student empowerment and skill building. One school system that was fortunate enough to have full-time peer counseling teachers in every school used them as peer mediation coordinators.

As you can see, peer mediators can apply their skills and energies within the school in many ways. But how will you fund these efforts?

FUNDING

Obtaining funding for a peer mediation program is yet another critical part of the implementation process. Because the amount of funding you raise determines the kind of program you can implement, you should consider the issue of funding as soon as you begin to explore peer mediation.

How Much Money Is Needed?

Budgets for peer mediation programs range from only a few hundred dollars to well over $40,000, depending upon the design of the program. There are four categories of expense:

1. **Coordinator's Compensation.** The most common form of compensation is to provide *time* to an individual who is already on the school payroll. This "in-kind" compensation sometimes means that the school does not have to raise additional funds. Other programs raise funds either to hire a coordinator who is not already part of the school system, or to underwrite a percentage of a school employee's salary. The amount of money involved ranges from a small stipend for a teacher ($500) to a ten-month salary for a full-time coordinator ($20,000 to $40,000). This last option usually occurs only when an outside agency or grant monies provide funding for the program. Although some schools use community volunteers as coordinators, it is still necessary to have someone at school oversee these volunteers.

2. **Training Expenses.** Training costs are often the largest out-of-pocket expense incurred when starting a peer mediation program. Training expenses include trainer's fees, travel expenses (for trainers to come to you or for you to go to them), materials, refreshments, and substitute coverage for staff who participate. The total cost can run from only a few hundred dollars (if training services are donated or there is someone on staff who can conduct the training) to many thousands of dollars. The best training programs have a high trainer-to-trainee

[20] A promising trend in this young field is to offer *all* applications of mediation—juvenile justice, victim-offender, school, community, and family mediation services—under one umbrella program. The school-based program becomes an affiliate of this larger effort.

ratio to ensure that trainees receive appropriate feedback, but this increases training expenses. Training costs can drop dramatically after the first few years if school staff assume this responsibility.

3. **Operating Expenses.** Operating costs are quite small in most programs. Included in this category are forms, paper, copying, curricula, field trip expenses, and outreach materials (brochures, T-shirts, posters). Many of the operating needs can be donated by the school at little expense.

4. **Evaluation Costs.** Some programs are able to raise the funds to hire an outside agency to evaluate their peer mediation effort, but the costs involved usually make this prohibitive. More often than not, programs are either evaluated by the coordinator, or a university or public agency evaluates the program at no cost.

There are a few things to remember when budgeting for a peer mediation program. The first is to plan ahead. Although the ultimate goal is always to have your school system fund this program itself, you may not achieve this level of institutional support after one, three, or even five years of program operation. Look down the road: How much money will the program need it if expands in six months? next year? in two years? Strive to raise money for the first three years, not only the first one.

A second consideration concerns using an economy of scale. If an entire school system rather than an individual school implements peer mediation programs, you can save a great deal of money by not duplicating services. One school system employee could conduct all of the trainings, for example, or educators who become experienced trainers in their own school can conduct trainings in other schools. You save money in the long run if you think big. (See Appendix D for more information on implementing peer mediation programs in many schools simultaneously.)

Where Is the Money?

At first glance, locating funding appears to be the greatest challenge to implementing peer mediation programs. But for a variety of reasons, funding is not always the obstacle that people assume it will be. First, it is acknowledged at all levels of the educational establishment that something needs to be done about conflict and violence in schools. Second, peer mediation has a unique appeal: it is effective; it is visible; it works directly with young people; and it has a potential long-term impact on society. Finally, as of this writing, the concepts of nonviolent conflict resolution, mediation, and violence prevention are undergoing an explosion of interest and support in American society. The result is that a diversity of funding sources have been willing to underwrite this program.

Funding for peer mediation comes from one of four sources. The first is *money taken directly out of the school system's budget.* As previously mentioned, it is critical that your school system eventually pay for the costs of peer mediation. If it does not, chances are slim that peer mediation will survive over the long term. Initially, however, it is difficult to gain access to these funds. Most schools are only willing to donate staff time to the effort, or "match" funds from outside sources at the start.

The three other sources of funds are generally more accessible during the first years of a peer mediation program. The most commonly used funds are *public money available through grants.* Numerous government agencies at the federal, state, and local levels have provided funding for peer mediation programs. (In fact, the federal government and

One of the best things about peer mediation is that you have the opportunity to solve your problems through peaceful and open communication. Many times the parties resolve their disputes and leave the mediation session with a new or renewed friend.

Middle school mediator

many states have recently passed legislation or have legislative initiatives pending that will fund peer mediation and related violence prevention programs.) Sometimes this money is dedicated specifically for programs like peer mediation. At other times, this money is not dedicated for peer mediation, or even for schools, but educators have been able to show that they will spend it in a way that furthers the goals for which it is designated. Keep a watchful eye for "Requests for Proposals" circulated by these agencies, many of which can be found in the central office of your school system.

The third source of money is *private foundations*. Countless peer mediation programs have been funded by private foundations which distribute grants to institutions that meet their requirements. As with public grants, private foundations must be convinced that you will use their money effectively to promote the aims they have adopted. Some cities have grant libraries that will help you learn which foundations might be interested in funding you, how much money they award in grants, and when and how to apply for a grant. Before you do the hard work of writing a proposal to a foundation, contact them to ensure that they will consider funding your program.

A fourth and final source of money is *private companies and individuals* who underwrite peer mediation programs in their local schools. The money is tax deductible; it supports a worthy cause; and the public relations benefits alone are worth the cost of funding this effective program.

Strategies for Raising Money

After you have identified potential sources of funding, you must then set about obtaining it. In most cases this means one thing: writing proposals. A proposal should clearly demonstrate your school's need for peer mediation, the degree of support that exists for the program, and the benefits you expect from implementing it. (See Appendix B for suggestions for writing grant proposals.) A few suggestions for proposal writing include:

- **Practice the fine art of telling funding sources what they want to hear.** To receive a grant from a foundation, agency, or corporation, you need to convince them that peer mediation will meet their goals. Although a small (but increasing) number of funding sources include "promoting effective conflict resolution" as one of their goals, most do not. You must therefore present peer mediation in terms that each funding source can understand. For a foundation whose goal is to promote innovation in the schools, highlight how peer mediation transforms the way schools resolve conflict. For a grantor interested in improving race relations, stress peer mediation's ability to enable students from different races to solve problems together. For a corporation whose aim is to keep students in school, discuss peer mediation's ability to reduce the suspension rate, motivate at-risk students, and improve school climate. Peer mediation programs have been awarded monies devoted to many purposes, including:

  - School improvement and innovation
  - Drop-out prevention
  - Peace education
  - Increasing student self-esteem

- School restructuring
- Substance-abuse prevention
- Violence prevention
- Delinquency prevention
- Special education
- Desegregation and racial tolerance
- Teacher training
- Law-related education
- Child-abuse prevention
- Attendance improvement

- **Show the funding source that you won't need them for long.** Stress to funding sources that you won't be dependent upon their money indefinitely. Time and experience bring increased financial independence to peer mediation programs. As school-based staff members develop the ability to train mediators on their own, one of the biggest expenditures—training—disappears. In addition, some programs are able to arrange for their school system to underwrite the cost of the program in future years. When you show a foundation that its money will have an impact far into the future, your program becomes a much better investment.

Community Partnerships

Even better than writing proposals yourself is having someone write them for you. You may be able to accomplish this by joining in partnership with an outside agency that can oversee fund raising and other aspects of program implementation. The clear first choice in this regard is a community mediation program (if you are lucky enough to have one in your area). Many community programs have joined with local schools to start peer mediation programs, and some can even provide training at little or no cost.

You are not limited to community mediation programs, however. Any organization devoted to school improvement, community empowerment, public health, or social change will find something of interest in the peer mediation concept. Local community groups, hospitals, social service organizations, courts, state agencies, universities, law-related education programs, and counseling services are all potential candidates. These groups have access to funds that schools alone are not eligible to receive. And if they can do the work to raise the funds, it takes one responsibility off the already burdened shoulders of the coordinator and his or her allies.

Even though fund raising is always a necessity when implementing a student mediation program, it is important to remember one thing: *Money is not the key to a peer mediation program's success.* Some of the most successful peer mediation programs operate on a shoestring budget. Having a skilled and committed coordinator, finding the right niche for the program, gaining the support of every segment of the school community, conducting an excellent training—all are more important to a program's success than money. If a school truly wants this program, it almost always finds a way to fund it. And in the end, you will design an effective program within the limitations of your budget.

At the risk of getting slightly off track, we will now explore an important design issue that is often overlooked when implementing peer mediation programs: program evaluation.

My mother and my sister were in a fight. Both said their feelings were hurt. I listened to their stories and recognized a communication problem. I asked if they were willing to solve their problems at that moment. They said yes and I helped them through the process of mediation. By the end they realized what had happened between them. They apologized and thanked me. I felt very accomplished.

High school mediator

PROGRAM EVALUATION[21]

It is advisable to consider how you are going to evaluate your peer mediation program from the earliest stages of program planning. This enables you to include the cost of evaluation in your fund-raising goal. But more importantly, effective evaluation requires so-called baseline data: information about what students and the school are like *before* the mediation program is implemented. It is too late to obtain this data after you have started the program, and without it, you can never know for certain whether specific changes are attributable to the mediation program.

This section outlines how to design and implement evaluations that produce useful results.

Why Evaluations Are Important

Evaluating your peer mediation effort is both necessary and desirable for many reasons. They involve your most immediate concern—the success of your program—as well as related interests such as the health of your school and the advancement of the mediation field. The most important benefits of conducting evaluations follow:

- **Evaluations build ongoing support for peer mediation.** Everyone involved with the program—from administrators to teachers to funding sources—will be curious whether the time and money invested in this effort was well spent. An evaluation provides proof positive of the impact that peer mediation has upon student mediators, parties, and the school as a whole. This leads to continued financial as well as administrative support. Evaluations are often required by both public and private funding sources.
- **Evaluations help you improve your program.** An evaluation can isolate the strengths and possible deficiencies in the way your program is working. Are mediation sessions resulting in sound, long-term solutions? Are certain mediators, or certain types of mediators, more effective than others? Are particular groups of students using the program while others are not? Learning the answers to these questions from an evaluation will enable you to strengthen your peer mediation effort.
- **Evaluations help you improve your school.** A successful peer mediation program becomes the central conduit for interpersonal conflict in a school. By analyzing the program's caseload, you therefore learn not only about the mediation program, but about the school as a whole. In this way, an evaluation can become a catalyst for institutional change, uncovering larger, systemic problems. Perhaps conflicts are occurring in a certain hallway, between members of certain races or cliques of students, or in a certain cluster of the school. Use this information to make appropriate changes in your school. A few examples of schoolwide actions that have resulted from peer mediation evaluations include formation of multiracial student panels to discuss issues and develop programs; creation of a "buddy" system in which entering students are assigned an older "buddy"; scheduling changes to minimize disruptive traffic patterns in specific corridors.

---

[21] This section was written with expert assistance from Dr. Julie Lam, Yale University.

■ **Evaluations contribute to the peer mediation field.** Evaluations build a body of evidence to demonstrate the effectiveness of peer mediation. This evidence assures that school-based mediation will continue to achieve credibility and grow.

Measuring Your Program's Objectives

Evaluations are intended to answer two basic questions: What happened? Why did it happen? To answer these questions, evaluators need to know what you hope to achieve. What are the goals and objectives of the program? *Goals* are general statements of desired states in human conditions and social environments. *Objectives* are specific, measurable statements that relate to the accomplishments of a program. Objectives are stepping stones that lead to the achievement of goals. For a peer mediation program, a goal might be to make the school a more effective place for learning; an objective toward that goal might be to reduce the suspension rate by 50 percent. Determining the degree to which a program meets its goals and objectives is the purpose of evaluations.

It is crucial for an evaluation—and in many ways for the success of your program—that objectives be clear, concise, and most important, measurable. Many of your program's objectives will be generated during your early outreach and support-building activities: the needs assessment surveys, the presentations and workshops, the private discussions with school leaders. The following are typical objectives of peer mediation programs and the ways that these objectives can be measured:

Objective 1. Decrease the number of detentions in the school. Measure this objective by counting the number of detentions (usually available from school records) over a defined period of time for the years before the program began and after the program is in place.

Objective 2. Decrease the number of suspensions. Measure this objective as above. You might also look at the average length of suspension before and after the program is implemented.

Objective 3. Improve school climate. Use a questionnaire completed before and after the program is implemented that asks students and staff to agree or disagree with statements about their school, such as "students have a lot of pride" and "there are a lot of fights among students in our school." In addition, use detention, suspension, and truancy rates to measure school climate.[22]

Objective 4. Decrease the time teachers and administrators spend on disciplinary matters. To measure this objective, teachers and administrators keep a daily log of the time they spend in activities related to discipline. Educators must be trained in a standardized approach to keeping records and must share a common definition of "discipline-related activities."

---

[22] A school climate questionnaire as well as a number of other evaluation instruments are included in the *School Mediation Program Evaluation Kit* by Dr. Julie Lam, available from the National Association for Mediation in Education, in care of Mediation Project, 205 Hampshire House, Box 33635, University of Massachusetts, Amherst, MA 01003-3635.

Objective 5. Improve students' self-esteem, communication, and conflict resolution skills. Administer questionnaires measuring student attitudes and skills before the program is implemented and then at specific intervals after the program is in place. You must decide whether this objective is to be achieved schoolwide, for student parties and mediators, or only for student mediators.

Objective 6. Improve relations among culturally and ethnically diverse groups. Again, administer questionnaires assessing attitudes toward and interactions with members of other groups before and after the mediation program is implemented. In addition, monitor incidents of racial, ethnic, or other cultural problems.

The Challenge of Evaluation

To *evaluate* is defined as "to ascertain the value or effectiveness of something." To determine the value of one thing, it usually has to be compared with something else. With peer mediation programs, evaluators compare one school to another; one group of students to another (either from within the same school or from different schools); even a single group of students with themselves at various times during the course of program implementation.

Effective evaluations maximize the "comparability" of the groups being compared. Groups should be as close to identical as possible with the exception of the variable in question. For example, to evaluate the effect of a plant food on plant growth, one would first find a number of identical plants: same species, same age, same level of health, same growing conditions, and so on. Then one would feed the food to some plants and not to others. The former plants are called the *treatment* group; the latter are the *comparison* group. Finally, one would evaluate by analyzing differences between the plants that received the food (treatment group) and the plants that didn't (comparison group). The greater the original similarity of the groups, the more differences can be attributed to the variable being evaluated (in this case, the plant food).

Three factors make it challenging to achieve a high degree of comparability when evaluating peer mediation programs. One is that each young person and school is so unique that it is difficult to assemble comparable treatment and comparison groups. Finding groups of students who have similar maturity levels, teachers, and social and family pressures is not an easy task.

The second complicating factor is that young people and schools are complex, and many things influence their behavior in unforeseen and uncontrollable (from the evaluator's perspective) ways. Suspensions may be reduced after the implementation of peer mediation, but a new administrative philosophy or the fact that students are waiting until after school to fight could account for this change. It is difficult to limit these other influences for the purposes of evaluation.

A final reason for the difficulty in evaluating peer mediation programs is economic. Even when you can find groups of students or schools to compare, it requires substantial human and financial resources to conduct an effective evaluation. Peer mediation programs usually don't have such resources to spare. Evaluating a program is not a high priority when more basic programmatic needs are pressing.

These three factors combine to leave the emerging peer mediation field with few competent evaluations and research studies. Given how young this field is, the paucity of credible evaluations is not surprising. As ever-increasing numbers of educators and academics become involved with peer mediation, however, this is beginning to change.

Evaluation Methods

Methods for evaluating mediation programs range from complex and labor-intensive schemes to simple designs that can be conducted by a part-time coordinator:

- **Program Monitoring.** Even though this first approach is the easiest to execute, it is often overlooked in favor of designs that measure the impact of peer mediation upon individual students. Here the goal is to describe the program not just as it was *proposed*, but as it is actually *implemented*. The basic question this design seeks to answer is: What really happened? Evaluators monitor the number of mediations, outcomes of the mediations, types of conflicts mediated, characteristics of disputants, characteristics of mediators, and whether mediated agreements are holding up at designated follow-up times. Beware that the number of disputes mediated can be an unreliable indicator of the success of the mediation program. A decrease in the caseload, rather than implying a diminishing of the program's effectiveness, may signify that students have integrated conflict resolution skills into their lives and do not need mediation services as often. Program monitoring also measures the extent to which peer mediation is institutionalized. Here evaluators look to evidence such as whether mediation is part of the school code of conduct or formal disciplinary procedures. Is the mediation program a line item in the budget? To what extent are students, teachers, and parents knowledgeable about and supportive of the program? The more institutionalized a program is, the more likely it is to thrive.

- **The Experimental Design.** The experimental design is the most sophisticated way to measure the impact of the peer mediation program upon students. It requires that students be *randomly assigned* to groups. One of the groups receives peer mediation training; the other serves as the comparison group. This approach can also be applied to measuring the impact of peer mediation upon schools rather than upon individual students by comparing schools randomly selected to have mediation programs to schools not selected. Random assignment to groups is the only way to be certain of equivalence at the time that baseline data is collected. This experimental design requires the greatest effort prior to program implementation. But because the groups have a high degree of comparability, this approach provides the most credible argument that the mediation program is responsible for differences between them.

- **The Matching Design.** Using the experimental design is often not possible. As an alternative, comparisons can be made between schools with peer mediation programs and comparable schools without programs (or peer mediators with comparable students who are not mediators). Every attempt should be made to establish the comparability of the schools and students by matching group members on important characteristics (for example, sex, race, age, socioeconomic background, and academic record).

Peer mediation has changed our school by giving the students an alternative way to solve conflicts. Students feel comfortable sharing problems with people who will listen intently to them. I think that peer mediation allows students to look deeper into problems with their peers.

Middle school mediator

- **The Pre-test/Post-test Design.** In this basic design, no other schools or students are used as comparisons. School or student mediators are simply compared to themselves prior to the program and at specific intervals after the program is implemented. Although this method identifies whether or not a change took place, it cannot determine with certainty whether a change was due to the effects of the peer mediation program. Because of its simplicity, the pre-test/post-test design has been used the most to evaluate school-based mediation programs.

- **The Post-test Only Design.** An even less sophisticated design is the post-test only design. Here, evaluators ask students, teachers, and administrators to describe any changes they have observed since the initiation of the peer mediation program. Respondents are also asked to what degree they attribute those changes to the program. This weak design should only be used where peer mediation has been in operation before the decision is made to evaluate.

Funding Evaluation Efforts

Finding the necessary funding is the biggest obstacle to carrying out a comprehensive evaluation of your program. If you hire an outside evaluator who uses a rigorous design involving comparison schools, it is certain to be expensive. Of course, if you are able to raise the money for such an extensive evaluation, that is wonderful.

More often than not, you will have to find low-cost ways to evaluate your peer mediation program. A good place to start is local colleges and universities. Collaborating with a nearby university is an inexpensive, win–win approach to evaluation. You get your program evaluated, and faculty and graduate students get data for their papers. Faculty in disciplines such as legal studies, criminology, sociology, psychology, and education may be interested in conflict resolution and peer mediation, and internal university research grants are often available to fund small-scale preliminary studies.

It is most common for peer mediation coordinators to do their own program evaluation. The case forms in the appendices of this book and surveys available for purchase make a good starting point for designing an evaluation, and people without evaluation training can easily use them. You can analyze the data solicited by these forms on your own, or farm it out to graduate students at nearby universities.

Regardless of the approach you take, it is wise to plan your evaluation as you plan your program.

PEER MEDIATION AND SCHOOL DISCIPLINE

Another focus of program design is the relationship between peer mediation and school discipline. *It is of the utmost importance that the school population perceives these very different school functions as separate entities!* Peer mediation offers students the opportunity to resolve their own conflicts without outside interference. The disciplinary system, in contrast, is essentially punitive, using institutional power to force students to comply with school norms.

Problems arise because students in conflict may have contact with one, the other, or both of these approaches. As a result, they can lose sight of the differences between them.

If peer mediation appears to be a part of discipline, it destroys its reputation as a student-controlled process. And if mediation seems to make disciplinary consequences negotiable, the effectiveness of the disciplinary system is reduced. The integrity of both approaches is threatened when the distinction between them is blurred.

Which Issues Are "Mediatable"?

The first question to consider when defining the relationship between peer mediation and school discipline is: Which conflicts are "mediatable"? That is, when students get into conflicts, which will be deemed appropriate for mediation alone, which will require traditional disciplinary measures, and which will require a combination of both approaches? It is important to note at the outset that the overwhelming majority of student-student disputes result from incidents of gossiping, name-calling, poor sportsmanship, and boyfriend-girlfriend difficulties. These issues usually do not require disciplinary attention, and administrators in charge of discipline can refer these conflicts directly to mediation. Indeed, in the early stages of program development, the disciplinarian refers the majority of mediation cases.

Some issues clearly require a response from the school disciplinary system, however. If a conflict involves serious physical violence, racial or sexual harassment, weapons, or drugs in school, then appropriate consequences must be assigned swiftly and authoritatively.

The challenge rests in handling cases in which it is unclear whether peer mediation, school discipline, or some combination of the two best serves students and the school. An example illustrates this clearly:

Maryanne and Keisha have been good friends for three years. During study hall, Keisha confronted Maryanne and accused her of spreading rumors about her. Although a physical confrontation followed, a teacher was able to break the girls apart just after Keisha pushed Maryanne. No punches were thrown, and neither of the girls were hurt. Both were sent to the disciplinarian's office. This is the first time either of them has fought in school.

Determining how to handle conflicts like this one is a daily dilemma for disciplinarians. We can assume that the school's disciplinary code prohibits fighting and assigns some punishment for the first offense. In many schools, that punishment is either in-house or out-of-school suspension. But how should the disciplinary code be applied given the unique characteristics of this conflict? Should Maryanne, Keisha, or both girls be suspended for fighting on school property? Let's analyze the options.

If a disciplinary system is to deter students from breaking the rules, disciplinarians must apply it consistently, regardless of individual circumstances. Keisha did break school rules by pushing Maryanne. If the disciplinarian doesn't assign her the appropriate consequences, it sends a message to Keisha as well as to the entire student body that they can break school rules with impunity. From this perspective, then, it seems that Keisha, if not both girls, should be suspended.

Most disciplinarians, however, prefer not to suspend students unless it is absolutely

Peer mediation works because of the peer part. I think that kids feel more comfortable talking out their problems with other kids who understand. The parties aren't as threatened talking to people their own age.

High school mediator

necessary, and many factors suggest that suspension is not the best option for Maryanne and Keisha. First, they have never fought before, and so their behavior is not habitual and in need of correction. Second, their friendship increases the likelihood that they will be able to resolve their conflict by speaking directly with one another. And finally, Maryanne and Keisha were not engaged in a serious physical fight. They did not actually come to blows, and neither girl was hurt. Applying a strict interpretation of the disciplinary code in this situation might benefit neither the students nor the school. Sending them to peer mediation seems to be the best alternative.

This difficult decision would be handled in a variety of ways by different educators. But one distinction is essential to understand when considering how to respond to conflicts like this one: *The issues in a conflict, and the actions students take in response to those issues, are different things and require different interventions.*

Even when students take actions that are prohibited and require a disciplinary response (such as fighting), the issues at the core of their conflicts are usually typical student concerns. Keisha may have physically assaulted her friend, but she did so because Maryanne allegedly spread rumors about her. Though suspending one or both of these girls may deter them from fighting, it will not resolve their concern about rumors. That issue is best resolved in a forum like peer mediation. Increasing numbers of schools therefore recommend mediation to help students resolve their conflicts *in addition* to giving them disciplinary consequences for their behavior. Most disputing students, no matter how heinous the actions in question, benefit by participating in mediation.

When Peer Mediation and School Discipline Overlap

Important logistical questions are raised whenever mediation and school discipline are combined. Determining how to integrate these two approaches causes debate among educators even within the same school. (One ancillary benefit of implementing a peer mediation program is that it motivates educators to analyze and streamline their approach to discipline.) To understand this, let's look at three routes that disciplinarians can use to refer students to mediation.

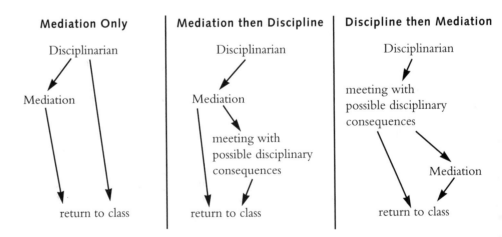

In the first option, the disciplinarian decides that the conflict in question does not require disciplinary action. Students can choose to go to the mediation program for assistance or return to class. This is the most direct referral route between the disciplinary system and the mediation program. If the students do not choose to go to mediation, the disciplinarian might do some informal mediating on his or her own before returning students to class.

In the second option, the disciplinarian recommends students attend mediation first, but requires that they return to meet with him or her afterward. When the mediation process is concluded, the disciplinarian decides what action, if any, to take. The disciplinarian may take the outcome of the mediation session into consideration when making a determination.

In the third option, the disciplinarian meets with students first and assigns whatever consequences he or she deems necessary. Only after students have received their punishment—in some cases only after they have returned from suspension—are they required or invited to take advantage of the peer mediation process.

With each of these three options, administrators make referrals to mediation without compromising the integrity of the disciplinary system. The first approach, "mediation only," is by far the most common. In many schools, every conflict except those involving weapons, drugs, or serious physical violence goes to peer mediation as a first resort.

The "mediation then discipline" option is more controversial for a number of reasons. One concerns whether students are told that the outcome of peer mediation will affect disciplinary consequences. Some administrators find it effective to use mediation as an incentive, informing students that if they work out an agreement in the mediation session, their punishment will be lessened. This motivates students to utilize and become invested in a process that they might not otherwise take seriously. Most disciplinarians, however, prefer to tell students that the outcome of peer mediation *will have no effect* upon their determination. They feel such an effect would compromise the disciplinary system, and enable students to break the rules without facing the appropriate consequences. These administrators also fear that this approach might lead students to create unsound agreements just to avoid being punished.

A second concern expressed about the "mediation then discipline" option is that it can make students confused and resentful about receiving punishment *after* they have worked hard in mediation to resolve their dispute. Some coordinators report that student parties misdirect their anger at the seemingly unfair system back at each other. Taken together, these concerns support the idea that whenever it is unclear if disciplinary action is required, disciplinarians should make no promises regarding peer mediation's effect upon their punishment. Most students will be able to resolve their disputes in mediation sessions; as long as they perceive a disciplinarian's subsequent actions to be fair, facing consequences after mediation will not threaten their resolution.

When it is certain that students will be receiving punishment for their actions, the third, "discipline then mediation" option is the best. These students are thereby encouraged to talk out their dispute even after they have been punished. If suspension is involved, the students can be asked to return to school during their suspension to attend the mediation session (at which point the number of days they are suspended can be reduced), or to participate in mediation on their first day back to school. Many schools now include peer mediation as part of their formal reentry process.

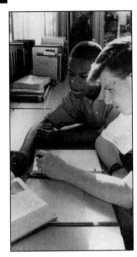

Here are a few other suggestions to aid in integrating peer mediation and school discipline:

- **Design the peer mediation program in conjunction with the administrator in charge of discipline.** Include the disciplinarian in your planning from the start. One key issue to discuss is how the disciplinarian will be informed about cases that have gone to mediation.
- **Maintain ongoing communication with the disciplinarian.** To a large degree, you will discover the best approach to integrating mediation and the disciplinary system through trial and error. This is true regardless of the policy you decide upon at the start. The peer mediation coordinator (along with the advisory council) and the disciplinarian should maintain close contact, continually reevaluating as the program moves forward. Try analyzing cases together to determine if there are better ways to structure this relationship.
- **Practice how you present each other.** One common mistake disciplinarians make when they introduce peer mediation to students is to make it seem like an involuntary punishment. ("You have to go to peer mediation. Now!") Help them learn to describe the program to students in a way that you feel is appropriate. By the same token, ensure that student mediators are not giving parties the false impression that mediation is a substitute for school discipline.
- **Never stop advocating for peer mediation.** Disciplinarians, like everyone else, fall back upon what they know and feel comfortable with. They can be overly cautious in referring cases to mediation for fear that students cannot handle the issues involved. You must therefore gently and continually remind disciplinarians to refer students to peer mediation. Students have successfully mediated all kinds of cases, including those involving gangs, racism, homophobia, and serious physical violence (after parties have returned from suspension).

One final note: Peer mediation programs are generally not well suited to handle conflicts in which the parties can be characterized as student vs. the institution. These common conflicts involve things like absenteeism, chronic tardiness, poor academic performance, or not abiding by school prohibitions (wearing hats, chewing gum, smoking, playing radios, and so on). The mediation process requires the participation of at least two interested parties, and school representatives usually have neither the time nor the inclination to attend a mediation session to discuss such "non-negotiable" issues. Using peer mediation for these conflicts also risks reducing it to a method of enforcing the status quo.

Some experimenting has been done with modifying the mediation process to handle student vs. school conflicts, however. Mediators meet individually with students in these situations, listen to them, and help them to create solutions that are acceptable to all involved. In some instances, school counselors represent the school's interests in mediation sessions. Parents have been involved in these sessions as well. To date, this approach has been most useful in handling issues of tardiness and truancy.

The mediation program and the disciplinary system serve different functions in the school. Peer mediation is of, by, and for the students that it serves. The disciplinary system, regardless of the extent to which it has the well-being of the students at heart, ultimately represents and promotes the interests of the school. But when they work together, everyone benefits.

DO I HAVE TO GO?
VOLUNTARINESS AND PEER MEDIATION

Reflecting the program's roots in the community mediation movement, *voluntariness* has been a fundamental principle of school-based peer mediation since its inception. The mediation process is completely dependent upon the parties' willingness to take responsibility for resolving their conflict. "Involuntary mediation" is an oxymoron. Indicative of this philosophy is one of the first questions that student mediators ask parties: "Are you willing to try mediation?" If the answer is no, and the mediators cannot convince the parties to change their minds, then the session ends.

From the beginning, however, subtle and not so subtle forces have been used to "encourage" students to try peer mediation. Although often disguised as a choice between alternatives created by the school, it is coercion nonetheless. (When presented with the option of either going to peer mediation or having a disciplinarian decide one's fate, who would not "voluntarily" choose peer mediation?) Some schools go beyond this more subtle pressure and, under certain circumstances, require that students attend a mediation session.

Educators and school-based mediators offer a number of reasons to justify compelling students to try mediation. One is that because mediation is so unfamiliar to students, they would never choose to participate in it without a push in that direction. Another is that characteristics of young people—their fear of the unknown, their need to save face, their contemporary inclination to fight first and talk later—predispose them against choosing mediation.

Both of these arguments are weak, however. With a comprehensive outreach and education campaign, with a supportive staff, and with a wise selection of student mediators, school-based mediation programs should be able to overcome these obstacles. The kind of "young people don't know any better" philosophy built into these arguments contradicts the premise that accounts for peer mediation's success: that given the opportunity, in a safe setting, students will choose to do the right thing.

A more compelling argument for coercing students into mediation is a more practical one: it works. In large numbers of cases, students who have been forced to attend a peer mediation session end up working together and resolving their conflicts. Not only that, these same students write in confidential evaluations that they appreciated the chance to do so. Many coordinators report that students who initially were required to go to peer mediation voluntarily seek out the program's services in the future. Far from turning them off, forcing students to try mediation usually turns them on to the process.

A key distinction explains why this is so—the difference between choosing to *attend* a mediation session and choosing to *participate in it* once there. The former is affected by the coercion discussed above. The latter, although initially overshadowed by circumstances that bring students to mediation, nevertheless remains completely in their control. From the start, coordinators (the front line of "guaranteeing" voluntariness) and mediators inform parties that "The administration may have sent you here, but we are separate from them and we will not force you to do anything that you do not want to do." At every turn, student parties see that *their* concerns are pivotal. Sitting face-to-face with their adversaries in a mediation session, assisted by peers earnestly trying to understand

[After you've been in mediation] you realize most people should know this way of communicating . . . . You realize the other person thinks a different way and there is usually a reason why they acted a certain way. Some of the people I thought I would never like or even understand, I do. Even now we are friends. If not friends, we speak and are pleasant to one another. It changed my whole outlook on them.

High school party

their stories and help them resolve their conflict, students become invested in spite of themselves.

The best argument for coercing students to attend a mediation session, then, is that mediation provides students with an opportunity for learning and for conflict resolution that we would prefer them not to miss. Once in the session, if students will not or cannot take advantage of this opportunity, that is up to them. But at least they have been given the chance.

In the end, schools use three approaches to encourage students to try peer mediation:

1. **Encouraging students to choose to participate voluntarily.** Students come forward on their own to seek mediation services, or the coordinator is instrumental in convincing them to try the process. This approach emphasizes the benefits of peer mediation to students. Most students become involved with the mediation program in this way.

2. **Using subtle forms of coercion to get students to choose to participate.** This involves emphasizing the consequences of *not* choosing mediation: the vice-principal will have to decide what to do; the situation will be out of students' control; students might be suspended. The operative word here is *subtle*. If not handled effectively, parties will *feel* coerced into participating and will be angry at the system and the mediators. This approach is usually taken by an informed and skilled disciplinarian or teacher, and only rarely by a coordinator or other students.

3. **Using the power of the institution to require that students attend a mediation session.** Because requiring students to try mediation supports the perception that peer mediation is an arm of discipline, this approach should be used sparingly and only under specific circumstances (after suspension is the most common). This is only used by disciplinarians and other high-level administrators.

Voluntariness is an ideal that every peer mediation program should strive for. All school staff must understand that encouraging students to choose to mediate is always preferable to telling them to do so. Explore the issue of voluntariness with teachers, administrators, and students so that you can create an acceptable policy. If you do an effective job of educating the school community about the mediation process, most students will try mediation with little prodding.

CONFIDENTIALITY

Students appreciate mediation because it is private. The mediators' guarantee of confidentiality enables students to talk freely in the session without fearing that their personal business will course through the school rumor mill when they are finished. This enables the process to work.

Creating your program's policy regarding confidentiality is therefore another central task of program design. Fundamentally, mediators discuss information they learn in a session only with their coordinator. Coordinators are part of the mediation program, and mediators can and should tell them everything that happens in a session.

But some interests within schools require that not all things that transpire in mediation remain confidential. Administrators—responsible for students while they are on school property—need to be apprised of certain information. Parents have the right to be informed if their children are in harm's way. And there are times when it is in the best interests of students themselves for information to go outside the mediation program. A few examples: a student who says that she wants to commit suicide; a student who admits to having a gun; a girl who is being abused by her boyfriend.

Your program's policy on confidentiality must accommodate these competing interests. The way mediation services are delivered and the relationship of the program to the rest of the school will both be affected by your approach to this issue. And regardless of what you decide, your policy must be applied competently and consistently. One major breach of confidentiality can damage the reputation of a program beyond repair. Consider two issues in this regard:

1. **What information discussed in a mediation session will not be kept confidential?**
   As a rule, no one beyond the student mediators and the adult coordinator knows what transpires in a peer mediation session. In most mediation programs, the only exceptions are made when the issues involve a serious potential for harm such as with drugs, weapons, and abuse. Other programs include anything that would be considered a reportable offense in the student handbook.

   It is essential that student parties understand all limitations upon the confidentiality of what they discuss. This ensures that later they will not feel they were misled into discussing things that they did not want to become public. At the start of every session, mediators inform parties about the exceptions to confidentiality with a statement like "Everything you tell us will be kept private unless it is illegal or might lead to someone getting hurt in the future." Knowing the rules in advance puts parties in charge of information leaving the session. It also enables coordinators to release essential information without jeopardizing the program's credibility among the students it serves.

   It is preferable to keep the exceptions to confidentiality to a minimum. The more limits upon confidentiality that parties hear at the start, the more hesitant they will be to trust the mediators and the process. As a rule, student parties will not discuss information that mediators do not promise to protect (unless, of course, they want that information released). If peer mediators say that talk of drugs in school will not remain confidential, for example, students will not discuss drug use during mediation.

   Many programs describe their exceptions to confidentiality using the catch-all phrase "life-threatening," as in "Everything you tell us in this mediation session will be kept private unless it is life-threatening." There are some advantages to using this phrase. It leaves parties informed and in charge, but it does not intimidate them with a long list of unprotected information. In addition, it allows the program flexibility in deciding what is life-threatening. Because this approach is somewhat ambiguous—reasonable people disagree, for instance, if drug use is life-threatening—it is important that student mediators, coordinators, and administrators clarify what they consider "life-threatening." When this is understood, this approach has been very effective.

I love being a mediator. It allows me to help people solve their problems and being a mediator helps me grow as a person. I have learned active listening skills, sensitivity, and teamwork. My life has been greatly enriched by this program because I have earned many new friends.

Middle school mediator

2. Who will know what transpires in a mediation session and to what degree?

Mediators *always* inform the program coordinator about what happens in a session; they do not usually tell administrators, teachers, and parents. Under what circumstances will these last groups be informed about the content of a mediation session?

In most schools, disciplinarians leave it up to the coordinator's discretion as to whether or not they need to be informed about a case. These disciplinarians are only informed of life-threatening issues that must be brought to their attention. This arrangement is ideal if all concerned feel comfortable with it, and it should be a goal of every program.[23]

Some program coordinators provide administrators and/or disciplinarians with a copy of mediated agreements and case paperwork, but do not discuss what transpires in mediation sessions. A few even inform disciplinarians about what occurs in every mediation session. Both approaches, especially the last, are far from ideal, and these schools should strive to move toward the arrangement described above. Of course, mediators must always disclose to parties the level of administrative involvement in the process.

Teachers are never informed about what transpires in a mediation session unless it is specifically requested by the parties. With the exception of life-threatening information, this is usually the case with parents as well. One school, attempting to keep parents informed and involved, started with a policy of informing parents whenever their child was involved in a mediation session. They quickly discovered, however, that this violated students' trust and discouraged them from utilizing peer mediation services.

In most peer mediation programs, confidentiality only applies to the mediators and the mediation coordinator. *The parties are free to inform anyone they want to about the session.* One party might request that the other party not talk publicly about the mediation session, and this can be included in the written agreement, but it is not required. A small number of programs require that parties refrain from discussing what transpires in the session, but because of the difficulty of ensuring that parties will live up to this commitment (and the problems that might result if they do not), this is not recommended.

It is important to note that although educators express concerns about students' ability to handle the responsibility of confidentiality, very few problems have occurred after the mediation of tens of thousands of cases. When the subject is covered properly in training, and when coordinators provide mediators with the support that they need, young people are very capable in this regard. In the vast majority of cases, confidentiality is not an issue anyway.

---

[23] One group of high school students felt uncomfortable informing the disciplinarian about life-threatening circumstances. They decided that in the event that the coordinator needed to go outside of the program, they would first consult with the school psychologist. The coordinator and the school psychologist would then decide together whether school administrators needed to be informed.

Training for student mediators should explore the issue of confidentiality in depth. Examples of topics for discussion include:

- Going outside of the program with life-threatening information is the sole responsibility of the coordinator. Student mediators should never tell anyone besides the coordinator.
- If mediators sense that parties are discussing something that is potentially life-threatening, they should immediately inform the parties of this. Parties usually welcome the help that results from telling others, as long as it can be done in a way that is comfortable for them.
- Mediators should not discuss cases with other mediators (aside from their co-mediator) outside of meetings facilitated by the coordinator.
- If adults approach the mediators and ask questions about a case, mediators should refer them to the coordinator.

Students have a visceral understanding of confidentiality. Most young people have firsthand experience of how secrets and rumors can tear friendships apart and even lead to violence. Still, it is important to be prepared. Plan well, and make sure that your policy is understood and supported by all segments of the school community. If you do, you should have few problems with this aspect of peer mediation.

WHEN AND WHERE TO MEDIATE

Because peer mediation sessions in middle and high schools are scheduled for a certain place and time, program designers must decide when and where to mediate. Although these are two of the more mundane issues you will consider, they are nevertheless crucial to your program's success.

At what time during the school day should mediation sessions take place? Every school has its own answer to this question. In the best programs, mediation sessions are scheduled according to the needs of the parties and the nature of their conflict. If the parties are ready to talk, appropriate mediators are located and a session held as soon as possible. Mediators sometimes miss classes, but teachers in these schools appreciate the educational value of mediating. No student mediator misses more than a few classes each month, and then only classes in which they are doing well and where they can make up the work that they miss.

Other schools do not have the flexibility to schedule mediations in this way. The most common limitation is the availability of a coordinator to oversee mediation sessions. If a coordinator has two periods a day to devote to the program, mediation sessions are only scheduled during those two periods. Teachers who have been trained as mediators can expand the times when mediations take place by co-mediating with students or supervising student mediators when the coordinator is unavailable. But coordinator availability remains a limiting factor.

Another reason programs do not conduct mediation sessions as needed is that administrators and teachers do not want student mediators missing classes. Such programs schedule sessions only during specified times of the day: before or after school, or during lunch periods, study halls, "electives" (music, art, gym), and so on. If a dispute is referred

From *Students Resolving Conflict: Peer Mediation in Schools*, published by GoodYearBooks. Copyright © 1995 Richard Cohen.

Before I was in a lot

of conflicts but now

I can handle some

things on my own

and being a media-

tor helps me to stop

being in conflicts.

Middle school mediator

mid-morning, student parties must wait until the next available mediation period to enter mediation. Because not allowing students to mediate during classes severely limits a program's ability to deliver services, it is preferable to create a policy in which students can occasionally miss classes.

What about where to mediate? If at all possible, your peer mediation program should have a room of its own within the school. At a minimum, a "mediation center" must be able to accommodate a small table and chairs for four to six people. Beyond that, the quality and size of peer "mediation centers" vary widely. Some schools have a suite of offices with a waiting area and separate rooms where two or more mediation sessions are conducted simultaneously. Other programs use a single room divided into the mediation area and the coordinator's office by a wall that does not go all the way up to the ceiling. With parties' permission, the coordinator inconspicuously listens from one side of the office while students mediate "in private" on the other side. Still other programs operate out of spaces no bigger than large closets. (Often these rooms *were* storage closets before the mediators cleaned them out!)

Having a "home" in the school has powerful benefits both for the student mediators and for the mediation effort as a whole. For the mediators, the mediation center is a physical manifestation of their efforts, a place where they go to feel their positive, collective force. Mediators can stop into the center between classes to get help with homework, to see if there are any cases, or just to relax. For the program, having a permanent and identifiable location gives peer mediation a tangible presence within the school. Students and teachers can go there to make referrals. And program logistics are much easier to manage when a space dedicated to mediation is familiar to everyone.

Mediation centers need to be private. Parties will not feel safe if their friends can walk by and see or hear what is going on inside. Windows should be covered, and sound should not be able to escape. Since mediators sometimes meet with one party in private, the mediation room should also have an anteroom or be close to another supervised area (such as administrative offices, coordinator's office, or classroom) where disputants can wait.

The mediation center should have a sign out front. It should also be decorated by the mediators to make it comfortable and inviting. If agreements and other confidential paperwork are kept in the room, the center should have a lock on the door and a locked file cabinet within. Only the coordinator and selected students should have access to these files.

If at all possible, locate the mediation center near the coordinator's office or classroom. This makes it easier for the coordinator to carry out other responsibilities while supervising a session. He or she can do paperwork in the office or even work with students in a classroom and still be able to keep an eye on the mediation. The mediation center should be separate from the disciplinary offices. Keeping a physical as well as a functional distance from the disciplinary system ensures that students will not confuse the two programs. (Too great a distance, however, makes it difficult for disciplinarians to refer students to peer mediation.)

Some schools do not have a room to devote exclusively to the mediation program. Although this puts the program at a disadvantage, coordinators have been able to come up with creative solutions that enable them to carry out their mission. Peer mediation programs have shared rooms with other programs (student council, yearbook, or other clubs), or used counselor's offices, empty classrooms, school committee rooms, and even the cafeteria when need be.

FINAL WORDS

Although the design and redesign of a peer mediation effort continue for the life of the program, it is important to address the issues covered here as early as possible. Solicit ideas from the school community by distributing written drafts of your design to key people and when appropriate, to the school-at-large. When you have arrived at a tentative plan with which you are comfortable, take the second part of the implementation readiness survey that follows. If you have addressed these issues adequately, then it is time to move forward to the next phase of program implementation: training and outreach.

Peer Mediation Implementation Readiness Survey

PART B. PROGRAM DESIGN AND PLANNING

1B. Coordinator's Availability

Our coordinator has the flexibility to schedule and supervise
    mediation sessions at any time during the school day.   +20

Our coordinator is available for only a few preordained periods each day.   +10

Our coordinator will have to fit this into other full-time
    responsibilities/we do not have a coordinator yet.   -100

2B. Coordinator's Commitment and Ability

Our coordinator has excellent communication skills and is excited
    about taking on this responsibility.   + 30

Our coordinator has average communication skills and/or is only
    moderately interested in peer mediation.   + 0

Our coordinator has poor communication skills and/or is not
    interested in taking on this responsibility.   -100

3B. Coordinator's Compensation

Our coordinator is compensated with money and/or time during the school day.   + 20

Two or more people are sharing the job of coordinator and doing it
    during their planning periods.   + 5

Our coordinator is donating her or his efforts to the program and is given neither
    time during the school day nor monetary compensation to do this job.   - 50

4B. Funding

We have all the funding we need for the next three years.   + 20

We have all the funding we need for this year.   + 10

We do not have funding to meet our needs at this point.   - 100

5B. Program Evaluation

We have arranged to have a professional evaluation conducted
    of our peer mediation program.   + 20

We will be conducting our own informal evaluation in-house.   + 10

We have no plans to conduct an evaluation of our program.   + 0

6B. Advisory Council

The implementation of our peer mediation program is overseen formally
    by an advisory council composed of students, teachers, and administrators.   + 20

The program is being implemented by only one or two people.   + 0

7B. Mediator Meetings

Meeting with mediators will be built into our school schedule
    (a mediator homeroom, a mediation class, and so on).   + 20

Meeting with mediators is not built into our school day but we
    will hold meetings with student mediators at least bimonthly.   + 10

We will not hold regular meetings with the student mediators.   – 10

8B. Relationship with Disciplinary System

The peer mediation program will work closely with the disciplinary system.   + 20

The peer mediation program will not work closely with the disciplinary system.   – 20

9B. Staff Training

The majority of our staff and administrators have participated in training on
    mediation and conflict resolution.   + 20

A core group of our staff and administrators have participated in training on
    mediation and conflict resolution.   + 10

None of our staff or administrators have participated in training on
    mediation and conflict resolution.   + 0

10B. Schoolwide Training for Students

All students in our school will receive training in conflict resolution
    through the curriculum.   + 20

Some students in our school will receive training in conflict resolution
    through the curriculum.   + 10

No students in our school will receive training in conflict resolution
    through the curriculum.   + 0

11B. Confidentiality and Voluntariness

We have formulated policies regarding voluntariness and confidentiality
    that administrators, teachers, students, and parents support.   + 20

We have not yet formulated policies regarding voluntariness
    and confidentiality.   + 0

12B. Availability of Mediation Services

As long as they keep up with their other responsibilities, our student
    mediators will be allowed to mediate whenever necessary, regardless
    of what time of day it is.   + 20

Our student mediators will only be allowed to mediate at a
    few specified periods during the school day.   + 10

Our student mediators will only be allowed to mediate before or after school.   – 50

13B. Space

We have an appropriate, dedicated space in which to conduct our
mediation sessions.   + 20

We have to use a space that is sometimes used for other purposes
to conduct our mediation sessions.   + 10

We do not have a space in the school to conduct our mediation sessions.   – 30

TOTAL:

Scoring

170–270 points: Excellent. You are ready to begin training peer mediators.

110–170 points: Caution. Try to improve your program design before
training peer mediators.

< 110 points: Poor. You are not ready to begin training peer mediators.

CHAPTER 6

Training and Outreach

Organizing a successful training program is the next stage of peer mediation implementation. This can be exhausting work for the coordinator, but it is well worth the effort. Training functions like the booster rockets that propel a spaceship into its destined orbit; whereas earlier phases get the program off the ground, training finally makes it operational. In this chapter we will discuss the range of issues involved in planning a successful training program. The chapter closes with a look at the important work of outreach and promotion.

APPROACHING TRAINING

When considering mediation training, two fundamental points must be stressed at the outset:

You cannot learn to mediate from a book. An individual's personality, habits, prior training, and beliefs all affect his or her ability to mediate. But we are too "close to ourselves" to judge when these are a help or a hindrance to this work. Mediation trainees depend upon others to make them aware of whether they are judging the parties, listening inappropriately, missing opportunities to build agreement, or forgetting issues. Most people learn to mediate through simulated and real mediation experience guided by the constructive criticism of skilled trainers. Written materials are an important supplement, but they can never replace this person-to-person process.[24]

You cannot train others to mediate unless you are a mediator yourself. This truism must be stressed to those considering peer mediation training. Although educators are sometimes required to use curricula to teach students material that they themselves are in the process of learning, this does not work well with mediation. Experienced mediators make dozens of discrete, strategic decisions during the course of a single mediation session, each made in reference to his or her understanding of the process, past experiences, and perceptions of the current mediation. Trainers must have a comprehensive understanding of mediation to guide trainees in the "real time" of role-plays and simulations. If they are only one step ahead of their students, they will not be able to conduct a dynamic and effective training.[25]

The bottom line is this: If you are not already an experienced mediator, you need to participate in mediation training before you can initiate your peer mediation program. Schools use two primary approaches to peer mediation training: *direct training* and *training*

---

[24] Educators with no formal mediation training—even counselors and disciplinarians who "mediate" informally all the time—are often humbled by their first mediation training experience. Usually they discover that they are far less skilled as mediators than they had assumed.

[25] The peer mediation training curricula currently being published are useful only to those who have already been trained as mediators. This author considers irresponsible those organizations that market their curricula—"buy our training guide to set up your peer mediation program"—to educators who are not trained as mediators.

Over the summer two kids got into a fight and the counselor was going to kick them out of the park but I told the counselor about mediation and they agreed to try it and when they saw how the kids talked out their problems they really enjoyed it and I got a certificate of leadership.

Middle school mediator

institutes. Direct training involves having experienced mediation trainers come to your school and conduct one or more trainings for students and staff. The training institute involves sending school staff to a peer mediation training for trainers, after which they return to school to conduct their own training for students.

Although open to debate, most experienced trainers agree that direct training is preferable for a number of reasons:

- Direct training ensures your trainees the benefits of working with experienced and skilled trainers. Because student mediators are the heart of a program, the quality of their training is crucial to your success.
- Direct training ensures that the training program and implementation assistance are geared to the unique needs of your school.
- Direct training is cost-effective because it trains more school-based staff and students for the money.
- In most instances, outside trainers lend an aura of respectability and professionalism that helps win support for peer mediation.

Two factors appear to make the training institute approach more appealing. It seems less expensive than direct training, and it promises to prepare school-based staff members to conduct their own student mediation trainings as soon as possible. This would move your school more quickly toward self-sufficiency and at the same time reduce the need to hire trainers, one of the biggest programmatic expenses.

A number of factors limit these benefits, however. One is that if the training institute is not local, the travel expenses of sending staff to the training can consume any savings. The cost of sending two teachers to an out-of-state training—it is always better to send teams of teachers so that they can support one another when they return to school—can equal the cost of training twenty-five people on site.

A far more significant limitation of the training institute approach, however, is that it usually requires trainees to learn how to mediate *and* how to train others to mediate simultaneously. Given that both mediation and training are complex sets of skills, and that both are mastered primarily through experience, many people simply feel unprepared to conduct their own training after completing these institutes. And often they *are* unprepared, especially if they have not arranged to gain experience as mediators before they begin to train. Only exceptional people are capable of returning to their schools after completing a training institute and conducting a credible peer mediation training on their own. (Training institutes are more effective for elementary peer mediation programs where the mediation process is simpler and easier to convey to students.)

Steps can be taken to make the training institute approach more effective. One is to send educators who have already been trained as mediators. This way they can devote their attention to mastering the training program rather than focusing on learning to mediate. Or, you might initially use graduates of a training institute to assist an experienced trainer.

Direct training—having experienced mediation trainers conduct a training at your school—should be the first choice for peer mediation programs in middle and high schools. This approach has one potential disadvantage, however. When trainings are conducted *for* school-based staff members, they become accustomed to others assuming this responsibility and reluctant to take it on themselves. Direct trainers should work with them from the outset—perhaps including them as "apprentice" trainers—so that they are psychologically as well as substantively prepared to assume responsibility for training students as soon as they are able.

SOURCES OF TRAINING

Regardless of whether you choose direct training or the training institute approach, there are a variety of potential training sources, including:

- **Organizations and individuals that specialize in conducting school-based peer mediation trainings.** Peer mediation specialists are the most commonly used and often the best sources of training for schools. The many advantages associated with them include their expertise, the high quality of their field-tested training programs, the ability of these trainers to travel to your school, the respect that experienced trainers can command in the school, and the ongoing support and follow-up training that these trainers provide for your program (especially if they are based in your area). If these trainers are providing direct training, make sure they plan to train school-based staff members to conduct their own trainings after they gain experience as mediators. Potential disadvantages of working with peer mediation specialists are that they can be expensive, and they might not be locally based.
- **Local community mediation programs.** Building links with the community strengthens your school-based effort in many ways. Using a community mediation program is therefore a wonderful option for training if it is available. By definition, the community program will be nearby, enabling it to provide ongoing support and engendering a special level of commitment to your school. Community mediation programs are also likely to have slightly lower fees than peer mediation specialists, and they may be willing to help you raise the necessary funds. In many areas, however, community mediation programs do not have experience working in the school setting. Their training, therefore, might not be as effective with young people. This option is also limited to those who have a local community mediation program. To find out whether your community has one, consult the yellow pages of your phone book under "mediation," or call your court system's administrative offices or state mediation association. Since community mediation programs regularly train volunteers to mediate disputes in the community, consider participating in such a training yourself. An excellent way to receive introductory mediation training, it can begin to prepare you to conduct your own training for students.
- **Local universities or colleges.** Increasing numbers of colleges and universities are starting peer mediation programs on their campuses. This process is quite similar to implementing a program in a primary or secondary school. Using college professors and their students to conduct your training has similar advantages and disadvantages to working with community mediation programs.
- **Staff and students from local schools that have peer mediation programs.** This is a very economical option if it is available to you. Students can train their peers or other students younger than themselves. The training will not be as polished as training from

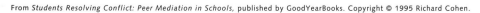

other sources, but if done effectively, students can make up in enthusiasm what they lack in experience. One major obstacle is the logistics: not only is it difficult for student mediators to find time to train that does not conflict with other responsibilities, it requires an enormous amount of time and effort to prepare students to be trainers. (Without adequate preparations, using students as trainers can be disastrous.) Largely because of these logistical challenges, this option is not often utilized.

- **Mediation training specialists on staff within your school system.** A few committed and forward-looking school districts have seen fit to hire in-house mediation specialists. These full- or part-time staff members provide schools within their district with training and assistance in all aspects of school-based mediation programs. If this option is available to you—and if the person hired to fill this position is capable—consider yourself lucky. Any school district that is making a systemwide commitment to this program would be wise to follow this approach.

EVALUATING TRAINING SOURCES

Having located potential sources of training, you must next choose one that best meets your needs. You will need to evaluate two factors: the mediation models that they use and the quality of their training programs.

The Mediation Model

Mediation processes used in peer mediation programs around the world are not identical. Some models ask each party to summarize the other parties' perspectives; others do not. Some approaches provide mediators with a detailed outline of steps to follow when mediating; others provide only a general structure to guide students. Some use two student co-mediators, while others use one, three, or even more. Part of your job is to select the model that will be most effective in your school.

Of course, it is difficult to evaluate such distinctions when you are new to mediation. Most schools end up implementing whatever model they discover first: perhaps one used by a neighboring school system or the one used by a trainer they want to work with. It should be comforting to note, however, that effective peer mediation models are far more similar than different. You should expect a mediation model to exhibit the following six characteristics:

1. **A structure.** The mediation process should be divided into stages that are easy for students to understand. Although the number of stages—and how closely students are encouraged to follow them—will differ, it is essential that the process incorporate definable steps.

2. **An emphasis on reconciliation as well as the creation of agreements.** Effective peer mediation models place as much importance upon restoring communication and healing relationships as on creating agreements to resolve substantive issues. The former accounts for a large part of the educational impact of mediation, and it is especially necessary in the school setting where parties always have at least a minimal ongoing relationship. Student mediators are trained to help their peers

collaborate to resolve their differences, and the mediation model should stress the *collaboration* as much as the *resolution*.

3. **The use of co-mediators.** Mediating is too difficult for one student mediator to handle alone. The overwhelming majority of peer mediation models therefore employ two student "co-mediators," and this seems to be ideal. Some models use three or more mediators, but the logistical problems and resulting increase in classes missed by mediators make this inadvisable.

4. **The encouragement of written agreements.** In middle and high schools, mediation sessions should result in written agreements. Written agreements are tangible, incontrovertible evidence that things have changed as a result of mediation. Writing an agreement forces parties to focus and commit themselves in a way that is lacking when agreements are only verbal. They also enable students to refer to the agreement more easily in the future.

5. **The use of private sessions when necessary.** Private sessions refer to the times when mediators meet with parties individually. Some models encourage mediators to take private sessions during the middle of every session, some begin every mediation session with private sessions rather than a joint session, and some frown upon using private sessions altogether. It is best to use a model that incorporates private sessions, but that trains student mediators to use them only when they feel they are needed. Although private sessions are an important tool, they are unnecessary in many student conflicts. (See Appendix C for more information on private sessions.)

6. **An ability to adapt to different cultural norms.** In the United States, the need to make adaptations of the peer mediation process is limited compared to other types of mediation. Nevertheless, it is important to use a model that is flexible in this regard. Perhaps eye contact is not advisable with the population in your school. Perhaps a written agreement or the direct expression of feelings would be out of place. Perhaps mediators should take a more active role in generating solutions. Your model should be able to incorporate these considerations and still be effective.[26]

It is interesting to note that most mediators—those with decades of experience as well as new trainees struggling to master the intricacies of the mediation process—become devoted to whatever mediation model they learn. There are many ways to mediate, however, and the criteria presented here should be used only as a guide for choosing a mediation trainer. All mediators should be taught to delight in seeing someone mediate differently, yet effectively. Only in this way will our knowledge grow.

The Quality of the Training Program

Having located potential sources of training and considered the mediation model that they use, the last step in selecting a training source is to evaluate the quality of their training programs. Before listing some criteria to help you do this, one essential point needs to be made: *You have every right to expect your peer mediation training to be of the highest quality.*

A friend and I had a disagreement. She seemed jealous of my relationship with my boyfriend. I gathered from her tone that we were growing apart. Rather than losing my closest friend over something that might not last, I talked it out with her. Without interruptions and name calling, we worked it out. There's proof that mediation does work for everybody if they're willing to cooperate.

Middle school mediator

---

[26] For more on this, see the book *Mediating the Tough Cases: Advanced Issues in Peer Mediation Case Work,* available from School Mediation Associates.

To create a dynamic learning experience for their students, most classroom teachers must overcome institutional restrictions like forty-five–minute class periods, mandatory curricula, standardized testing, and homogeneous groups. Mediation trainers, on the other hand, usually have the freedom to create ideal learning conditions within their training. They can

- work with students who are self-selected and want to be in the training;
- design their curricula to meet the needs of the students they are working with;
- use methods that are experiential and engaging to students;
- require students to take responsibility for their learning;
- present programs that concern the real-life problems that are important to students, thereby motivating them to learn;
- work with heterogeneous groups in a way that emphasizes cooperation rather than competitiveness and that highlights the unique talents of every trainee;
- pace the training according to the rhythm of each group of trainees rather than according to an external school schedule; and
- create a supportive atmosphere in which trainees can take risks without losing face and without worrying about their grades.

Because mediation trainers have this freedom, you should accept nothing less than an excellent experience for the students and staff who participate in their program.

The following criteria will help you evaluate potential training sources, and you will be best served by the trainers who meet the greatest number of them. Of course, you may need to factor additional considerations into your decision. Perhaps the benefits in terms of cost and convenience of working with less-qualified trainers justifies selecting them over trainers with more experience. But whenever possible, trainers should meet the following criteria:

- **Trainers should have extensive experience with mediation in general and with school-based peer mediation in particular.** The best peer mediation trainers have studied mediation for years, have mediated many cases within and outside of schools, and are familiar with the way schools work. In addition, they should have experience implementing peer mediation programs.
- **Trainers should have extensive experience as trainers.** A skilled mediator does not necessarily make a skilled mediation trainer; the two are wholly separate areas of expertise. Substantively, trainers need to have knowledge of and facility with an array of presentations, exercises, games, and role-plays that teach the skills of mediation. Trainers also need to be able to create a learning environment where diverse students and teachers take risks and feel increasingly comfortable with one another. Skill in guiding this "group process" is as essential to conducting effective trainings as imparting information about mediation.
- **Trainers should have experience working with young people.** Even if an individual knows how to train *and* how to mediate, it does not guarantee that he or she knows how to train young people to mediate. Working with students provides a unique challenge to the mediation trainer. Young people are quick to spot a phony, and they are even quicker to lose interest if the material or the presentation is not engaging. Peer

mediation trainers should have experience adapting material to the attention span and the developmental ability of the students with whom they work. They should also feel at ease and enjoy working with young people.

■ **Training programs should emphasize basic mediation skills and theory.** A specific set of theory and skills forms the core of all training programs. These include conflict resolution theory, communication and listening skills, negotiation and problem-solving skills, maintaining respectful control of the process, asking questions, winning trust, maintaining neutrality, and writing agreements. Programs may add information to supplement and inform this core (anger management, violence prevention, assertiveness training, prejudice reduction, music, and art), but of necessity, they should always emphasize the basics.

■ **Training programs should empower students and schools to be self-sufficient.** Training is an ongoing responsibility of school mediation programs. Student mediators graduate, and new ones need to be trained at least every other year. Given that training is also one of the biggest programmatic expenses, trainers should encourage schools to conduct their own trainings as soon as they can do so effectively. Training programs should also operate on the assumption that most people, with appropriate training and effort, will be able to mediate in a way that meets the needs of a school mediation program.

■ **Training programs should be tailored to meet the needs of each school.** Trainers should be willing and able to modify the structure as well as the content of their training program to meet the needs of your school. If your school wants to mediate special kinds of conflicts; if your system needs to train tenth-graders and seventh-graders simultaneously; if a large percentage of your student population is Southeast Asian—trainers should design the program accordingly. The best trainers will modify their approach—even in the midst of the training—in any way that will make it more engaging, more informative, or more effective for the trainees.

Training programs should emphasize evaluation and self-evaluation of trainees. Students, like everyone else, learn to mediate by trying it out and then receiving feedback regarding their performance. It is therefore imperative that training programs incorporate ample time for students to be evaluated and to evaluate themselves. This keeps trainees apprised regarding their progress as mediators, and perhaps more importantly, it instills in them the notion that mastering mediation is an ongoing process. Trainers should also provide coordinators with individual evaluations of student mediators at the conclusion of the training. This enables coordinators to create effective co-mediator teams and call only upon those students who are ready to mediate. One way to gauge a training program's emphasis on evaluation is to note its trainer-to-trainee ratio. The best will try to have as close to one trainer for every five trainees as possible.

Training programs should balance skill building with personal growth. There is a tension in mediation training between helping trainees grow personally on the one hand, and helping them develop effective mediation skills on the other. Facilitating personal growth and an internal reorientation to conflict is fundamental to making students effective mediators. But there is only so much time in a training and always more than enough skill-building work to be done. Too much emphasis on the former leaves trainees without the necessary skills. Too much emphasis on the latter leaves trainees

Being a mediator has changed my life. The training gave me skills I will use forever. I can now sort out my problems and figure out neutral solutions. I can better solve my disputes and will continue to.

Middle school mediator

om *Students Resolving Conflict: Peer Mediation in Schools,* published by GoodYearBooks. Copyright © 1995 Richard Cohen.

without a context in which the skills make sense. The best trainers find a balance between these two.

- **Training programs should have an ongoing interest in and commitment to working with your school.** A training program should maintain close contact with your school long after the training is complete, for follow-up training purposes as well as to offer technical assistance regarding program implementation. Obviously, this is easier to do if the training source is local. But whether they are across town or across the country, trainers should maintain regular phone contact, visit whenever possible, and provide you with materials and ideas for continued refinement of the process and the program.

- **Training programs should be of adequate length.** Peer mediation trainings for high school students are approximately fifteen to twenty-five hours, for middle school students twelve to twenty, and for elementary-aged students ten to fifteen hours. If you already have a curricular effort in your school, this can reduce the length of mediation training (because students have been exposed to basic communication and conflict resolution skills). You should be concerned if training programs are shorter than noted above.

In peer mediation training, a kind of "super" learning must take place in which every minute of time and every ounce of energy is devoted to the goal of learning to mediate. Training is not "forgiving" like the mediation process itself: unprepared and unskilled trainers can truly ruin a training and destroy your program's momentum before it begins. Training student mediators is wonderfully exhausting and demanding work, even for the most experienced trainers. Anyone who claims otherwise has not done it very much or very well.

A final caution is warranted: With the growth of the peer mediation concept has come a boom in the number of individuals and organizations that market themselves as peer mediation trainers. Because this field is so young, there are no standards that individuals must meet to call themselves mediation trainers. Some supposed trainers have little experience as trainers, and little if any experience as mediators. It is therefore advisable to be cautious when choosing a trainer. Conduct a thorough investigation into the background and experience of any training source before you agree to work with them.

CRITERIA FOR SELECTING TRAINEES

After you have determined how you are going to obtain training, the next task is to select your trainees. As previously mentioned, student mediators form the core of a peer mediation effort. Not only do they mediate cases, they are also your biggest resource for implementation, helping to design the program, conducting outreach campaigns, following-up on cases, and even training new mediators. A dedicated and skilled group that works effectively together will go a long way toward ensuring that your program is a success. Consider five main criteria when selecting trainees: diversity, personal skills and abilities, commitment, grade level, and availability.

1. **Diversity.** Student mediators should represent a cross-section of the school community. This includes diversity along the lines of race, ethnicity, physical capability, socioeconomic background, academic ability, grade level, sex, home neighborhood, cliques represented ("jocks," "nerds," and so on), and even personality types. A diverse training group benefits the program in many ways:

- It makes for a richer training experience because trainees work with those with whom they would not normally associate.
- It demonstrates to the trainees and to the school that diverse groups of students can work, learn, and have fun together.
- It prepares trainees for their work as mediators, when they will have to feel comfortable with and win the trust of all kinds of students.
- It provides the program with a resource to understand as well as reach out to all groups within the school. (People see that mediation is not just for this or that "type" of student.)
- It provides the program with greater flexibility and depth when assigning mediators to a case.

The greater the diversity of your trainees, the more energy and power they will have when they learn to work together. When schools make the mistake of stacking the training group with one type of student, they limit their program's effectiveness.

2. **Personal Skills and Abilities.** Trainees should have personal qualities that will make them good mediators. These might include communication skills, the respect of their peers, self-confidence, empathy, leadership potential, willingness to receive feedback, ability to speak in front of groups, and so on. Excellent mediators can spring from unlikely places, and so you should be open-minded in this regard. But especially in the initial year of the program, it makes sense to select students who show great promise as mediators.

3. **Commitment.** You should select mediation trainees according to the strength of their commitment to the program. With few exceptions, they should participate in the training voluntarily and be willing to serve as mediators for at least one year. Stress to potential trainees that a commitment to one thing often involves giving up other things, and mediators might have to stay after school or occasionally miss one of their favorite classes. Student mediators must also be responsible for attending all meetings and mediation sessions as well as for making up any schoolwork they miss as a result of the program. Some programs ask students to commit to a certain number of hours of work for the program each month, regardless of whether they are mediating or not.

4. **Grade Level.** To maximize your investment of time and energy, select a majority of trainees who will be enrolled in the school for at least one school year after the training is complete. Most programs train a predominance of students in the middle grades of their school. In a high school, a group of twenty trainees might include two freshmen, six sophomores, seven juniors, two seniors, and four staff. The same number of student trainees in a middle school might include three sixth-graders, nine seventh-graders, four eighth-graders, and four staff. These rough formulas will vary according to the design of the program and the time of year that the training is conducted. Even though in some schools being a mediator is a privilege reserved for the oldest students, this

I enjoy being a mediator because it has instilled positive, remedial qualities firmly into my character. Mediation has also given me an opportunity to work closely with a number of great people whom I otherwise may not have met.

High school mediator

approach is not advisable for a program's first year because it leaves the school with no skilled mediators after graduation.

5. **Availability.** The relative importance of this last criterion also depends upon the design of your program. If you are only going to mediate during study halls, you want to select trainees who have study halls scattered throughout the school day. If you are only holding mediation sessions before and after school, select a large number of trainees who can get to school early and who don't have commitments directly after school. The same concerns apply to the schedule of the training. If you will hold training predominantly after school, on weekends, or during the summer, you must find trainees who are available at those times. As a general rule, avoid selecting students who are already overcommitted and involved in many other extracurricular activities.

Noah's Rules

One guide you can use to create a strong group of trainees is "Noah's Rules." Like the biblical Noah who included all known animal species on his ark, you want to bring together as diverse a group of students in your training as possible. In addition, follow Noah's lead by striving to include at least two of each "type" of student in the training. Participating in mediation training is a risk, and if a trainee is the only representative of his or her self-identified group—the only Vietnamese, ninth-grader, athlete, teacher, metal head, and so on—that trainee is more likely to feel isolated and uncomfortable. (This is one reason why students drop out of peer mediation training.) Having someone else like oneself in the training provides an anchor in a sea of difference, and this helps trainees weather their initial discomfort until they are able to form relationships with other trainees.

Because of space limitations, however, sometimes you can only include one representative of a particular group in the training. In these cases, try to select someone with the fewest other unique characteristics that set him or her apart from other trainees. If you can only have one gang-affiliated student in the training, don't select an individual who would also be the only Haitian or the only eighth-grader in the training. Each additional difference will magnify his or her initial discomfort.

Group Size

Most school mediation programs include approximately twenty trainees in their initial training, although the number depends upon the setting, the type of program being implemented, and the philosophy of the trainers. The training group should be small enough to allow for the individual attention that mediation training demands, and large enough to provide the school with an adequate pool of qualified mediators. On average, 85 to 90 percent of trainees are ready to begin mediating upon completing the training. After the initial year, the size of your training groups will be determined by considering the caseload, the number of experienced mediators available from previous trainings, and the training resources at the program's disposal.

Sometimes one or two trainees drop out of the training for one reason or another. Because of this, either arrange for "alternate" trainees who can be called upon if someone drops out, or begin the training with a few more trainees than you'll need in the end.

Including "At-Risk" Students in Your Training

Of all the benefits attributed to peer mediation programs, those that accrue to student mediators are most impressive. Substantively, mediators learn valuable skills and new perspectives that serve them well inside and outside of school. In addition, mediators' self-esteem increases as they gain confidence in their abilities and appreciate that they have a special responsibility in the school. All students benefit personally from their participation in a peer mediation training.

In acknowledgment of this, many programs strive to include so-called at-risk students in the training. At-risk students are those who have behavioral and/or emotional problems that put them "at risk" of not succeeding in school. Giving at-risk students peer mediation training—giving them the opportunity and the skills necessary to make a positive contribution to the school—has a number of benefits. It can make a difference in these students' educational careers. Students who feel they are needed and appreciated in school are much more likely to continue to attend.

In addition to the benefits to the students, including at-risk students in your cadre of mediators helps the program as well. Although educators often assume that they are guaranteeing program success by training only well-adjusted students as mediators, at-risk student mediators strengthen a program immeasurably. Young people who have had problems with fighting in the past bring a unique perspective to their work as mediators. They know firsthand the language, the postures, the causes, the pressures, and the unsatisfying and sometimes even disastrous consequences of using violence to resolve conflicts. They have the experience not to be intimidated by parties in these situations. And they often have the respect of their peers that enables them to win the trust of even the most disaffected students.

Given the clear benefits of including at-risk students in your training, the only relevant question to answer is: How many? The number of these students should be relative to the other trainees. Because mediation training is so labor intensive, you cannot afford to train students who won't serve you well in the future, and you have precious little "extra" time to win students over and get them focused on learning the skills of mediation. Given these considerations, dedicate no more than 15 to 20 percent of your training slots to students who have behavioral problems themselves.

Regarding selection criteria, keep in mind that students can have behavioral problems in school and still have many if not all of the qualities necessary to be good mediators. In fact, good grades and good behavior do not guarantee that a student will make a good mediator, or vice versa. Mediation is a great leveler. Although coordinators sometimes include one or two students in the training for their own benefit (and with no expectations that they will become strong mediators), for the most part you should judge potential at-risk trainees by the same criteria you use to judge other students: diversity, personal skill and ability, grade level, and availability.

At-risk students may fall short initially in the quality of their commitment to the program. It takes extra effort both to get these students involved in the training and to keep them there once they join. At-risk students often come to the training initially either because a teacher or administrator strongly recommended that they do so, or because it gets them out of classes. If the training is conducted correctly, however, by the

I feel good when I mediate because I know I have done something good after each session.

Middle school mediator

I really feel proud of

myself that I am a

mediator. It brought

my self-esteem high-

er than it was. I am

really glad that I

have the qualities of

a mediator that can

help me out in the

future.

Middle school mediator

end of the first session they will be excited about becoming a mediator and will enthusiastically choose to return.

When recruiting at-risk students, then, find a balance between stressing the serious commitment that the program requires and letting them come for their own reasons. At-risk students may not write glowing essays about why they want to be mediators; they may not shine in a pretraining interview. By asking too much of them before they have firsthand experience of the program, you risk scaring them away.

Once the training has started and they are interested in continuing, ask more of these students. Remind them that they have been chosen to be leaders and perform a prestigious function in the school. If they are prone to fighting, ask for a commitment that they will not fight for the duration of the training and renew this commitment once the training is over. These students may also need extra help handling the other responsibilities involved in participating in the program. Personal reminders on the days of training sessions, for example, increase the likelihood that they will remember to come. Check with them about how they are handling their schoolwork during the training and help them get assistance if they need it.

It is worth the extra effort to include at-risk students in your training. Although every at-risk trainee will not be inspired by peer mediation training, many succeed in the training to such an extent that trainers will not be able to distinguish the students who have behavioral difficulties from the rest of the group.

Including School Staff in Your Training

Although peer mediation is ultimately designed to empower students, it cannot be successful without the support of teachers and administrators. Perhaps the best way to win this support is to include staff people in the peer mediation training, learning side-by-side with the students. The impact of this program can be fully appreciated only after it is experienced, and teachers and administrators who complete the training with students become the program's biggest boosters. They serve as ambassadors to the rest of the staff, and they are also an important source of referrals in the early days of program implementation.

Staff members benefit as much as the program does from their participation in the training. They learn new skills and gain confidence as facilitators of conflict resolution that serve them well in their classrooms, offices, and homes. They mediate occasionally for the program—usually teacher-student disputes along with a student co-mediator— which is always an enjoyable and educational experience. And perhaps most significantly, teachers are invigorated by spending time with students as "colearners." Teachers invariably cite working with students in this way as one of the most beneficial and enjoyable aspects of the training. Watching students—even those they had assumed did not belong in the training—act responsibly and with intelligence renews their faith in young people. Teacher mediators often return to the classroom with new enthusiasm.

When training teachers and students simultaneously, pay careful attention to the ratio of one group to the other. The most successful trainings include between 20 to 25 percent adult trainees and the balance students. Any less and teachers feel isolated; any more and students feel intimidated. As an easy rule of thumb, there should be a *maximum* of one adult to every three student trainees.

When selecting adults to participate in the training, apply similar criteria as those used to select students. Aim for a diverse group of staff with varied political connections within the school system (ties to the administration, to guidance, to the school board, to academic departments, to physical education, to school security, and so on). Select adults who have a facility for mediation, a sincere interest in the program, and the respect of their fellow educators. Although teachers don't often have the opportunity to mediate formally in school (which can be a disappointment to them), consider giving preference to those staff people whose schedules will allow them to mediate or coordinate if necessary. Make sure as well that the teachers selected feel comfortable learning "as equals" with their students.

If possible, include one of the school disciplinarians in the student training (unless students feel intimidated by him or her). A disciplinarian who understands and supports the program can become your biggest ally and your best referral source. Disciplinarians also find that the training provides them with a new perspective, a useful model, and some effective techniques for handling the conflicts that confront them every day.

To recruit staff, most schools ask for volunteers and also invite specific individuals whom they would like to participate. In addition to providing for substitute coverage, some programs have been able to arrange for continuing education credit for teachers. Although hesitant to miss their responsibilities in the classroom, more than enough teachers and staff are usually interested in participating.

Consider inviting parents to fill a few of the training slots reserved for adults. Parents can model conflict resolution skills at home, and when students see this approach outside of school, they are more likely to apply it in all areas of their lives. Developing mediation skills benefits parents both personally and professionally. After they have completed the training, parents can also help with program coordination and outreach.

THE PROCESS OF SELECTING TRAINEES

How should your program select trainees? The easiest approach is to train an already existing group of students in a classroom, a student club or committee, or the student government. Some schools train their peer counselors or their student council members if these groups meet the requirements of diversity, personal skills, availability, and commitment. A drawback of this approach is that such clubs and committees often comprise the core of active and assertive students in a school. Rather than training students who regularly receive special attention and training, it is preferable to "share the wealth" and honor students who are not already involved in school programs.

A more common method of selecting trainees, then, is to assemble a heterogeneous team of students who are not already part of an existing group. The most efficient way to accomplish this—and a way that includes staff in another element of the program—is to solicit recommendations from teachers and administrators. After an overview presentation or training, staff members complete nomination sheets that outline the qualities you are looking for in student mediators. (See page 223 for a sample form.) Teachers have a few days to return these sheets to the coordinator, who selects trainees from among the nominees. Some programs require that students receive two staff nominations to qualify for

selection. Disciplinarians are especially helpful in recommending at-risk students who might be appropriate for the program.

If time and energy permit, it is ideal to include the student body in the selection process as well. Students can be encouraged to volunteer themselves or nominate peers whom they feel would be suitable. As with the staff, the student body learns about the program through assemblies, presentations to classrooms, and articles in school newspapers. Students then nominate not the most popular students, but those to whom they go for help when they have a problem. (At-risk students may have to be actively recruited.) Mediation trainees are selected from among these volunteers and nominees. A drawback of this approach is that because so many students apply, the coordinator must spend time interviewing far more applicants than are needed.

It is important to note that the selection process can be used to strengthen other aspects of program implementation, especially outreach and education. The more that you can involve members of the school community in developing the peer mediation program, the greater the investment they will have in its success. An important and countervailing factor, however, is that coordinators have much to accomplish during the first year of a program, and they must use their time efficiently. This argues for making the selection process as simple and straightforward as possible. Whatever approach you choose, take both of these factors into consideration.

Once students have either applied or been nominated to be mediators, the coordinator (ideally with the assistance of advisory council members and peer mediators) must screen the nominees and select those who are most appropriate. Some schools use an empowering (but time-consuming) process in which students discuss the nominees in their homerooms and arrive at a consensus regarding who should be the mediators. But in the majority of programs, the ultimate decision regarding selection rests in the hands of the coordinator and those assisting him or her. In this way the training group can be tailored to meet the needs of the program as a whole.

There are a variety of ways to screen nominees including:

- **Hold a preliminary meeting for nominees.** During this introductory meeting, the coordinator (and helpers) discusses the commitment that mediators must make in terms of time, attitude, and behavior in school. In some programs, mediators must agree to uphold a code of conduct (attending class, doing homework, not fighting). These meetings screen out students who are not willing to make the necessary commitment.
- **Ask students to fill out a written application for the position of mediator.** This can include questions about logistical information (when are applicants' nonacademic periods, do they have after-school commitments, are they available on the training dates?) as well as questions about nominees' qualifications and their motivations for applying to be mediators. Because certain students who would make excellent mediators have very poor written skills and are intimidated by this process, some programs do without a written application.
- **Conduct individual interviews with nominees.** You will learn about the students from how they present themselves during the interview, from their answers to questions, and from their behavior in role-play simulations. (See page 224 for an outline of a sample interview.)

Typically, students selected to be mediators are required to have permission from their teachers *and* their parents or guardians to participate in the program. Students should approach each of their teachers and ask for permission to mediate occasionally during class. (See page 226 for a sample teacher permission form.) This puts the teachers in charge, and their responses clarify how much flexibility you will have in using a student as a mediator. This is most helpful for programs that will be conducting mediation sessions during class periods. If more than two teachers will not support a student's selection, it is best to select another student.

Asking for parent permission serves a number of purposes. It is an essential courtesy; it avoids problems with parents who might not want their children participating in the program; and it is a form of outreach to the community. Send a letter home that congratulates parents on their child's selection, reviews the nature of the program and the benefits it can bring to students and school, and clearly describes what is being asked of their child. (A sample letter to parents is included on page 225.)

When recruiting mediators, consider whether incentives can be offered to students who participate in the training. Some schools arrange for students to receive course credit for the training, while in other schools being a mediator fulfills the community service hours required for graduation. Incentives are not necessary, however; usually more than enough students will participate in the training without them. But there may be creative ways that you can compensate students for the time and energy they devote to the mediation program.

After student trainees have been selected, some schools require that they sign a contract with the program. The contract outlines the mediators' responsibilities and can include everything from the number of hours they must devote to the program each month to the code of conduct described above. Using a contract is instructive to students in that it is similar to the agreements that they help parties create. It also indicates the level of commitment that is necessary to be a mediator. Sometimes it is better to have mediators sign this contract—and formally commit to the program—*after* completing the training when they are most informed and excited about the program and its responsibilities. (See page 227 for a sample contract.)

It is usually quite easy to recruit students to be mediators; the hard part is turning students away.[27] Selecting mediators is most time-consuming during the first program year when students are not informed about the program. Later, you will find the program training many of last year's parties to be this year's mediators.

The best thing about peer mediation is that we have teachers and students willing to help kids solve their problems.

Middle school mediator

---

[27] Make sure you find a way to thank those students whom you do not select to be mediators so as not to alienate them from the program at this early stage.

From *Students Resolving Conflict: Peer Mediation in Schools*, published by GoodYearBooks. Copyright © 1995 Richard Cohen.

SCHEDULING TRAINING

You need to answer three questions when deciding how to schedule your peer mediation training. The first concerns the time of the calendar year to conduct the training. The second regards the extent to which training will be scheduled during the school day. And the third involves the length and configuration of the training sessions. Work closely with your training source to resolve these questions. Your advisory council can also be helpful when it comes to scheduling. Such a diverse group is likely to know when dances, field trips, standardized testing, and so on are planned that would conflict with the training schedule.

The Time of Year

Peer mediation programs successfully conduct trainings any time between August and April. The most common time is during the middle of the first semester, when students and educators have settled into the year's routine. (Any earlier and there are too many distractions related to the start of school.) Conducting the training at least six weeks into the first semester also provides more than enough time to select your trainees and manage training logistics.

Some programs prefer to train their mediators during the second half of the school year. This allows more time for recruiting and outreach before the training, and when the following school year begins, trainees from the previous spring are refreshed and ready to mediate. The only requirement for second semester training is that students be given ample opportunity to mediate cases (and develop their confidence) before the school year ends.

A few programs conduct their training over the summer break when students and staff have fewer competing responsibilities. In this scenario, teachers and sometimes students are financially compensated for participating in the training.

Keep in mind that the time of year you conduct the training will have an impact upon whom you recruit. Trainings offered at the beginning of the school year will include more students from upper classes. Those conducted at the end of the year should not include students who will be graduating that year.

The Time of Day

After determining the time of year you will conduct the training, you next have to decide how to schedule the requisite hours. This issue presents an early challenge to program initiators, for it is often a lightning rod for people's resistance to the program. Tensions result in large part because peer trainings are usually conducted during the school day, with students missing their regularly scheduled classes to attend. Even teachers and administrators who support the program can be justifiably concerned by this.

It is essential to note that scheduling peer mediation training during school hours has many advantages. Such a schedule is the easiest to devise logistically. It demonstrates the school's commitment to the program and its appreciation of the fact that learning to be a mediator is hard work and a valuable service. Finally, training during school expands the number and the types of students who will be able to participate. Many students have

jobs and other commitments during nonschool hours; others, though they might make excellent mediators and benefit from their participation in the program, lack the responsibility to attend training sessions that are not held during school. (No matter how dynamic the training program, if it is a choice between training or playing, these students will choose to play.) Staff members, too, are more likely to take part in the training if it occurs during the school day.

You can respond in a number of ways to teachers' concerns regarding the training schedule. Stress that students who participate in the training will be required to make up any work that they miss. If they do not, they will be put on probation and/or asked to leave the program. Explain to staff that students benefit from the training—learning essential skills, improving self-esteem, igniting excitement about school—in ways that help them grow academically as well as personally. Finally, try to schedule the training in a way that minimizes its interference with students' academic responsibilities. Here are just a few ways to do this:

- Vary the days of the week and the times of the day that the training is conducted to reduce the time that trainees miss any particular subject.
- Schedule some of the mediation training during days that are devoted to teacher in-service training.
- Inform staff members about the training schedule soon after you decide upon it. This way they can plan tests and field trips accordingly.
- Integrate peer mediation and conflict resolution into the academic schedule, so that students can be trained as part of a regular class. (This is usually feasible only if school-based staff conduct the training.)
- Combine training sessions during school hours with sessions after school, on the weekends, during vacation days, or during the summer.

The Length and Configuration of Sessions

The final aspect of scheduling has to do with the length of training sessions. Here especially, take your cues from your training source. Some trainers prefer short, intensive trainings in which mediators work together for two or three full days in a row. Others prefer to space the sessions out to give trainees time to digest and practice what they learn. Students may also find it easier to keep up with their schoolwork when they can return to their classes between sessions. Consider a couple of competing factors:

1. Mediation training is largely experiential and is best conducted during substantial blocks of time. Given that preparing, conducting, and then critiquing a single role-play can take over an hour, the typical class period is far too short.
2. Students have a limited attention span, and the younger the student, the more limited it is. Even though peer mediation training is dynamic and fast paced, you will need to take this into consideration when scheduling training.

The most common model for training is two to four day-long sessions, scheduled in a row or spread over the course of three weeks. Alternatively, five to seven two-and-a-half to four-hour sessions can be spaced over the course of a couple of weeks and scheduled at various times during the school day.

One final suggestion: If you must schedule portions of the training during nonschool hours, at least schedule the first session during the school day. In this way you will have access to all students and be able to get them excited about the program so that they are likely to return. If you begin the training on a holiday, a Saturday, or after school, you almost guarantee that certain kinds of students will not attend.

WHERE TO TRAIN

Being a mediator has taught me to always view both sides of a situation before making any type of decision.

High school mediator

Peer mediation trainings have been conducted in every conceivable space, from the storage closets in school basements to the mahogany paneled boardrooms of sponsoring corporations. Trainers usually require a room with movable chairs and enough space to allow the group to sit comfortably in a circle. The training site must either be large enough for four to five small groups to meet and not disturb one another, *or* it has to have nearby "break-out" rooms where small groups can work. (A typically sized classroom alone is not adequate.)

Finding a space within your school that meets these requirements can be difficult. Possibilities include classrooms, libraries, media centers, cafeterias, teachers' rooms, and auditoriums. Sometimes the training has to move to different locations on different days or even during a single day. When you conduct the training at school, you must make do with what is available.

Holding the training off site has two major advantages. Trainees are better able to give their full attention to the task at hand when they are away from the normal distractions of school life, and it makes the training experience special for students and staff when they are in a different environment. Holding the training off site does create some logistical obstacles—transportation, the extra time involved, and possibly even the expense. Training off site also makes it more difficult for key administrators to "drop in" to training sessions, something that can help build their confidence in the program. On balance, however, off-site trainings are preferable. Many schools use public libraries or community centers that are available at no cost and that are within walking distance. You should also consider conference centers, local colleges and universities, hotels, VFW halls, nursing homes, and even private businesses as possible sites.

DURING THE TRAINING

Once the training is underway, coordination work decreases as the trainers take over primary responsibility for the program. Nevertheless, many things still need the coordinator's attention during the training:

- **Managing training logistics.** This includes arranging for transportation to and from the training site, providing meals and refreshments, contacting the "alternate" trainees if they are needed, and coordinating the visits of administrators, sponsoring agencies, and the press. When possible, providing snacks and a pizza lunch greatly enhances the training experience for both students and adults.

- **Reminding students about the training sessions.** Students do not carry appointment books. When days or weeks separate training sessions, it is wise to remind them prior to each session. Make an announcement over the intercom, create a phone tree so that students contact each other, and seek students out personally to remind them.
- **Making sure students are keeping up with their school responsibilities.** Check in with the students about this. If a student is not making the effort to keep up with school-work, and you cannot convince him or her to do so, it is wise to have an alternate replace that student in the training. Sometimes relations between a student trainee and one of his or her teachers become strained, so you will need to help them negotiate these difficulties.
- **Evaluating the trainees.** Trainers cannot promise that every student will be ready to mediate after the training. Rather, at the conclusion of the training, trainers should evaluate each trainee and determine with them whether they are ready to begin. It is important that you have a preliminary sense of trainees' strengths and weaknesses after the training. Keeping your own notes on students as you learn with them during the training will serve you well when you begin scheduling cases.

Before you proceed to the next chapter—and before you complete the final section of the implementation readiness survey at the end of this one—let's look at how to publicize your program.

OUTREACH AND PROMOTION

Upon completion of the training, your peer mediation program enters one of the most crucial phases of its development. Promoting the program's services should now become the primary focus of all who are associated with it.

Before the training, outreach efforts were geared toward securing initial support for the program, encouraging input into program design, and recruiting mediation trainees. These tasks will continue for the life of the program (and your past efforts in this regard will serve you well). But now that the mediation program is about to "open for business," you have an additional set of goals:

- To inform everyone in the school that the program is ready to serve them.
- To promote the concept that is fundamental to peer mediation: It is in everybody's best interest to talk out conflicts rather then fight them out. The number of referrals received—and consequently, the impact that the mediation program will have upon the school—is directly related to the degree to which students and staff understand this idea.
- To remove any stigma attached to utilizing or being referred to the mediation program. Participating in mediation should be regarded as a sign of maturity, intelligence, and strength.
- To educate the school community about the kinds of cases that are appropriate for mediation.
- To publicize the way that students and staff can avail themselves of the program's services. They should know with whom to speak when conflicts arise, how they can make referrals, and when and where mediation sessions will be held.

Being a mediator

has changed my life

by giving me useful

skills. I have learned

to listen with an

open mind. My

friends also come to

me with their prob-

lems for a neutral

opinion.

Middle school mediator

- To establish a positive image for the mediation program. People need to see peer mediation as something that makes an essential contribution to school life.
- To remind students, teachers, and administrators continually that the program exists. When interpersonal conflicts arise, people need to think immediately "Should this be mediated?" If you do not remind them, they may very well forget.

Your outreach efforts at this stage also have an internal purpose: *You want to get students mediating as soon as possible.* Do not underestimate the importance of this. The mediation training has gotten your program's metaphorical spaceship into orbit, and mediating cases is the fuel that keeps it going. If students wait for months before mediating their first cases, they can lose their confidence and enthusiasm. As one coordinator summed this up: "If they don't use it, they will lose it." Not getting enough cases is also disheartening for mediation trainers and program coordinators.

Some time pressure is involved here. New mediators are justifiably nervous about conducting their first "real" mediation session, and their self-doubt only increases with the passage of time. Strive to have all your trainees mediate within three weeks of the conclusion of the training, and certainly no more that two months later. Once they mediate, students' confidence increases dramatically, and they understand that in many ways, the role-plays of the training were more challenging than real cases.

After the training is complete, a new resource exists for program outreach: the student mediators. With one or two cases under their belts, student mediators make the most enthusiastic and credible advocates for the program. They can reach their peers better than any adult. It is your job to involve students in program outreach as much as possible. Student mediators should feel like mediation is *their* program, and they need to be responsible for making the rest of the student body feel the same. Only if they are successful at reaching both their teachers and their peers will mediation have the kind of preventive impact upon school violence that it potentially can. Although all trainees should be responsible for helping with outreach, this work keeps students who are not ready to mediate actively involved in the program. They can direct their energy toward outreach activities—very useful and important work at that!—until they are able to improve their skills and begin mediating.

Students are not the only ones who can help with outreach. Use teachers, administrators, and parents to get the word out as well. The following is a list of twenty-three ways to promote your mediation program:

1. **Conduct outreach presentations that include role-play demonstrations.** The most effective way to generate support for and understanding of peer mediation is to conduct presentations that include role-play demonstrations. With a mix of relevant issues, adequate acting, and a little humor, role-plays engage students and staff alike. New mediators are very capable of enacting a role-play simulation in front of groups. Suggestions for making these presentations run smoothly include:

   - Encourage students to lead as much of the presentations as possible. Those who don't act in the role-play can deliver short presentations, run short games or exercises, and field questions.

- Practice the presentations and role-plays before you present them. This will ensure that everyone understands their roles. As effective as a well-prepared presentation is to your outreach efforts, a poorly delivered one can set the program back.

- Remember that you don't have to present an entire role-play. Five or ten minutes, with ample time for questions, is more than adequate.

- Include as part of the role-play a teacher referring the case to mediation so that staff members understand how referrals are made.

- Whenever possible, seek out students who have been parties in mediation to participate in your presentations. Ask former parties in the audience if they would be willing to speak about their experiences in mediation. These testimonials are very effective.

- Presentations to small groups (ten to thirty people), though more labor intensive, are generally more effective than presentations to auditoriums full of people. If you do present to assemblies, make sure that you have adequate amplification. More than one assembly has been ruined by poor sound.

Be creative about finding an audience for your presentations. Some programs go to every homeroom in the school, rotating groups of mediators each time. One program did a live presentation over the school television station which was viewed by all homerooms simultaneously. Other schools conduct presentations for students who are detained in "in-house" suspension. You might want to offer promotional presentations at administrative meetings, assemblies, faculty meetings, school-board meetings, and PTO or PTA meetings.

2. **Make a promotional videotape.** Videotaped presentations can be shown to a variety of audiences. Although not as effective as a live "performance," a videotaped presentation is time efficient and allows for greater flexibility.

3. **Use the training graduation for outreach purposes.** Mediator graduation can be held during an assembly of the entire student body; mediators can take the oath of confidentiality with their peers as witnesses; special guests from the community can be invited; and the local media can interview students and broadcast the graduation ceremony.

4. **Create an effective name for your program.** Creating a name that mediators feel proud of and that the student body can identify with can be a boon to your outreach efforts. Students should come up with this name themselves. Some names from other programs include J.A.M. (Just Agreements through Mediation); Project Peace; R.A.P.P. (Resolve All Problems Peacefully); Beef-Eaters ("beef" is slang for fight); S.M.A.R.T. (School Mediator Alternative Resolution Team . . . Get S.M.A.R.T.!); Common Ground; and Fuss Busters.

5. **Use the school and community press.** At school, place articles in the student newspaper and parent newsletter, and stories on schoolwide TV if available. (One group of students produced and acted in a peer mediation "commercial" shown on school-based television.) Use the announcements and the daily bulletin for outreach purposes as well. One program offers students the "mediator tip of the week" over the intercom, while another thanks students (with their permission) who used mediation services. Peer mediation as a human-interest story appeals to local newspapers and television stations as well. Consider sending them press

releases, inviting them to the training graduation or other special events, or offering tours of your program.

6. **Print peer mediation business cards.** Business cards should include information about mediation and how to make a referral to the program. Distribute these to the mediators and all program supporters. Students enjoy handing out these cards to their friends and to others whom they think might benefit from mediation services.

7. **Encourage mediators to be role models.** Some of the most effective public relations result from the way that mediators carry themselves after the training. If they resolve their own conflicts nonviolently, and if they encourage their friends to do the same, this will make a lasting impact upon adults as well as students. Stress the importance of this to your mediators and help them live up to this responsibility.

8. **Teach student mediators effective ways to present mediation to their peers.** Student mediators know that mediation is a viable approach to solving conflicts. And they know how to mediate. But often they don't know how to encourage their peers to try the process. A simple question—"Why should I go to mediation?"—can stop them in their tracks. Spend time with mediators simulating conversations with peers and practicing the most effective arguments for trying the process.

9. **Use teachers to present the program to students.** Teachers and support staff can also get the word out to students. Provide teachers with an outline of a brief presentation so that they can discuss the program with their classes, with their advisees, or in their homerooms. If they desire, a student mediator can assist with these presentations. One school discussed peer mediation during its monthly "reading period": a time when the regular schedule was suspended to enable all students to read about and discuss a topic of importance.

10. **Conduct a poster ad campaign.** One school conducted a very effective marketing campaign using simple 8-1/2-by-11-inch posters with provocative phrases about mediation such as: "Mediation Works," "Nobody Loses in Mediation," "Mediation Is Private," and "In Mediation, You Are in Control." By blanketing the school with these posters at regular intervals, they were able to get teachers and students talking about the program. Another effective use of posters is to remind disciplinarians to refer cases. Put a sign across from the vice-principal's desk that reads: "Think of Mediation First!"

11. **Hold a logo or poster contest.** Some programs organize contests that encourage students to design a logo and/or a poster for the program. You can also ask the art teacher to assign this task to his or her students.

12. **Create peer mediation T-shirts or caps that student mediators can wear.** This is a very popular outreach tool. Make sure the students themselves have a hand in designing these, or you risk that they will not wear them. You can print the logo from the contest on these items.

13. **Check in regularly with the administrator in charge of discipline.** One creative way to do this is to assign a different mediator to stop into the disciplinarian's office each day and inquire whether there are any cases. Not only does this visit remind the disciplinarian about the program, it impresses him or her with the commitment of the student mediators.

14. **Organize a dramatic or musical presentation about peer mediation and violence prevention.** Some peer mediation programs encourage student rappers, musicians, and actors to create and present dramatic presentations about violence, conflict resolution, and peer mediation.

15. **Create a peer mediation bulletin board.** Display news about the program, information about student issues, and pictures of the student mediators here.

16. **Keep referral sources informed about the status of cases they refer.** Within the limits of confidentiality, make sure that referral sources know what happened to the students they referred to peer mediation. Every time they learn that a conflict was successfully mediated, it makes them more likely to think of mediation in the future. At the end of the year, write a note to teachers and administrators thanking them for making referrals.

17. **Keep the school-at-large informed about the progress of the program.** Some programs circulate monthly reports and a year-end evaluation that outline the number and the types of cases handled. Others hold open houses and invite everyone in the school community as well as members of the board of education, local politicians, foundation representatives, and state education department officials to attend. It is in your interest to alert everyone to the difference that peer mediation is making in your school.

18. **Have an "Each One, Reach One" Week.** Each mediator makes a list of five people that he or she knows in school who are not mediators. The mediators then seek out one of their people each day during the designated week and explain peer mediation to them. At the end of the week, the program will have personally reached more than a hundred people.

19. **Conduct ongoing workshops for teachers, support staff, and parents who want to learn about mediation and conflict resolution.**

20. **Have a "Name-Tag" Day.** This simple idea—designating a day when all mediators wear a name tag similar to the one that they wore during training—is very effective. When people ask them about the name tag, they use the opportunity to inform them about peer mediation.

21. **Work with directors of curricula or curriculum committees to integrate conflict resolution into the curriculum.**

22. **Present peer mediation at orientation sessions for incoming students.**

23. **Send letters announcing the opening of the program to all parents and community agencies.**

FINAL WORDS

In all of this outreach work, it is important to keep one thing in mind: Peer mediation should be preventive. If your outreach and education efforts lead students to resolve their own conflicts before they make it to mediation, that is all the better. If students use mediation services to prevent conflicts from escalating, that is fine as well. In one sense, you are trying to put your program out of business at the same time that you are building it.

With the training complete and outreach underway, the time has arrived for you to do what you have been working toward from the start: mediate cases.

Peer Mediation Implementation Readiness Survey

PART C. TRAINING

1C. Trainee Screening

Our student mediation trainees have been screened. They are well informed
about mediation, and they have each made a personal commitment to
the program for one year.   + 20

Our student mediation trainees have not been through a formal selection process,
and they have not made a commitment to the program prior to training.   − 10

2C. Trainee Diversity

Our student mediation trainees will represent a diverse cross-section of the school.   + 20

Our student mediation trainees will be a homogeneous group.   − 20

3C. Trainers

Experienced peer mediation trainers will conduct the training at our school.   + 20

One of our staff is being sent to learn how to mediate and train others to mediate;
he or she will conduct our student training.   + 0

We are going to buy a training curriculum and train our own students.   − 10

4C. Trainer-Trainee Ratio

We will have one mediation trainer for every four to six trainees.   + 20

We will have one mediation trainer for every six to twelve trainees.   + 0

We will have one mediation trainer for the entire training group.   − 10

5C. Training Schedule

Our student mediators will be trained during the school day.   + 20

Our student mediators will be trained both during the school day and
after school or on weekends.   + 10

Our student mediators will not be trained during any school time.   − 10

TOTAL:

Scoring

80–100 points: Excellent. Your training program will be very effective.

60–80 points: Caution. Try to improve your training design before you move forward.

< 60 points: Poor. Your training approach is not adequate to meet the needs of a peer
mediation program.

CHAPTER 7

Mediating Cases

I t may take only a few days, it may be a matter of weeks, but soon after the training is complete, your program will begin to mediate cases. This chapter outlines the important role that the coordinator plays in this process. After presenting this synopsis of a typical peer mediation case, we will discuss each aspect of casework in detail.

The adult peer mediation coordinator receives word that two students are having a dispute that might be appropriate for mediation. This coordinator contacts and meets briefly with each student to see if both are willing to mediate. If they are, he or she schedules a session and assigns two student mediators to co-mediate the case later the same day.

When the time arrives to mediate the case, the coordinator briefs the mediators, and then either sits in a corner of the room, or leaves and waits in an anteroom. The formal mediation session begins once the parties arrive at the mediation room. Student mediators conduct the session on their own, but if they have special questions or problems during the session, they call on the coordinator for assistance. The mediators are usually able to help their peers resolve the conflict within one class period. After the parties return to class, the mediators meet with the coordinator and evaluate the session. In the days and weeks that follow, mediators and/or the coordinator check back with the parties to make sure the agreement is working and to offer assistance if needed.

RECEIVING REFERRALS FOR MEDIATION

All members of the school community should be encouraged to make referrals to peer mediation. During the initial weeks of program operation, most referrals come from disciplinarians and other administrators who redirect students who have been sent to their offices. After a short while, teachers begin to make referrals directly to the mediation coordinator. Peer mediators are another source of referrals, recommending the process to any student whom they feel would benefit from it. It is especially satisfying for mediators to work on a case from start to finish—identifying the parties, getting them to try mediation, mediating the conflict, and finally following up on the case. And as the student body accepts the program as its own, increasing numbers of mediation sessions result from students who refer themselves or their friends. This is ideal: students taking preventive, proactive steps to resolve conflicts *before* they escalate into violence.

It is preferable for referral sources to encourage parties to contact the mediation program themselves. But since this is not always possible or effective, individuals referring cases often take the lead by informing the program about a potential case.

Referral sources use a number of avenues to bring cases to mediation. One is to seek out the coordinator directly. If your program coordinator works out of a designated mediation center, then people can go to this location and speak with him or her. Such direct contact provides the coordinator with an additional opportunity to educate referral sources about the program. If these individuals have misconceptions about the process—a

I think peer mediation works because I personally have seen the changes that have come about in people's lives after the mediation session; you can see the violence literally dissipate as an agreement is reached between disputants. Our halls are filled with a more calm atmosphere now that students have an alternative to fighting.

Middle school mediator

teacher refers students to mediation so that they will "stop their rude behavior"; a student wants mediators to "tell my friends" to return a stolen object—coordinators can take the time to explain how mediation works.

Coordinators are not always available to receive referrals, however, nor do referral sources always have the time to find them. As an alternative method of referring cases, many programs use referral forms. (See page 229 for a sample referral form.) These forms are distributed to students and staff at the start of the year, and they can always be obtained at the front office, the mediation center, and in classrooms. People fill out their own names, the parties' names (if different), the date and time of the referral, the nature of the dispute, the degree of urgency, and as much of the parties' schedules as possible. They then deposit the forms at designated places such as the mediation center, the coordinator's mailbox, or locked referral boxes located throughout the school. The coordinator, sometimes with the mediators' assistance, collects these forms regularly. In addition to creating a peer mediation referral form, some schools add a section onto their standard disciplinary form that enables teachers to request mediation for their students.

Most programs require that referral sources identify themselves, but a small number of schools allow people to refer cases to mediation anonymously. This approach enables students who otherwise might not have come forward to make referrals. In one school that initiated this policy, the mediation caseload increased and the program learned of potentially explosive conflicts before they escalated into violence. The concern that students would take advantage of the process, referring their peers to mediation as a joke or as a form of harassment, did not materialize.

INTAKE INTERVIEWS

One of the last questions that student mediators ask parties before they begin to mediate is, "Now that you have heard about mediation, do you want to try it?" This is a critical juncture in the process. If the parties answer yes and agree to mediate, it is often the first time they have agreed upon anything since their conflict began.

Significantly, parties usually answer this question in the affirmative. The fact that they do is attributable to perhaps the least appreciated aspect of the peer mediation process: the *intake interview.* Intake interviews are preliminary meetings that coordinators hold with each party, usually in private. Lasting anywhere from three to thirty minutes, these interviews take place after the case is referred to the program and before the parties come together to mediate. Considering that once students agree to try mediation, they are able to resolve their differences almost 90 percent of the time, the importance of the intake interview is clear. It is one of many reasons why the peer mediation coordinator must be highly capable.

Goals of the Intake Interview

During the intake interview you should attempt to

- introduce the mediation process;
- build the student's trust in the mediation program;

- determine the nature of the conflict. (How do parties perceive the situation, what are the issues, what is the relationship of the parties, how urgently does the situation need attention?);
- determine whether the conflict is appropriate for mediation. (Are there identifiable parties, is there potential for violence, are there negotiable issues, are parties capable of making age-appropriate commitments, can the conflict be resolved without mediation?);
- convince students to try mediation if their situation seems amenable to it;
- refer students to other people and programs that might help them.

Setting Up the Interview

.The logistics are the first challenge of conducting intake interviews. Unless the parties come to you directly or are sent by a staff member, you must first arrange to speak with them. It is often difficult to locate the students in the building, and you must be sensitive in how you approach parties once you have found them. If you embarrass students in front of their peers, they will not want to participate in the program.[28] In schools with no designated peer mediation office, the challenge of setting up the interview is even greater. You can make it easier to set up these interviews if you

- encourage referral sources to note the schedule of parties on the referral form;
- use the school intercom to page students. (To maintain privacy, you can request that they report to the main office rather than to the mediation center.);
- use the same form that the main office uses to call students out of class;
- ask other students to find parties and escort them to you. Not only do students, especially younger students, enjoy this role immensely, they often have the best information as to where parties might be.

Conducting the Interview

When coordinators finally meet with them, student parties exhibit varying degrees of interest in participating in mediation. We can delineate three general levels:

1. A small percentage of students become involved with the program upon reentering school after a suspension or because an administrator "asked" them to participate. With these potentially resistant students, it is not a question of whether they will physically attend the session. They have no choice. The question is whether they will choose to commit themselves to the process once they are there.
2. A larger percentage of students will already be committed to participating in mediation. Perhaps they have heard from their peers about the process, or they may have had a positive experience with peer mediation in the past. It is easier to meet your goals in these intake interviews. If it makes sense to move ahead and set up a session, these students will be more than happy to participate.

Peer mediation has cut down on the number of suspensions we have had. It has made the worst enemies into best friends. Now, if kids have any problems they can't solve, the first thing they do is ask to be mediated.

Middle school mediator

---

[28] This is not always a concern. Some mediation coordinators have such a wonderful reputation in their schools that students are happy to have the coordinator take them out of class in front of their peers.

3. The largest percentage of potential parties will fall somewhere in the middle: they may be interested in resolving their disputes, but they may also have misgivings about participating in mediation. Perhaps the parties have been referred by a teacher, or the student with whom they are in conflict has approached the program and asked for help. If these students are going to try mediation at all, you will have to convince them to make that choice.[29]

Strategies for Convincing Students to Try Mediation

The strategies that coordinators employ to convince students to try mediation are reminiscent of those used to win initial support for the peer mediation program. Here are the most effective:

- **Listen, Listen, Listen.** Listening is the foundation of the intake interview. Coordinators use their skills and their unique position in the school to win students' confidence and elicit their needs, feelings, and concerns. In this way, you demonstrate peer mediation's respect for students and its ability to help them achieve what they want. If you can make students feel that they are truly understood, then regardless of the outcome, the intake interview will have been a success.

- **Strive to help students above all else.** You must remember during the intake interview that your primary goal is to help the student that sits before you. Because mediation is so effective, because it is unfamiliar to students, and because they want to get cases, coordinators can lose sight of this and put the needs of their program first. If during the course of the intake interview you can assist students to resolve a conflict on their own—or direct them to a more appropriate program or person for help—that is all for the better.

- **Stress the benefits of mediation.** Stress the advantages of the mediation process during intake interviews: it is effective; it is confidential; it gives students complete control of the outcome; it can preserve a friendship; it can help them find out what really happened; and in most cases, no parents, teachers, administrators, or other students need be involved. Students usually have nothing to lose by trying mediation. When they describe their conflict during the interview, you can honestly say, "Mediation has helped other students who were involved in situations just like this one."

- **Stress the hazards of not mediating.** It is important to clarify what the consequences will be if students do not try mediation. Will the issues remain unresolved indefinitely? Will they lose a friend? Will they have to live in fear and always watch their backs? If an administrator is involved, will they lose control over what eventually does happen? Coordinators should help students answer these questions for themselves. After considering the consequences of not trying mediation, students are often more willing to give it a try.

---

[29] In spite of excellent outreach efforts, many students will still think they are "getting in trouble" when first asked to try mediation.

- **Stress that the other party is willing to mediate.** This underscores the hesitant party's control of the situation, and it indicates to him or her that the "adversary" wants to resolve the conflict. That the other party is willing to mediate can be seen as a gesture of conciliation. If you have not spoken with the other party yet, ask, "If I speak with the other party and they agree to try mediation, would you be willing to try it as well?"

- **Allow students to make their own decision.** If coordinators pressure students in the intake interview to try mediation, students, in turn, will resist this pressure. The best coordinators conduct intake interviews with subtlety. Instead of pressuring students to mediate, they use students' own desires and concerns to guide them toward choosing to mediate of their own volition. When students feel the coordinator's concern yet also feel free to make their own decisions—when they feel supported yet in control—then they are most likely to choose to mediate. Students will sometimes choose not to mediate when you feel certain that it would help them. But this is one of the risks of empowering young people to make their own decisions.

- **Ask students to "review" their conflict for the mediators.** This is an irregular strategy that has been used with some success. When students claim during intake interviews that their conflict is already resolved, ask them if they would be willing to review the situation so that the mediators might practice. Parties will often agree, feeling a greater degree of psychological control because the session won't be "for real." During these sessions, parties invariably explore their conflict in greater depth, uncovering issues and information that they had not previously discussed. As a result, they are able to create a more profound and enduring resolution to their conflict. This approach should only be used when you sense that a conflict is not as resolved as students claim it is.

It takes practice and skill to apply these strategies effectively and conduct successful intake interviews. A final and essential caution: Coordinators need to be careful not to begin to mediate during the interviews. If you spend too much time with the parties, it makes the eventual mediation session seem redundant. Once it becomes clear that students are willing to participate in mediation, schedule a session with the student mediators and conclude the intake interview. You might have to fight temptation if, like most coordinators, you enjoy mediating as much as the students do. But this must be done for the benefit of the program.

Determining Who Is a Party to a Conflict: "Bob told me that Janine said that Rakeem was saying . . . "

Most student conflicts directly involve only two parties. Even large-group disputes can usually be reduced to a collection of interpersonal conflicts. But during intake interviews, students often claim that additional people are directly or indirectly involved. This person did this, another one told them that, and on and on until the parties generate a long list of students who are peripherally connected to the situation. And it is common for parties to request that these other students join them in their mediation session.

As a general rule, coordinators should strive to involve as few people as possible in the mediation session. Nonessential parties are a distraction; they have a negative influence upon the key players; they make the process more difficult for mediators to control; and they waste precious time. Always ask yourself: Can the parties resolve their differences without these others present? If the answer is yes, then schedule the session to include only the key parties. Parties can always inform witnesses and other hangers-on about the results of the session after it is finished. If the answer is no, or if the parties insist upon including other people in the session, then you must choose whether to schedule the session or not. If you decide to do so, the mediators can usually ask nonessential participants to leave during the session without negative repercussions.[30]

Deciding Whether a Conflict Is Appropriate for Mediation

Just yesterday, my two good friends had a big argument and as much as I wanted to take sides, I stayed neutral. I helped them work out their differences.

High school mediator

Almost all students referred to mediation can benefit from participating in the process. Because of this, you will more often be trying to determine whether a situation is *not* appropriate for mediation than whether it is. The following is a list of the most common reasons for not mediating:

- **The issues in the dispute are not suitable for mediation.** Programs usually have a policy that prohibits mediation sessions that involve drugs, weapons, and abuse, or at least prohibits them until after disciplinary action.
- **One of the parties is unwilling to mediate.** In these cases there can be no mediation. This should not reflect poorly upon the program, the coordinator, or the party. Sometimes it is legitimately in the best interests of a student not to mediate. It may be worthwhile, however, to meet with the student who is willing to mediate and help him or her decide how to proceed.
- **There is too great a potential for violence.** Refer these students to the disciplinarian first and hold a mediation session later if the parties are willing. Beware of becoming overly cautious, however, as these disputes are the exception in even the most troubled schools.
- **Parties are not committed to the process.** Students will occasionally try to set up a mediation session as a joke or to get out of class. Clearly, a session should not be scheduled in these cases. For students who are willing to participate in mediation but who have misgivings, however, it is preferable to set up a session. Once these students become involved in the session, their commitment to the process usually increases.
- **One or both parties appear incapable of mediating.** Although they are the exception, some students have emotional problems that render them incapable of keeping commitments or controlling themselves in the session. These students cannot mediate. (The majority of students labeled with "moderate special needs" have been able to participate in mediation sessions.)

A final reason *not* to accept a case has to do with larger, programmatic concerns: When you first begin to mediate cases, it is very important that you are successful. During the initial weeks of operation, circumstances are unique:

---

[30] Use only the most skilled mediators for multiparty disputes. For more on this, see the book *Mediating the Tough Cases: Advanced Issues in Peer Mediation Case Work,* available from School Mediation Associates.

- Your mediators are novices.
- You have the attention of the school in a way that will rarely be repeated.
- Skeptical students and staff will be looking at the program to see if it really can work.
- Administrators and teachers might refer students with the most chronic behavioral problems in the school—students who have been troubling them for months—to mediation.

These factors advise caution about the kinds of cases you accept at the start. At first, accept only those that will likely result in a satisfactory resolution. In this way you ensure that people's first impressions of peer mediation will be positive. Cases that seem inappropriate can be referred back through the usual channels until you feel more confident. But don't be squeamish for long. Peer mediation has been effective even with the most difficult student disputes. As soon as you are off to a good start, accept the challenging cases.

The best thing about peer mediation is that sometimes we make a friendship better than it was before.

High school mediator

SCHEDULING THE MEDIATION SESSION

Once student parties have agreed to try mediation, you must determine the best time to schedule the session. The simple answer to this question is *as soon as possible.* Your goal is to provide students with conflict resolution services quickly and efficiently, whether you hold a mediation session immediately upon receiving a referral, or schedule it for sometime within twenty-four hours.

But this is easier said than done. Delay in scheduling is a common problem in peer mediation programs. By the time the referral is made, the parties are contacted, intake interviews are conducted, peer mediators are located, and the session is scheduled, two days to as much as a week can pass. By this time, tensions may cool to such a degree that even though the situation is not resolved, the parties lose interest in mediation. Programs should take every step they can to avoid this potential obstacle.

There are two good reasons to delay scheduling a session, however. The first concerns the design of the program. Not every program has the flexibility to mediate whenever the service is needed. Most can only mediate during specific times of the day as determined by the availability of the coordinator and the student mediators. Because there is no way to prevent this, at least a small delay between the initial referral and the mediation session is almost always unavoidable.

The second reason to delay scheduling a mediation session concerns the parties'—rather the program's—readiness to mediate. Many parties are incapable of mediating as soon as a session can be scheduled. If an incident has just occurred, they need time to calm themselves and reflect upon the situation before they can discuss it constructively. Venting of emotions is a welcome part of the mediation process, but if parties are extremely angry, they may be unable to sit in the same room much less listen to one another. Scheduling mediation sessions under these circumstances is an unnecessary risk, and it is wise to wait a number of hours or even days before mediating such conflicts.

When there is a lapse between the time students are referred to mediation and the time of their session—either because of logistical factors or because of the need for a "cooling-off period"—your main concern is to prevent parties from escalating the conflict prior to the session. There are a number of ways to accomplish this. See if the parties can agree to avoid each other until the mediation session. Help students think through the ramifications of such an interim agreement: Are they likely to come into contact with each other? Do they have any of the same classes? How will they handle it if they see each other? What will they say to their friends until the session is held? Students should make this agreement only if they can clearly uphold it.

When students are not willing or able to commit themselves to an interim arrangement, then try the second approach. Have parties wait in a neutral, supervised area—the mediation center, the disciplinarian's or counselor's office—until a mediation session can be conducted. (Some students in this situation will be expected back at the disciplinarian's office anyway.) Of course, this approach is feasible only if the mediation session can be scheduled within a reasonable period of time.

In those rare instances when neither of these methods works, and the coordinator is unable to mediate the situation on the spot, then it is best not to schedule a session at all. Inform students that unfortunately, the mediation program will not be able to help them this time. Wish them luck and refer them back to the disciplinarian.

One final note: Some peer mediation programs, most commonly in middle schools, find themselves with too many referrals to handle at once. Coordinators therefore have to prioritize cases and focus on those that need immediate attention. This problem can be managed by referring to the information on the referral form concerning urgency, and by having students agree to return later or wait in the disciplinarian's office.

ASSIGNING MEDIATORS TO A CASE

Having come this far, it is now time to assign mediators to the case. Depending upon the number of years that your program has been in operation, you should have between fifteen to forty qualified peer mediators to choose from. Before describing the methods used to assign mediators, we must first discuss a tool that is essential no matter which method of assigning mediators you decide to use: the mediator master schedule.

The Mediator Master Schedule

The mediator master schedule is a document that details when each student mediator is available to mediate. Create it by first assembling all of the mediators' schedules during a typical week of school. You want to know where each of your mediators is at any period of the day, what classes they are in, and when they have lunch, study periods, free periods, preparation periods (for staff), and so on.

This information should then be organized in a way that highlights when students and staff are available to mediate. For some coordinators this is a simple task of noting when students have nonacademic subjects or study halls. In the many schools that allow students to mediate during classes, however, it is more complicated. Coordinators regularly update the master schedule according to students' academic standing in each class. If a student mediator is having trouble in math class, he or she will not be pulled out of that subject; if another shows improvement in English, then that student might be asked to mediate occasionally during that period.

Basic Criteria for Assigning Mediators

Regardless of the method you use, four basic criteria guide the assignment of student mediators: availability, relationship to the parties, fairness, and age or grade level. Determine the first one, availability, by referring to the mediator master schedule. Regarding the second—relationship to the parties—most programs strive to assign mediators only to those cases in which they do not know the parties. The reasons for this include:

- If student mediators know the parties, it is difficult for them to restrain their biases.
- Parties might be ashamed to speak honestly about their situation in front of peers with whom they have an ongoing relationship.
- Even if mediators do their job well, it gives the appearance of partiality if they have a relationship with one party and not the other.
- Parties who do not understand or accept the constraints of the mediator's role can become upset with a mediator-friend who does not "stick up for them" in the session.

In small schools where it is difficult to find students who do not know each other, coordinators try at a minimum to assign mediators who only know the parties peripherally.[31] Mediators are encouraged to withdraw from a case whenever they feel that their prior relationship with a party (be it positive or negative) will hinder their performance.

The third criterion for selecting mediators, fairness, simply means trying to give every mediator an equal number of chances to mediate. It is unfair if some mediators get to mediate many times while others are rarely selected.

The final basic criterion is the age or grade level of the mediators. Most programs only assign peer mediators to work with students who are in their grade or below. To do otherwise makes it unnecessarily difficult for mediators to win the trust of the parties.

Methods of Assigning Mediators

Coordinators use two approaches to assign peer mediators to cases: open assignment and fixed assignment.

1. **Open Assignment of Mediators.** In the "open" assignment process, mediators are assigned on a case-by-case basis. This approach allows coordinators the flexibility to choose whichever mediators they think are best suited for a particular case. In addition, the open assignment process enables mediators to co-mediate with a variety of their peers, hopefully learning new things from each. By strengthening the interpersonal relationships among the mediators, this method makes the program stronger.

   In addition to the four basic criteria for selecting mediators just discussed, consider these additional criteria when using the open assignment approach:

---

[31] There are notable exceptions to this rule. A few coordinators assign mediators who know the parties because they feel it helps build their trust in the process. Of course, the parties are asked when the session begins whether they are uncomfortable with the mediators. If they are not, they report no problems.

[Participating in mediation] made me a better person. . . . You learn to open up to the experience of others. . . . You can come in here with maybe a Vietnamese guy and a Hispanic girl and a black guy, and those may be races while you are in school you don't think you can get along with. But if you come here and share problems with them, you find that you really can. You can relate not just socially but with problems.

High school party

- **Skill.** Mediators should be selected according to their level of skill. If the case is a difficult one—perhaps involving strong emotions, complex issues, or a history of violence—assign more experienced and proficient mediators. If the conflict is more straightforward, you can assign mediators who are less skilled. As your program mediates cases, you will become familiar with each mediator's strengths and weaknesses and can confidently assign them to appropriate cases.

- **Mirroring.** Mirroring refers to the practice of matching personal characteristics of the mediators to potentially important characteristics in the parties. Because people generally feel more comfortable with others who are like themselves, mirroring is used to put parties at ease and facilitate trust building and communication. If the dispute is between a boy and a girl, try to arrange for male and female co-mediators; the same principal applies if the parties are Caucasian and Hispanic, a freshman and a junior, a teacher and a student, or a "jock" and a "rocker." Even if the parties are similar—both burly football players, both Chinese, both "shop rats"—it often makes sense to mirror them in the selection of mediators. Of course, even though mediators may be more similar in certain ways to one party than the other, they must still maintain their neutrality.[32]

- **An Effective Team.** Although peer mediators should be skilled in all aspects of the mediation process, they nevertheless have unique strengths and weaknesses. Coordinators therefore try to select mediators who complement each other. You might assign a mediator who is assertive and able to control the session with a mediator who is quiet but good at eliciting feelings. Or, schedule a student who speaks well with one who takes accurate notes and writes excellent agreements.

- **Specific Knowledge.** Sometimes it is important to select mediators who have specific knowledge about the issues in dispute or about the culture in which the dispute arose. If both parties belong to a specific clique in the school, choose a mediator who is familiar with that clique. If a dispute concerns the application of school policy on such things as grading, class selection, or school government, you will want mediators who are familiar with these policies.

- **Mediator Growth and Development.** A final consideration when choosing mediators should be the personal and "professional" growth of your mediators. Consider assigning mediators to a particular case because they will learn something from the case. A mediator who used to get into physical confrontations over minor issues can be reminded of the benefits of talking things out by mediating a case with this profile. Two shy mediators who are often overpowered by strong partners might be scheduled to mediate together so that they become more assertive. Many schools also use a "mentor" system—pairing new or less-skilled mediators with more experienced co-mediators.

The major drawback of the open assignment method is that it is time consuming. With each new case, the coordinator must select and then locate the appropriate mediators. When things get hectic in school, this can be difficult to do well.

---

[32] Although mirroring is essential when the conflict involves issues of prejudice, some research indicates that it is not as important as had previously been thought. Experienced student mediators can win the trust of all kinds of people and overcome the barriers created by personal difference.

But take heart. In reality, open assignment is often more haphazard than this discussion might lead you to believe. Who is chosen to mediate might simply be determined by which student mediators are in your office when you are scheduling the case. Thankfully, most mediators can adequately mediate most cases.

2. **Fixed Assignment of Mediators.** An alternative to the open assignment method can be called *fixed assignment*. Teams of mediators are assigned to particular periods each week, and unless there is a concern that the team is not appropriate for a case, they mediate whatever is scheduled during their time slots. This method does not allow you the flexibility to select just the right mediators for each case, but it does have some advantages. It facilitates the scheduling process because you know that teams of mediators will always be available at specific times. Mediators report to the mediation room at their designated time, pick up their cases, and begin mediating (sometimes without the coordinator having to be involved). Fixed assignment also enables mediators to develop a close working relationship with their regular co-mediator.

Of the two methods used to assign student mediators to cases, the open assignment approach is most common in middle and high schools. A few peer mediation programs allow parties to select their own mediators. This approach poses numerous potential difficulties, including that parties might disagree on the mediators, that the chosen mediators won't be available when needed, and that the mediators selected will be unsuitable for the case. But if the logistics are manageable, and if control over this aspect of the process will convince students to participate in mediation, then it might be worth a try.

Using Adult Mediators

Because peer mediation programs are designed to empower students, and because teachers and administrators have many other responsibilities, adults do not mediate often in peer mediation programs. Coordinators must be sensitive to the fact that some cases are too difficult for students to handle, however. When you encounter such a difficult case, or when a conflict involves an adult as a party (student-teacher, teacher-teacher, student-administrator, and so on), make sure that at least one of the co-mediators is an adult. Whether this adult is the coordinator or some other trained staff member, the assistance of adults in these instances is invaluable.

Do not make the mistake of becoming dependent upon adult mediators, however. Some programs decide to use student and adult teams to co-mediate during the initial phase of implementation, rationalizing that this will help students gain confidence and at the same time guarantee a high quality of service. But it can be difficult for these programs to wean themselves of their reliance upon adults. Because students sometimes do not mediate with the sophistication of adults, coordinators become unable to trust students to do the job on their own. Remember: If properly trained, students can mediate most conflicts among their peers with great success *without* adult intervention.

From *Students Resolving Conflict: Peer Mediation in Schools*, published by GoodYearBooks. Copyright © 1995 Richard Cohen.

SUPERVISING MEDIATION SESSIONS

At long last, your mediators finally begin to mediate cases. Do not think that your work is done, however. The coordinator has an important role to play even during the mediation session.

At the Start of the Session

Most coordinators provide some background information to student mediators before the session begins, including the names of the parties, the number of parties expected, and how the parties ended up in mediation. Because mediators should learn everything they need to know about a dispute from the parties themselves, provide only the bare essentials, as well as any special circumstances such as

- underlying issues that mediators should look for;
- special instructions from an administrative referral source that mediators need to tell parties. (Perhaps the disciplinarian has requested that parties return to the office after the mediation, or maybe he or she has promised that the suspension will be reduced if the parties reach an agreement.);
- special time limitations. (Maybe one party has an unexpected commitment in thirty minutes.);
- it is the parties' second mediation session;
- because of the level of hostility, mediators should begin with private sessions or have parties sit on opposite sides of a table.

Coordinators might also give mediators a pep talk that includes general as well as mediator-specific reminders. Remind a mediator who often talks too much to be aware of this in the session. For new mediators, a reminder that they do not have to come up with an agreement is helpful. (Otherwise the pressure they feel to do so can have a negative impact upon their performance.)

There are a number of ways to gather parties in the mediation room. You can deliver passes to students the morning of their mediation session. These passes enable mediators and parties to leave their regular assignments and proceed to mediation at the designated time. Or, have the mediators escort parties to and from the mediation session. Peer mediators check the case referral form to locate the parties, pick them up, mediate the case, and then escort students back to class when the session is over.

Some coordinators post a flow chart in the mediation center to guide mediators through the process. This helps them take charge of the entire process. The steps on a flow chart might include:

1. Pick up a referral form.
2. Take an agreement form, two note sheets, and two questionnaires.
3. Pick up the parties and have them sign in.
4. Mediate and write an agreement if possible.
5. Congratulate the parties.

6. Ask parties to fill out the postsession questionnaire.

7. Have parties sign out and escort them back to class.

8. Fill out the case data sheet.

9. Discuss the case with your co-mediator and fill out a self-evaluation.

During the Session

When all parties are together in the room, the formal session begins under the leadership of the student mediators. The important question now is: Where should the coordinator go? Should you sit in on the sessions, or should you leave the room altogether? School-based mediation programs have contrasting policies in this regard, and mediators and coordinators will usually argue for whatever they are familiar with. Compelling arguments support both perspectives.

In many programs, the coordinator leaves students alone in the mediation room. These coordinators assert that peer mediation is first and foremost a *student* program, and having adults in the room compromises its effectiveness. Student mediators in these schools agree, claiming that their peers feel more comfortable and are more likely to invest themselves in the process if no adults are present. Not sitting in on the session has some logistical advantages as well. The coordinator can get other work accomplished during the session. And because you are not tied to a single session, the program can mediate several sessions simultaneously (with the coordinator available to assist all the mediators if they need help).

In contrast, some schools feel it is essential that an adult be in the room to supervise mediation sessions. They cite a number of reasons for this, the most compelling of which is that when adults observe the sessions, they are able to critique the mediators' performance and help them improve their skills. In addition, coordinators who observe a session can offer assistance and guidance to mediators while it is underway. If the mediators make a serious mistake, or if they are stuck, the coordinator can intervene to ensure that the process runs smoothly. Some schools' concerns for the safety of students (and legal liability) lead them to require that the coordinator be in the room. If coordinators screen cases appropriately, however, this should not be an issue. See the appendices for a discussion of legal liability.

In the end, the best approach is one that is flexible and enables the coordinator to consider the dynamics of each case. In the majority of student disputes, the coordinator's presence is unnecessary if not a hindrance, especially after the mediators have gained experience. Student mediators can always take a break and meet with the coordinator if they need assistance. But until you have confidence in your mediators, and in those cases where it seems important to have an adult in the room, coordinators should not hesitate to sit in on sessions.[33]

When you do decide to sit in on a session—either to observe and assist unpracticed mediators or to supervise difficult cases—you *must* do a number of things. Let the parties know that you will be observing. There is no need to overemphasize this fact, just mention that you will be at your desk or you will be working on the other side of the office.

---

[33] Some programs strike a balance by requiring that each student mediator be observed by a trained adult during their first three real mediations, after which they mediate without an adult in the room.

Participating in mediation gave me confidence about myself since for once I was taking responsibility by not acting immature. . . . Listening to someone's story, understanding where the mistake was, and learning to forgive. These things are very useful to me because it has helped me to take it easy on others and not believe everything people say.

High school party

You can see when mediation works because the people you are mediating start to feel like: "Wow this is working!" They feel as if they can trust us. Then they start to think of peer mediation in a different way. They don't think it is stupid. They think it's a really good program.

Middle school mediator

Be as inconspicuous as possible. Sit as far away from the session as you can and make sure that you are behind the line of sight of the parties. Some coordinators sit in the corner at their desks with their backs to the session. Others sit on the opposite side of a partition.

A final and most important recommendation for the coordinator sitting in on sessions is to keep interruptions to a minimum. Each time you intervene, you chip away at mediators' credibility and confidence. Student mediators are far from perfect, and chances are good that they will make mistakes. But the process of mediating involves feeling stuck and having to think on your feet, and there is no way to learn this without experiencing it. Only intervene when the mediators ask for help, or when you perceive them to be making a mistake that jeopardizes the entire process. Or, as one trainer bluntly puts it to coordinators: "Your most important job while supervising sessions is to *keep your mouth shut!*"

Remember as well that if you do not sit in on the sessions, you should nevertheless remain accessible in case the mediators need your assistance. They may need advice to help them create a strategy to move the process forward. They may need you to locate an additional party and bring him or her to the session. They may need a suggestion regarding where to refer student parties for more help.[34] If for some reason you will not be accessible when mediation sessions are underway, arrange for another trained adult to be available.

The last way coordinators can help mediators during a session is to facilitate the use of private sessions. One unintentional yet beneficial aspect of the mediation process occurs when coordinators wait with one party while the mediators hold a private session with the other. During these breaks, you can often help parties reflect upon what is happening in the session in a way that moves the process forward.

At the Conclusion of the Session

When the mediation session comes to a close, the coordinator is involved in still other ways. If an agreement was reached, you can help with logistics like photocopying the agreement and administering a post-session questionnaire. If the parties were not able to resolve their situation in mediation, you can inform them of their options and ensure that they return to class promptly and safely. (One of the few fights on record occurred when parties were going back to class after not reaching an agreement.)

Most importantly, the coordinator should be a sounding board for the mediators, helping them learn from their experience. Mediating real cases is the most powerful teaching tool there is. Peer mediators should receive feedback from each other as well as from the coordinator, discuss any discoveries they made about the process or about themselves, and analyze questions that were raised by the case. These discussions also provide the coordinator with information that can be used to evaluate the mediators and determine their suitability for various types of cases. Realistically, most programs have little

---

[34] Though most referrals are made with the assistance of the coordinator, programs should always inform peer mediators about the other services that are available to help students within the school and community. These include school counselors, groups designed to prevent suicide or substance abuse, mentor programs, and even programs that help students with schoolwork or assist them in finding jobs.

time for post-session critiques, and much of this work is done when mediators convene as a group. But always allow at least a few minutes after each session for student mediators to collect themselves and receive some positive feedback before returning to the normal school day.

CASE FOLLOW-UP

The mediation program's involvement with the students it serves does not end when the session is over. The best programs remain in contact with parties for weeks if not months. Mediation programs conduct follow-up interviews with student parties for three reasons:

1. **To support students in upholding their agreement.** By staying in touch with parties, the program demonstrates that it cares about and wants to support them. Contact with the program serves as both reminder and inspiration to students to uphold the commitments they made in their mediation session.
2. **To offer continuing assistance to students.** This assistance usually takes the form of either conducting informal negotiations to help parties modify their agreement, or scheduling a second mediation session. If problems unrelated to the interpersonal conflict exist, students can be directed to other programs or people that might be of help.
3. **To collect data on the effectiveness of the program.** Having data to document the positive impact peer mediation has upon the school is essential to win continued support for the program. This data also provides valuable information regarding how the program is working and who it is serving that can lead to design changes.

Schools approach the task of follow-up in a variety of ways. One common formula suggests that programs should check in with parties two days, two weeks, and finally two months after their mediation session. This can be modified depending upon the specifics of each case. It might be less than twenty-four hours before you seek out parties that were especially hostile in the session, while students who leave the session friends you may not contact for ten days. Some programs include the clause: "If this agreement is not working and we are having problems, we agree to come back to mediation first" on every agreement. Others require that parties agree to a date and time for a follow-up meeting at the conclusion of each session. This makes the logistics of follow-up much easier.

What occurs during follow-up contact varies among programs as well. In most schools, the mediation representative and the party have a brief, informal conversation about whether the agreement is working. This can literally take just a few minutes. Some programs also ask that parties fill out a written questionnaire. Although the coordinator usually does the follow-up, many programs arrange for the mediators themselves to meet with the parties.

One point is important to emphasize regarding follow-up. Contact with parties should be conducted with the same sensitivity to confidentiality as the mediation session itself. Meetings should be held in the mediation office, and when informal contact occurs, mediators should take their cues from the parties. If parties don't say hello when they pass in the hall, mediators and coordinators should take this as a sign that they should only speak with them in private. On the other hand, many students will not hesitate to discuss the details of their session in front of their classmates.

RECORD KEEPING

In addition to arranging for follow-up contact with parties, you should also keep accurate records of the program's activities. The paperwork involved in running a peer mediation program is what coordinators like the least, but if you create an efficient system, it can be quite simple. A few forms can take care of all of your needs. Each case should generate a file, numbered in chronological order. By the time the case is closed, it will contain most of the following forms. (See pages 229–235 for samples of all of these forms.)

1. **Peer Mediation Referral Form.** These forms are used to refer cases. If you transfer the information onto the case summary form, it is not necessary to save them.

2. **Case Summary Form.** This form has space for all information relevant to a case including who referred the case, who mediated the case, the nature of the dispute, the nature of the agreement if one was reached, any referrals made by the mediators, and case follow-up information. It can also include other information that you need for your funding source regarding the age, grade, race, or gender of the parties.

3. **Peer Mediation Agreement Form.** Mediators write up agreements on this form. The original usually remains in the case file, while copies are given to the parties. Some programs print their agreement form on carbonless copy paper that automatically produces two to three copies of the agreement.

4. **Post-mediation Session Questionnaire.** This questionnaire is usually administered to parties immediately following the session and before they return to class. It asks for their impressions of the mediators, of the process, and of their agreement, and it takes less than five minutes to fill out. It can also help recruit future mediators by asking parties whether they would like to participate in the next training. Post-mediation session questionnaires provide you with immediate feedback about your work. Comments are usually positive, but sometimes problems with the mediators or the process surface and can be corrected. This form also provides the program with quotes that can be used for outreach and fund raising. ("Mediation allowed us to talk it out rather than fight . . . everyone should use it rather than get into trouble"; or "I always thought mediation was stupid, but it really helped me.") Some programs administer the questionnaire at the first follow-up meeting instead of directly after the session.

5. **Mediator Post-session Self-Evaluation.** This form helps mediators reflect upon and analyze their performance. Create a file where each mediator can keep his or her self-evaluations, so they can refer to them before they mediate.

Programs keep records and report data to the school community in other ways. Some programs create monthly and then yearly reports outlining the number and the kinds of cases that were mediated. These reports can be distributed to everyone within the school as well as to the local press and funding sources. Other programs create peer mediation journals in which anyone connected with the program can write down his or her comments. The entries in the journal can later be used (with permission) for reports, year-end evaluations, and public presentations. Finally, an excellent system for referencing students who use mediation is to create an alphabetized listing of all parties' names. Next to each name write the number of the case that they were a part of. This makes it easy to find case information if it is requested by an administrator or the parties.

All of the records of the mediation program must be kept confidential under limits decided upon by your program. They should be stored in a locked file cabinet to which only the coordinator and specified students have access. Administrators, teachers, and students should not be able to see these files unless they have the permission of the parties or an exception is prescribed. Old case files should be destroyed after students graduate.

One mediation program reported an interesting use for its case records. A parent of a mediator complained to the school administration that her child was doing poorly in a number of classes because she mediated too much. The meticulous records of the program showed, however, that her child had only mediated three times that semester, and not once during the classes in question.

As always, make students responsible for as many aspects of record keeping as possible. They can collect referral forms, note follow-up information on the case summary form, write comments in the program journal, and so on. Many programs design their record-keeping processes so that student mediators can do the lion's share of the work. One middle school student even created a computer program especially for mediation records.

By being a conflict mediator I get a lot out of it such as seeing the smiles of others who have been in mediation and who feel really satisfied with the agreement they've reached. It's an all-natural high.

Middle school mediator

FINAL WORDS

No small amount of preparation surrounds the mediation of cases. This work—however removed from the "glory" work of mediating—is nevertheless essential to making the program run effectively. Do not be daunted by all the details. As you gain experience in the role of coordinator, the logistics become second nature and you will discover many ways to make your job easier. Know as well that your contributions as coordinator make possible the important work that goes on behind the door of the mediation room, where students help their peers improve the quality of their lives, the quality of their school, and perhaps in the long run, the quality of their world.

CHAPTER 8

Mediator Meetings and Program Maintenance

Mediating cases is exciting and gratifying. If peer mediation programs are to remain effective over the long term, however, they must be given ongoing attention and care. This maintenance work has three major focuses. The first is *program design*. Adapting your peer mediation program to the unique needs of your school continues for months and even years after you first begin. Through day-to-day experience, you will discover many ways to improve your original design. Perhaps the scheduling system needs to be revised; or new developments necessitate a change in the relationship between discipline and peer mediation. Use referral sources, the advisory council, mediators, and even parties to help you evaluate the program and solve problems. Mediators should take the lead in this work as they are often aware of difficulties even before the coordinator.

The second focus is *outreach*. The importance of continued outreach to the success of peer mediation efforts cannot be overestimated. Always strive to broaden your program's base of support by educating the student body and winning new allies among the staff. At the same time, maintain good relations with those who do support the program: keep them up to date on the status of referrals they make, send them thank-you notes, and so on. Both program design and outreach have already been discussed at length in Chapters 5 and 6 respectively.

The third vital aspect of maintaining your program concerns *the development of your mediators.* Apart from providing them with cases to mediate, the best way to cultivate the talents of peer mediators is to meet with them regularly throughout the year. So-called mediator meetings are essential to maintaining a healthy program. These meetings have a number of objectives, including

- providing time for mediators to discuss cases;
- developing mediators' skills through advanced training;
- maintaining group cohesion, interest, and excitement;
- planning and implementing special projects;
- handling internal disciplinary matters.

CASE ANALYSIS AND DISCUSSION

Most programs encourage mediators to discuss cases with their co-mediators and with the coordinator immediately after they finish mediating. Because experience is the best teacher, these discussions are invaluable to the development of student mediators. But the need to minimize interference with academics usually prevents students from spending the necessary time on this. In mediator meetings, however, peer mediators can explore their casework experiences in depth.

In the meetings, students can take turns presenting cases that they have found interesting or challenging, or the coordinator can ask students to present cases that illustrate relevant and timely issues. Portions of sessions can be role-played to help mediators learn alternative strategies for dealing with difficult situations. When appropriate, mediators should also be encouraged to consider the substance as well as the process of cases. Discussion of a recent mediation might lead the group to ponder why so many fights occur during third lunch, or to explore the state of race relations in the school. These inquiries are welcome.

Encourage mediators to be each other's best teachers during case analysis. Giving constructive criticism not only builds a supportive atmosphere within the group, it is an important skill in and of itself. The "supportive yet detached" attitude necessary to give such feedback is similar to that of the mediator.

Remind mediators to be aware of the bounds of confidentiality when discussing cases; one mediator might be friendly with the parties in a case mediated by another. In general, ask students to change the names of the parties when they discuss cases. The information learned during these meetings should be treated with the same level of confidentiality as information disclosed during a session. Mediators should not discuss the details of the cases they mediate with each other except in these meetings.

I love being a mediator. I thought kids wouldn't listen, but after all the cases I solved, I realized that this program could really work.

Middle school mediator

ADVANCED TRAINING

Ongoing, advanced training is a second focus of mediator meetings. Initial mediation training covers the basic skills necessary to enable students to begin mediating cases. But mastering those skills, and learning more complex ones, only happen as a result of experience as a mediator, reflecting upon those experiences, and advanced training.

If your initial training was well conceived, a variety of training techniques were used: role-plays, written and experiential exercises designed to teach a specific skill, short presentations, games, and so on. All of these can be used in ongoing training. Topics for advanced training generally do not follow a prescribed agenda but rather arise from the needs expressed by the mediators or from your observations of them. Mediators might need more practice in asking questions, writing agreements, finding the issues, using neutral language, or any other aspect of the mediation process. Consider bringing in students who are not mediators to act as parties in role-plays. In addition to making role-plays more exciting and realistic, this helps the program reach more students.

Advanced training can concern other issues besides mediation skill building. Mediators might want to learn how to facilitate meetings so that they can take more responsibility for the functioning of the program. Presentations about specific cultures or about prejudice and diversity are always appropriate. Other programs that operate in the school (drug and alcohol awareness, suicide prevention, peer counseling, peer leadership) can also make presentations about their work. Anything that will help students grow as people and as mediators is welcome.

The coordinator, not the initial training source, facilitates the bulk of advanced training. Your training source should provide follow-up training and consultation, but it is usually not possible or advisable to continue to rely exclusively upon their help. Trainers should offer you materials to use on your own or direct you to published conflict resolution and mediation curricula that will meet your needs.[35] Guest presenters and even the student mediators themselves can also deliver advanced training.

Periodic evaluations are another essential part of advanced training. These include both self-evaluations as well as evaluations by peers and coordinators. Year-end evaluations, when mediators review their progress and set their goals for the following year, are especially useful.

BUILDING GROUP COHESION AND MORALE

Mediators' enthusiasm and ability to work effectively as a team are important ingredients in the success of any peer mediation effort. But since their work is done almost exclusively in pairs, student mediators rarely get to spend time with each other as a group. It is easy for them to lose touch with each other. Mediator meetings can therefore rejuvenate students and remind them that their work is part of a larger effort to make the school a better place.

Group cohesion and morale are especially important when programs are young and referrals may be few and far between. Sometimes students do not have the opportunity to mediate their first cases until many weeks after the training is complete. Regular meetings maintain the program's momentum and prevent mediators from losing their enthusiasm.

You can do a variety of things to maintain an excited and effective peer mediation team. At the very least, you need to ensure that mediators are committed to treating one another with respect and caring. Beyond that, the possibilities are limitless. Try to make at least a part of every meeting fun. Use exercises that build trust and develop the group's ability to work together as a team. Plan games, special breakfasts, pizza parties, field trips, and recognition assemblies. Many programs have year-end celebrations or picnics. The more you can do to make mediators feel like their work is appreciated, the better.

SPECIAL PROJECTS

Mediator meetings are also a time when the team can plan and implement special projects. There are countless ways mediators can operate as a force for positive change in the school, and special projects do not even have to be directly related to students' work as mediators. Some ideas include

- offering mini-courses in conflict resolution and mediation for their classmates;
- conducting workshops for students in "in-house" suspension;
- leading discussion and awareness groups with their peers on subjects such as violence, race relations, substance abuse, and AIDS (after receiving appropriate training);
- conducting mediation trainings at other schools;
- visiting courts, community mediation programs, or private mediators to expand their knowledge of mediation;

---

[35] One curriculum, *On-Going Training Activities for Student Mediators*, by Dan Meyer (available from Our Town Family Center in Tucson, Arizona) was written expressly for this purpose.

- planning and/or participating in regional conferences for student mediators;
- organizing fund-raising events such as talent shows, movie nights, bake sales, and car washes.

INTERNAL PROGRAM DISCIPLINE

A final objective of mediator meetings is to create and enforce a program's internal disciplinary policy. Though the need for a disciplinary code is infrequent, in some instances mediators need to be put on probation or even suspended from the program because of inappropriate conduct. Examples of such conduct include not making an effort in school, starting a fight, sharing confidential information, and not attending mediation sessions or meetings. A disciplinary code should

- clearly inform students regarding what is expected of them as mediators;
- outline consequences for prohibited behavior that are fair and predictable; and
- protect committed mediators—and the program as a whole—from students who do not live up to group standards.

Because peer mediation disciplinary policies stress the responsibility of each student for maintaining a successful program, students should take the lead in both formulating and enforcing this code. One of the best ways to do this is to make a group contract. Students first list the types of behavior they expect of their fellow mediators and those they want to discourage. Then together they create a series of progressively serious consequences for each instance a member behaves contrary to their mutual expectations. Each mediator signs the group contract, understanding that he or she must either live up to it or expect the designated sanctions. Mediator meetings help students maintain their commitment by providing a forum where they can discuss their own conflicts and get assistance and advice from their peers.

It is worth noting that although the objectives of mediator meetings have been discussed separately, they are all closely related. Activities designed to meet one will have a positive impact upon the others. An engaging advanced training session might excite the group; resolving an internal disciplinary problem can improve students' ability to work together; discussion of cases might uncover a need for special training.

MEDIATOR MEETINGS: WHEN AND WHERE?

Although mediator meetings are an important part of program maintenance, many programs hold them infrequently, if at all. When coordinators become busy, mediator meetings are easy to sacrifice. In addition, there seems to be no "good" time to hold the meetings. Before school is almost impossible, especially if students are bused. During school means students miss more class time, something that every program strives to avoid. And after-school scheduling runs into the same problem with busing as well as conflicts with students' commitments to extracurricular activities and jobs. In the end,

coordinators usually hold meetings during the school day but vary the times of meetings so that students don't miss the same classes. Or, they look for opportunities unique to their school's scheduling system. Some of these options include

- creating a special homeroom for mediators so that they can meet together briefly every day;
- making peer mediation a student club or organization so that mediators convene during the time built into the schedule for club meetings;
- manipulating mediators' schedules so that all mediators have the same lunch period and can meet then;
- holding meetings starting the last period of the school day and continuing thirty to forty-five minutes after school. This minimizes classes missed and it enables students to fulfill other commitments (or make it to a late school bus);
- holding breakfast meetings before school and providing food for the mediators (and whoever helps them get to school).[36]

The frequency of meetings varies from school to school. Although bimonthly meetings are generally recommended, some programs meet with mediators for a few minutes every day, and others meet once a month or less. The need for meetings will obviously depend upon the stage of your program development and the projects currently underway.

Meetings should ideally be held in the mediation room (if your program has one and if it is large enough). When this is impossible, programs hold meetings in any suitable space: empty classrooms, the library, cafeteria, gymnasium, or even off campus on special occasions.

FACILITATING MEDIATOR MEETINGS

There are many parallels between facilitating meetings and mediating. Both mediators and meeting facilitators guide the *process* (the way the group interacts, who speaks when, the time devoted to each topic) to help participants manage the *substance* (issues to discuss, decisions to be made, materials to be presented). Experienced mediators already have many of the skills of a facilitator, and your initial trainer likely modeled many of these skills during the training. Here are a few suggestions for facilitating meetings:

- Create an agenda for every meeting that outlines your goals and the amount of time allotted for each item. Use input from the student mediators; check to see whether the agenda is acceptable with them before you begin each meeting.
- Strive to keep the meetings engaging at all times. Plan activities that use a variety of different learning modalities (discussion, role-play, written work, dyads, and small group sharing). Sit in a configuration that is congruent with your goals (a circle, for instance, encourages communication within the group). Include breaks and energizing activities like games, awards, and refreshments whenever appropriate.

---

[36] It is a good idea to provide food at every meeting, regardless of the time of day. Eating together helps to create a warm, "family" atmosphere among the mediators.

- Pay close attention to the group process at all times. If students wander from the designated topic, guide them back to it. If they do not behave in a way that promotes trust and teamwork, point this out. If they are not engaged, ask them why and modify the agenda accordingly. It is better not to have meetings than to have meetings that are boring and deflate students' enthusiasm.

- Allow students to "pass"—to choose not to participate in activities—whenever possible. Giving participants this control helps them feel both respected and comfortable.

- Work toward having the students facilitate their own meetings. With a little training and guidance, students can run these meetings very effectively.

FINAL WORDS

If you do the hard work outlined in this book, chances are good that you will create a strong and effective peer mediation program. In the years ahead, peer mediation and collaborative conflict resolution should become an integral part of educational institutions around the world. You will have been one of the leaders in this work, not only demonstrating the potential of peer mediation, but more importantly, enabling young people to demonstrate their potential.

Part III: Tools

CHAPTER 9

Peer Mediation Session Transcripts

The two transcripts that follow will provide you with an intimate view of the mediation process. Both are fictionalized versions of actual school-based cases. In the first case, The Basketball Throw, the high school students reconciled their differences despite the prejudice that was one of the sources of their conflict. It is generally easier to achieve reconciliation and agreement when the parties have been friends, as in this case.

In the second conflict between middle school students (The Hollywood Club), the parties had not been friends. Although it is not as easy to bring parties together under these circumstances, it is nevertheless usually possible to help them create an agreement that resolves the dispute and leaves the door open to a more intimate relationship. Before you read the transcripts, three important points must be made:

1. These cases are not meant to be perfect examples of peer mediation. All mediators make mistakes, get confused, and have difficulty guiding the process at times. As long as they don't make a major blunder, however, things usually work out fine in the end. The transcripts are an accurate representation of what real peer mediation sessions are like.

2. Be advised that these are just two representative cases. The issues in your school may be slightly different or may appear more or less serious than the two examples here. Pay more attention to the process than the issues involved. It is the process that is almost universally transferable.

3. The mediators in these transcripts use a mediation model that is one variant of the peer mediation process. The opening remarks, the order of questions, the degree to which parties are asked to paraphrase each other's remarks, the way agreements are written—all will vary slightly from school to school. But fundamentally, effective programs use a mediation model similar to the one used here.

Transcript 1:

THE BASKETBALL THROW

Parties:
Hector Ramos and Tommy Nguyen, eleventh grade
Mediators:
Ricardo Espinal, eleventh grade, and Patty Chau, twelfth grade

Background

Hector Ramos and Tommy Nguyen have been friendly for the past couple of years. They are both juniors in a multiracial public high school in an urban area. Hector is Hispanic and although he was born in the United States, he speaks Spanish fluently. Tommy is from Vietnam, where he lived until he was nine years old.

Tommy and Hector were recently about to fight in the hallway in school. There was some pushing before a teacher separated them and sent them to the disciplinarian.

After letting them cool off in the office, the adminstrator in charge of discipline encouraged the boys to try to mediate their dispute. They agreed. The mediators were Ricardo Espinal and Patty Chau.

Ricardo: Hello and welcome to mediation. My name is Ricardo and this is Patty, and we are going to be your mediators today. What are your names?

Hector: Hector.

Tommy (*mumbled*): Tommy.

Patty: Excuse me, I didn't hear you.

Tommy: Tommy.

Patty: Okay, thanks. Well, welcome. We are glad you came to mediation and we hope we can help you. Before we get started, we want to tell you how mediation works and see if you have any questions. Mediation is voluntary and so you don't have to try this if you don't want to. What we try to do is help you come up with a solution to this situation that you guys like. We don't tell you what to do or judge you or say who is right or wrong or anything like that. We just try to help you come up with your own agreement to this thing.

If you can come up with an agreement, we will write it down, have you each sign it, and give each of you a copy. If you can't come up with an agreement, that is alright too. But many people are able to figure something out that they like, and we think you might be able to too.

One more thing I want to say. Nothing you say in this mediation will leave this program unless it is life threatening. We won't tell other kids, teachers, parents, even the principal. What is said here, stays here.

Do you understand that?

Hector and Tommy: Yes.

Patty: Alright, Ricardo has a few more things to say before we get started.

Ricardo: Yes . . . uh . . . we take notes sometimes, but that is just so we remember stuff. We'll rip them up at the end of the session. You can take notes on the paper in front of you too.

Try to listen to each other as much as you can. If you interrupt too much, we will ask you to speak one at a time.

We have two main rules in mediation: There are no put-downs and there is no physical violence. Can you agree to these rules?

Silence

Ricardo: . . . uh, we can't mediate unless you both agree to the rules.

Tommy: I agree.

Ricardo: Good . . . How about you, Hector?

Hector *(to Tommy):* I was willing to squash this whole thing, but you kept it going. If you want to go at it, we'll be there, you just name the time and the place . . . .

Tommy: Yeah, right. The last . . . .

Ricardo *(interrupting):* Listen, Hector. First of all, we can't have threats like that in mediation. We will just have to end the session. And second of all, mediation is a way to work this out so that you really *can* squash this thing. But you have to follow the rules. . . . It is up to you. Do you want to continue?

Long pause

Hector: I guess so.

Patty: And so you will follow the rules of no put-downs and no physical violence during mediation?

Hector: Yes.

Ricardo: Great. That's really good. Just one more thing I need to tell you then. We might want to meet with you each separately later on in this mediation. We will see how things go.

Okay. Do you guys have any questions?

Hector and Tommy: No.

Ricardo: Do you want to try mediation?

Tommy: Sure.

Hector: I guess so.

Ricardo: Remember, Hector, you don't have to do this. It works well, and we have been able to help other students solve things like this, but it only works if you want to do it.

Hector: I'll do it, man.

Ricardo: Great, then let's get started. Who wants to speak first?

Hector: I'll go first. The problem started because he was going to get his boys from Chinatown to come down and jump me. I was . . . .

Tommy: What about *your* boys? . . . How come Franklin was saying that you and your friends were going to wait until I got off from work tomorrow and beat me up?

Hector: What are you talking . . .

Patty: Wait a second. We can't have both of you guys speaking at once. Let's let Hector finish his story, and then Tommy you will get a chance to say everything you want to say when he is finished. Is that okay?

Tommy: *(nods)*

Silence

Patty: Go on, Hector.

Hector: Okay . . . well . . . that is basically it. He was going to get his friends to jump me, and so today we got into a fight in the halls . . . well we almost got into a fight but Mr. Samuels broke it up.

Ricardo: So you are saying that you heard that Tommy was going to get some of his friends to beat on you. What started this thing, do you know? Why would Tommy want to do this?

Hector: I don't know really. We actually used to be kinda friendly . . . I guess it was a couple of weeks ago when things started to turn bad.

Patty: What happened then?

Hector: We had a situation outside the gym. Tommy took a basketball that I had and he threw it down the hall. He was acting like some stupid tough guy, trying to impress his friends, I think. When I asked him to go get it, he wouldn't.

Tommy *(under his breath)*: Why don't you tell them what really happened?

Ricardo: Tommy, you have been great at not interrupting. Let's let Hector finish, and then you will get your chance, because we really want to hear from you too . . . and Hector, remember what we said about put-downs.

Hector: Okay, sorry. That's it really. It started with the basketball thing I think, and since then it has gotten out of hand. Everyone is telling me he is getting his friends to jump me. And so I was getting my people together in case we had to go at it.

Ricardo: Hector, how did you feel when he wouldn't get the basketball?

Hector: Uh . . . well. . . at first I thought he was just kidding but then when he wouldn't get the ball I started getting angry. I felt like: Why is he being so ignorant? Is he just trying to impress his friends?

Ricardo: And that was how . . . .

Patty: So after this situation . . . .

Ricardo *(to Patty)*: Oh, sorry, go ahead.

Patty: . . . So after this situation with the basketball, you started hearing a lot of rumors about a fight?

Hector: Yeah, everyone has been talking about it. People have told me to watch my back because Tommy's Vietnamese friends are in this gang and everything.

Patty: Did you and Tommy ever talk to each other after the incident a couple of weeks ago?

Hector: Not really.

Ricardo: And so what happened today?

Hector: I don't really know. We were walking down the hall, and I heard somebody hiss at me and so I turned around and Tommy was there with some of his friends and pretty soon we were yelling and about to fight. Then we were sent to the office.

Ricardo: I see . . . okay, is there anything else you want to say, Hector?

Hector: No.

Patty: I have one more question. Hector, you said that you guys used to be kind of friendly. What did you mean?

Hector: Well, we weren't good friends or anything like that, but we used to be cool, joke around and stuff . . . we are in some of the same classes. We are both on the football team too.

Patty: And you guys were getting along until that thing with the basketball?

Hector: Yeah.

Silence

Ricardo: Do you have any more questions, Patty?

Patty: No.

Ricardo: Alright, let me see if we understand what you are saying, Hector. You and Tommy used to be friendly up until a couple of weeks ago. At that time, something happened where he threw your basketball down the hall and he wouldn't go get it. You were angry with him for this, especially because you thought you were friends. After that a lot of rumors started flying around that Tommy was going to get his friends and jump you. And so you started to get your friends together in case there was a fight. And then today, you were both in the halls and you were about to fight but a teacher sent you to the office. Is that right?

Hector: Yeah.

Ricardo: Did I leave anything out?

Hector: No, but like I said before, we weren't really good friends or anything, we were just alright with each other.

Ricardo: I see.

Patty: Great. Thanks, Hector. Okay, Tommy, it is your turn. Why don't you tell us about this situation from your side? And thanks for waiting your turn, by the way.

Tommy: He left out a lot of stuff. First of all, I don't have any friends that are in gangs or anything that I am going to get after him. That is just stupid.

Hector: What about Quang?

Tommy: I don't even hang out with Quang anymore. He likes to shoot off his mouth but I didn't ask him to fight you or anything. All of these rumors just were growing. I didn't start them. And another thing . . . before that incident happened in the gym last week, I was standing there and Hector walked up with a couple of *his* friends. I called to him: "Hey Hector, throw the ball!" And Hector said: "Why should I give it to you—you people can't play basketball." And so . . . .

Hector: I was just kidding, man. Can't you take a joke?

Silence for a short while

Ricardo: Hector, remember what we said about no interruptions. The same as it was for Tommy, if you have something you want to say, just write it down and we will come back to you. Anyway . . . uh . . . Tommy, please go on.

Tommy: I don't know what I was saying.

Patty: You were saying that Hector said something like: "Your people can't play basketball."

Ricardo: Oh . . . and one other thing, Tommy. You don't just have to answer what Hector said first. We want to hear about this thing from your side from the beginning.

Tommy: Oh . . . yeah . . . well . . . anyway, it was after he said that that I took the basketball and threw it down, kind of as a joke. I didn't mean it to go all the way down the hall like it did. But he seemed really angry, and then I got angry and I didn't want to get it for him.

Patty: Were you feeling upset by what he had said, about "you people can't play basketball"?

Tommy: I don't know . . . I guess.

Silence

Ricardo: Is there anything else you want to say, Tommy?

Tommy: Not really.

Ricardo: Do you agree with what Hector said about your being friendly before this happened?

Tommy: Yeah.

Short pause

Ricardo: *(nods to Patty)*

Patty: So what you are saying, Tommy, is that you agree that you used to be friendly. But when that incident happened in the gym, Hector had said something that kind of upset you. And when you threw the ball, you didn't mean it to go that far down the hall, but you got angry and so you didn't want to get it after you threw it. Is that right?

Tommy: Yeah.

Ricardo: And you also said that you haven't been trying to get your friends after Hector, including this guy Quang?

Tommy: Yeah. Quang is kind of a goon, man. He was thrown out of his last school because he almost knifed somebody, and so I can see how Hector was, like, you know, didn't want him to be involved. But I had nothing to do with that.

Patty: Alright. Is that it?

Tommy: Yup.

Ricardo: Okay, thanks Tommy. Before we move on, is there anything you want to say, Hector after hearing what Tommy said?

Hector: Yeah, I want to know why, if he wasn't trying to get his friends against me, why did he have this big meeting after school the other day with all the Vietnamese guys. I heard about it and a friend of mine saw them meeting. Everybody in school was talking about the "Vietnamese War Council." It was crazy. People have been writing "VWC" on the walls and stuff.

Patty: Tommy, you want to say something about that?

Tommy: The "VWC" thing was just kind of a joke. But we had heard that the Latins were all going to fight with us, and so this friend of mine called that meeting. I wasn't even really involved in it. It was stupid . . . .

Ricardo: Okay.

Patty: Hector, what do you say to that, to what Tommy just said?

Hector: I don't know, man.

Ricardo: Alright . . . so it seems like there are a lot of things happening that are, like, maybe, miscommunication or something. And rumors too. Each of you thought the other was organizing his friends to fight. And even back in the incident with the basketball, you both were, uh, neither one of you wanted to hurt the other one but you kind of took it the wrong way maybe. Is that possible?

Tommy: *(nods slightly in agreement)*

Hector: Yeah, but I only talked to one person about this whole thing, and we speak in Spanish, so I didn't start any rumors.

Patty: Tommy, do you have any questions for Hector about what he said?

Tommy: No.

Patty: Okay . . . well . . . this might be a good time to talk about how to solve this situation. How do you guys want to solve this thing: what are you willing to do, and what do you want from each other?

Tommy: I just want this to be over.

Hector: That's fine with me.

Patty: Great, so you both agree on that. What needs to happen in order to end this?

Hector: Well, I would like to not be suspended for the fight because I can't afford to be suspended again. By doing this mediation does it mean we are not suspended?

Ricardo: We don't have any control over suspension and things like that. That is up to Mrs. Domenico. Sometimes this can help, I mean, if you come up with an agreement, she might think that is a good sign. But there is no guarantee. It is totally up to her.

Hector: Oh . . . .

Patty: Is there anything you guys want to say to each other? Like maybe about that situation with the basketball. An apology or anything?

Tommy: Uh . . . like I said before, I wasn't planning on throwing the ball all the way down the hall. It just happened and then it seemed like things got worse because of it.

Hector: That's cool, but you don't need to act tough in front of your friends.

Tommy: I really wasn't. I . . .

Hector: Hey, I know, because it is the same way with Latin guys and stuff. Trying to show you are strong.

Tommy: But I didn't mean it that way. That is not what I was doing there.

Hector: But your friends were there and everything. C'mon, man . . . .

Patty: It seems like you guys disagree about this. Tommy is saying that he really wasn't trying to impress his friends by what he did. You thought and maybe still think he was, Hector. We really can't prove anything here for certain. You kinda have to take each person on their word, and that's it. Do you guys understand that?

Hector and Tommy: *(nod)*

Patty: Would you like to put something about this sort of thing in the agreement if you can come up with one?

Tommy: What do you mean?

Patty: I don't know. Something about the way you act with each other . . . .

Silence

Hector: You mean like we won't act different in front of our friends.

Patty: I don't know. It is up to you. How does that sound to you, Tommy?

Tommy: That's okay, but I really don't think I was doing that.

Patty: Well, maybe we can put it in the agreement for the future, that you both won't do it in the future.

Tommy: I guess so.

Patty: But . . . I mean, it's up to you, Tommy. I mean it is up to both of you.

Ricardo: Tommy, what about that comment that you said that Hector said about "your people can't play basketball"? Does that fit in?

Tommy: Well . . . it pissed me off . . . .

Ricardo: How come?

Tommy: Because he was putting down my people. I can play basketball. He was just being ignorant.

Hector: Yeah, but c'mon. Vietnamese guys are short. Name one Vietnamese basketball player, I mean professional player.

Tommy: I don't know . . . but still, there could be. It is just ignorant to put someone down because of their race or something.

Patty: Watch the put-downs, Tommy.

Hector: Anyway, I didn't mean it in a bad way. I was just kidding around.

Long silence

Ricardo: But, Hector, do you see how Tommy took it?

Hector: Yeah, he took it like I was being prejudiced, and I'm sorry about that, but I wasn't being prejudiced.

Ricardo: So you are, kind of like, apologizing?

Hector: I don't know . . . *(to Tommy)* I meant what I said, I am sorry that you thought I was being prejudiced.

Pause

Patty: How do you feel about that, Tommy?

Tommy: It's alright.

Patty: Do you accept his apology?

Tommy: Yes.

Ricardo: Would you want anything about this in the agreement?

Tommy: No.

Ricardo: Are you sure?

Tommy: Yeah.

Ricardo: But . . . uh . . . you are sure you feel resolved about this?

Tommy: Yeah, I see what he means. It is just that there is a lot of prejudice in this town, and I didn't expect it to come from him, even though now I see that it really wasn't . . . coming from him I mean.

Hector: I hear ya on the prejudice thing.

Patty: Well, this is great! We are making real progress here. This might have been another one of those miscommunication things. Is there anything else that we need to talk about?

Silence

Hector: No, it seems like this is over.

Tommy: Yeah.

Ricardo: What about your relationship?

Hector: What do you mean?

Ricardo: Do you guys want to be friends again, go back to the way you were before, or do you want to have nothing to do with each other, or whatever you want . . . it's up to you.

Hector: I think just go back to the way it was before.

Patty: How about you, Tommy?

Tommy: I guess so.

Patty: You guess so?

Tommy: Yeah, I mean we weren't good friends before, and because of what happened I don't think we can all of a sudden be like before, but . . . you know . . . later.

Patty: So you mean kind of moving back to being friends.

Tommy: Yeah.

Patty: How does that seem to you, Hector?

Hector: Alright.

Patty: How should we say that in the agreement?

Hector: We will just be cool with each other.

Patty *(to Tommy)*: Is that okay with you?

Tommy: Sure.

Patty: Great! I think we are coming to the end. Is there anything else?

Patty takes out paper and starts to write an agreement.

Tommy: I think he should tell his friends that this is squashed, so they don't just keep this thing going on.

Hector: And you should tell your friends too.

Ricardo: Do you both agree to that?

Tommy and Hector: Yeah.

Silence

Ricardo: You know, it seems like one of the reasons this got all out of control was that there were rumors going around. Do you think maybe we should put something about that in the agreement?

Hector: If he hears something, I just want him to come up to me to check it out.

Ricardo: Yes, that's what I mean. What do you think of that, Tommy?

Tommy: That is good because that is how this whole thing got started.

Patty: But I wonder . . . I mean . . . If one of you comes up to the other about a rumor, couldn't that lead to another fight?

Hector: In a way, yeah . . . but I think, like, you have to do it in private.

Tommy: Yeah.

Ricardo: So you both agree, how should I say it, that "if you hear rumors, you will check them out directly with each other in private"?

Hector and Tommy: Yeah.

Ricardo: Is there anything else you guys want to add?

Tommy: This whole thing just seems so stupid. I wish it didn't have to happen.

Hector: Yeah, me too. I think we thought we were outlaws or something for a while.

Tommy: *(laughs quietly)*

Ricardo: Alright, then maybe we should write the agreement. Patty, are you writing it?

Patty: Yes, let me just finish here.

Silence as Patty writes

Ricardo: Do you guys think this agreement is going to work?

Hector: Yup.

Tommy: *(nods his head)*

Pause

Ricardo: So you guys got beat on Saturday?

Tommy: Yeah, we got destroyed.

Ricardo: I thought Jefferson's team was hurtin'.

Hector: Yeah, but we played like the worst we have ever played.

Patty: Okay, I have the agreement. Let me read it. It says:

1. Hector and Tommy agree that the situation is resolved between them.
2. Tommy and Hector agree not to act differently in front of their friends.
3. Both agree that if they hear rumors, they will check them out directly with each other in private.
4. Both Hector and Tommy agree to tell their friends that the fight is squashed.
5. Hector and Tommy agree to be cool with each other in the future.

How does that sound?

Hector: Good.

Patty: How does that sound to you Tommy?

Tommy: Fine.

Patty: Okay, why don't you both sign it at the bottom then.

She hands them the agreement and they both sign.

Ricardo: Alright, and now we will sign it too.

Both mediators sign the agreement.

Ricardo: Okay, well, thanks for coming to mediation. Do you have any final questions?
Tommy and Hector: No.
Ricardo: We really hope this works out for you.

Mediators shake both parties' hands.

Hector: Alright.
Patty: Yeah, thanks. Good luck, and come back to see us if you have any problems or need more help.
Ricardo: Alright, let's walk out and we will give you each a copy of this, and then we have to walk you back to Mrs. Domenico's office.

All stand up and leave.

Transcript 2:

THE HOLLYWOOD CLUB

Parties:
Susan Black and Linda Harshburn, seventh grade
Mediators:
Kalila Jones and Jeff Sipperstein, seventh grade

Background

Susan Black and Linda Harshburn are in the seventh grade. Although they are in the same class, they do not know each other well and they have different groups of friends.

Recently Susan went to the mediation coordinator, Mr. Johnson, and asked if she could mediate with Linda. The coordinator met with Linda and she agreed to try mediation.

The mediators were Kalila Jones and Jeff Sipperstein.

Kalila: Hello. I am glad that you have come to mediation. My name is Kalila and this is Jeff and we are going to be your mediators. What are your names?

Susan: Susan.

Linda: Linda.

Kalila: Hi. During this mediation we'll try to help you resolve your conflict. We will do this by helping you talk together and listen to each other.

Jeff: We try to help you come up with an agreement that we can write down and have you each sign and we sign it too. You get a copy and Mr. Johnson gets a copy and he puts it in a locked file cabinet. That is it. Do you understand?

Susan and Linda: Yes.

Kalila: As mediators, we are nonjudgmental.

Linda: What does that mean?

Kalila: It means that we don't say who is right or wrong in mediation. We don't take sides or judge you. Also, everything in mediation is private, including any notes that we take. We rip them up at the end. The only time we have to tell someone other than Mr. Johnson is if you talk about something like drugs or weapons or something where one of you might get hurt. *(Looks to Jeff to continue.)*

Jeff: We have a few rules in mediation. There are no put-downs allowed and there is no fighting allowed. Can you agree to that?

Linda and Susan: Yes.

Jeff: Also, you should try to listen to each other and not interrupt when the other person is talking. Okay?

Linda and Susan: Yes.

Jeff: Finally . . . we might take a private session later which means that we meet with each of you separately . . . . Now that you have heard all about mediation, do you still want to do it?

Linda and Susan: Yes.

Jeff: Do you have any questions?

Linda and Susan: No.

Kalila: Okay, who would like to speak first?

Linda: I would like to.

Susan: No, I want to. I am the one who wanted this mediation.

Kalila: Well, there is a rule in mediation. If you guys can't decide, we start with the person sitting on our left. We are not taking sides or anything. That is you Susan. Will you begin and just tell us about this situation?

Susan: Good. Well, I came to mediation because she has been calling me names and I can't stand it anymore. I have tried to tell her to cut it out but she doesn't. She just wants to bug me. My teacher told me I should take her to mediation.

Jeff: Okay. So you say that Linda has been calling you names and you want her to stop. Is that right?

Susan: Yes.

Jeff: What kind of names?

Susan: Well, they usually call me "dingbat," and sometimes there are other ones but I don't want to say.

Jeff: Alright. Is there anything else?

Susan: Not really.

Kalila: How did it make you feel when Linda called you names?

Susan: I felt bad because sometimes other people laugh, too, and I hate it. She has gotten all of these kids to get after me.

Kalila: What do you mean?

Susan: Well, they have formed this club and part of it is that they tease people. It's called the Hollywood Club.

Linda *(interrupting):* You don't know anything about that. The club has nothing to do with this.

Kalila: Linda, we want to hear what you have to say too, but can you wait until Susan is finished like we talked about before?

Linda: Alright.

Susan: See. She knows that I am right. Don't you think it is wrong that she is teasing me all the time?

Jeff: Well . . . uh . . . we can't take sides. What we want to do is help you and Linda solve this in a way that you both like. Is there anything else you want to say?

Pause

Susan: Oh yeah. I also think that she is making calls to my house on the weekends. She hangs up when I pick up the phone. My mother is really mad about this too. That is all I have to say.

Jeff *(to Kalila):* Do you want to summarize or should I?

Kalila: You can.

Jeff: Okay. So you are saying that Linda has been teasing you, and this makes you feel bad and you want her to stop. You also are saying that you think she is making prank phone calls to your house on the weekends. And she is part of this Hollywood Club and that has something to do with it. Is that right?

Susan: Yes.

Kalila: What is the Hollywood Club?

Susan: It is some kind of club where they watch movies, I think.

Linda: Can I say something?

Kalila: Just a minute. Susan, is there anything else that you want to say?

Susan: No, that's it.

Kalila: Okay. Thank you. Linda, do you want to say what is going on in your words?

Linda: Well I was teasing her, right? But it has nothing to do with the Hollywood Club. That is just stupid. The Hollywood Club is just a bunch of girls that watch movies together on the weekend.

Kalila: I see. Well, what do *you* think is going on?

Linda: Susan just bothers me. She is always making these stupid jokes in class and just, like, getting on my nerves. She sits behind me in class. Like the other day she was playing with the erasers and she got the chalk all over my shirt. It is just rude.

Susan: That was a mistake, and I said I was sorry.

Linda: Yes, but still it was annoying. I don't know what to say. She just kind of bothers me.

Pause

Kalila: Are there other ways that you feel like she bothers you?

Linda: Well, for a while now she has been spreading rumors that the Hollywood Club just sits around and drools over movie magazines. She also says that we all have a crush on this boy John Sampson and she calls us the "John Lovers' Club." It's stupid because a couple of weeks ago Susan came up to me and asked whether she could be in the club and I said no and I think that is *really* why she is angry.

Jeff: Okay, is there anything else you want to add?

Linda: No.

Kalila: And so how do you feel about this whole situation?

Linda: I just want to end this. I don't know. I am just, I don't know, frustrated.

Kalila: Alright, so Linda you feel like Susan is bugging you in a few ways. There was something with the erasers and getting chalk on you, and she is spreading rumors about your club. Also she asked to be in your club but you didn't want her to be. And the situation makes you frustrated. Is that a good summary?

Linda: Yes.

Jeff: Do either of you want to ask each other questions or anything?

Susan and Linda: No.

Jeff: Well, then, how do you want to solve this situation? Why don't you go first, Linda, because Susan went first last time.

Linda: I just want this to be over, that's all. And she should stop calling the club names.

Kalila: And you, Susan?

Susan: I want her to stop calling me names and stop making calls to my house and apologize for what she has done.

Kalila: Were you guys ever friends before?

Linda: No.

Susan: Not really.

Jeff: Alright, so the thing is that you both feel like you are bothering each other and you both want it to stop. Especially the name-calling and calling the club names. It seems like we might be able to solve this.

Kalila: I have one question. About the thing with the erasers. Susan said she apologized for what happened. Is that right Linda?

Linda: Yes.

Kalila: Did you accept that apology?

Linda: I guess so, at that time, but I was still mad.

Kalila: Okay. I just wanted to know.

Jeff: Well, we can't really solve this for you. What would you each be willing to do to solve this? Actually, Susan, were you calling her club names and saying those things about it?

Susan: I guess so.

Jeff: Do you want to say why?

Susan: I don't know.

Jeff: Was it maybe because you wanted to be in it?

Susan: Yes.

Pause

Kalila *(to Linda)*: And were you teasing Susan?

Linda: I already said I was!

Kalila: Well . . . .

Long pause

Jeff: Uh . . . like I said before. How do you want to solve this?

Susan: I'd be willing to stop calling her club names if she does the things that I want.

Kalila: How does that seem to you Linda?

Linda: That's okay. I'll stop calling her names too.

Kalila: Well, that's great. That means we have some agreement. I was wondering, Susan, about the phone calls. Do you really know they are from Linda?

Susan: I don't know for sure, but I hear all this laughing and it sounds like her.

Jeff *(to Linda)*: Do you know anything about this?

Linda: No, but I can make sure that the girls in the club don't do it.

Jeff: What do you mean?

Linda: I will just tell everyone not to do it, if they are, and that will stop it.

Jeff *(to Susan)*: Is that okay with you?

Susan: I guess so.

Kalila: Are you sure?

Susan: Yes.

Kalila: Well, that takes care of the name-calling and the phone calls. Does this feel like it is getting solved to you two?

Susan: A little, but I still want her to apologize.

Linda: Then you should apologize to me too.

Pause

Jeff: Could you . . . uh . . . both apologize?
Susan: What should I apologize for?
Linda: For calling the club the "John Lovers' Club."
Susan: Okay, but you apologize first.
Linda: No way.

Pause

Kalila: You are close to working this out. You could both do it at the same time, or . . . .
Linda: Okay, I apologize.
Susan: I apologize too.
Jeff: Do you both know what you are apologizing for?
Linda and Susan *(simultaneously)*: For calling each other names!
Jeff: Do you both accept the apologies?
Linda and Susan: Yes.

Jeff takes out an agreement form and begins to write the agreement.

Kalila: Alright. That seems like everything. Do you guys want to be friends?
Susan: I don't know, we really weren't friends before.
Linda: We could be like "hi–and–bye" friends, where we don't hang together but we
  don't bug each other either.
Susan: That's fine with me.
Kalila: Do you two think this is solved then?
Susan: Yes, but what about the other girls in the club?
Linda: I can't control them.
Susan: But you could tell them that we are hi-and-bye friends and we have solved our
  problem.
Linda: Sure.
Jeff: Is that all right with you, Susan?
Susan: Yes.
Jeff: Well, I have written this up in an agreement. I just need a minute to finish it.

Pause

Susan: How do you get to be a mediator?
Kalila: Well, we went through this training to teach us how to do it. If you want I can
  tell Mr. Johnson that you want to be a mediator.
Susan: Okay.

Silence while Jeff finishes writing.

Jeff: Alright. Here is the agreement. It says:

    1. Linda and Susan agree to treat each other nicely and not call each other names or the club names.

    2. Susan and Linda agree to be hi-and-bye friends.

    3. Linda agrees to tell her friends that she and Susan are hi-and-bye friends and that they shouldn't make prank calls to her house.

    4. Susan and Linda have apologized to each other and their apologies were accepted.

Can I add that if you have other problems you will come back to mediation if you can't work them out on your own?

Susan and Linda: Yes.

Kalila: Alright. Are you sure this is going to solve this?

Susan: Yes. I feel better.

Kalila: How about you, Linda?

Linda: Yes, I feel like it is solved.

Jeff: Well then, thank you for trying mediation because I know this can be scary. I had to come to mediation once like you, as the person in the fight.

Kalila: Yeah, thanks.

Linda: Okay.

Susan: I think I would like to be a mediator.

Jeff: It's fun . . . I mean . . . to help other kids.

Kalila: We will get you a copy of this, and then you have to sign out and go back to class.

All stand up and leave.

CHAPTER 10

Twelve Conflict Resolution Lessons

INTRODUCTION

The following lessons are designed for two purposes:

1. **To enable classroom teachers to begin to teach conflict resolution skills to their students.** If you teach students skills to manage their own conflicts effectively, your classroom will become more conducive to learning and growth.
2. **To serve as an introduction to conflict resolution that can be delivered to an entire student body prior to the implementation of a peer mediation program.** These lessons will build the conflict resolution skills of all students in a school, creating a common conflict resolution "language" that will lay a foundation for the peer mediation program.

CREATING A FORMAT FOR THE LESSONS

When presenting these lessons, create a standard format that sets them off from the normal school day. The format you use will differ according to the context in which you are teaching: do the students know each other already; are the lessons being taught separately or as part of an academic subject? Ideally, you should

1. **Begin with a game or other fun activity.**
    This gathers the group together and sets a positive, exciting tone.
2. **Review important points from previous lessons.**
    Reviewing previous lessons enables students to integrate and build consciously upon what they have already learned.
3. **Go over the agenda for the upcoming lesson.**
    This tells students what they can expect from you and what is expected of them. Inform students of the goals for the lesson whenever this will not compromise the teaching methodology.
4. **Do the lesson.**
5. **Close with a review or evaluative activity.**
    This helps students transfer what they have learned beyond the classroom. It also gives you feedback on what students are learning and how they feel about the lessons.

Some other suggestions that will deepen the impact of these lessons include:

■ Create an environment where students feel safe by expressing appreciation for students who take risks (smile, say thank you, clap), supporting students who make mistakes, encouraging students to express minority opinions, and allowing students who feel uncomfortable with an exercise to "pass" and not participate in that exercise.

- Reinforce the material that is covered in these lessons during the school day. Use both the subject matter you teach (the way characters in a novel are behaving, for example) and classroom management (using an I Message to ask students to pay attention) to make connections. The more that you can model these skills in your interactions with students, the better.

- Pace the lessons according to the feedback you receive from students. You will want to eliminate some sections because of apparent lack of interest; you might want to extend other sections into longer units.

- Instead of answering students' questions, encourage them to wrestle with and answer their own questions whenever appropriate.

- Make the lessons your own by adding personal anecdotes and examples that will engage your students.

- When dividing students into small groups, try to make groups as heterogeneous as possible.

- When students are working in small groups, spend time with each group to observe and offer assistance.

- Participate in the exercises and games yourself whenever possible.

- Be mindful that the way that students are seated in the room affects their levels of interest and participation. It is usually best to sit students in a circle. This enables every student to make eye contact with every other student, and it encourages participation and group discussion.

- Have fun and use humor whenever appropriate. Your enthusiasm will be contagious!

- Read Chapters 2 and 3 before you begin to teach these lessons. Much of what is covered here is explained in more depth in those chapters.

Remember that these lessons are only a beginning. You can improve your ability to have an impact on your students by participating in training in conflict resolution, mediation, or violence prevention. There are also an increasing number of curricula available in these areas.

Lesson 1.

CREATING A GROUP CONTRACT

Purposes:
To enable students to create their own norms for classroom conduct
To begin to create a safe and supportive atmosphere within the classroom

Materials:
Newsprint and markers

Time:
15 minutes

1. Explain that you and the students are about to begin an exciting series of lessons on conflict resolution.

2. Explain that to learn together, students will need to pay attention not only to what they are learning, but to *how* they are learning it—to the process of learning as well as to the substance. Students will need to feel comfortable with one another for this work to be successful.

3. As a way to begin this process, you are going to do the following exercise. Ask students to think of a secret about themselves; a secret that most people in the room do not know. The secret can be something that they did, that they believe, that they like, that happened to them, or something about their personality. Ideally, the secret should be something that is not the most positive thing about them. (*Do not mention whether or not students will have to tell this secret to the rest of the group!*) Give students a minute to think about this, during which they will feel apprehensive about having to tell their secrets to the rest of the group.

4. Inform students that they will not have to tell their secrets to anyone in the group; they just need to think about them for themselves. Wait until everyone has thought of a secret.

5. Ask students, "If you were going to tell this secret to the people in this class, what would you need from them? How would you want them to behave?" Explain that there are no right or wrong answers. They should call out anything that they think of.

6. Write their responses on newsprint. Responses may include:

   keep it a secret, don't laugh at or tease me, try to understand,
   listen well, put yourself in my shoes, try to help me,
   don't judge, I would have to trust them, be kind,
   you tell me a secret too, and so on

7. When students are out of ideas, ask them to put aside their secrets and think about a time when they were part of a group of people who worked well together. It might have been a sports team, a religious group, their family, a class, and so on. Ask them

what qualities these groups had that made them work so well. List these qualities on the newsprint. Responses may include:

a common purpose, help each other, everyone added their own strengths, we worked hard, had a good leader, we had fun, we trusted and respected each other, and so on

8. Ask students if they would be willing to make the lists they have generated a group "contract": something that they will try to live up to whenever you do the conflict resolution lessons. Encourage students to raise concerns about the list and explore together whether they can really live up to each item. Can they trust each other if they don't know each other well? (They can work toward this.) Can they keep everything a secret that goes on in the class? (They can keep people's private business a secret.) Do they think this will work? What will prevent it from working?

9. After discussing students' objections, ask each student to sign the list as an indication of his or her commitment to try and live up to it. Tell them that they should only sign it if they are going to live up to it. At this point, all students should sign the document. You can also give them time to decorate the contract with drawings or artwork.

10. Thank the students for working on the contract. Ask them how it feels to have paid attention to the *process* of how you are going to work together. Are there other areas of their lives where they might want to do this?

11. Display the document and refer students to it at the start of every lesson. Or, post it permanently in your classroom.

To extend the lesson:

- Ask students if they would be willing to abide by the contract at all times during your class, not only during the conflict resolution lessons.
- Spend time with students working out penalties that can be imposed if they do not follow the contract. (Students who tease someone else will not be allowed to participate in games, students who arrive late will have to clean up the room after class, and so on.)

Lesson 2.

CONFLICT IS NORMAL

Purposes:

To teach students what conflict is

To teach students that conflict is a normal part of life

To enable students to get to know one another more personally

Materials:

Newsprint and markers, Personal Conflict Sheet handout for each student

Time:

30 minutes

1. Put eight dashes on the board and play the game Hangman with the word *conflict*.
2. Congratulate students, and tell them that this word, *conflict,* is key to all of the work that you are going to be doing together.
3. Ask students to define the word *conflict*. Students usually offer synonyms like *fight, disagreement, argument,* and so on.
4. Offer this definition: *A conflict occurs any time people, ideas, or forces are in opposition or work against one another.*
5. Ask students how many people are needed to have a conflict. Most students will say two, a few will suggest that one person can have a conflict within him- or herself.
6. Highlight that people can have conflicts even within themselves. Ask students what their internal conflicts are about. Likely responses will be whether to do homework, what to wear, resisting peer pressure, whether to listen to parents, and so on.
7. Ask what kinds of people commonly get into conflicts. Provide a few examples: students and teachers, parents and children, and so on. Students might respond:

   > *teachers and teachers, teachers and parents, neighbors,*
   > *husbands and wives, sisters and brothers, bosses and employees,*
   > *teachers and principals, store owners and consumers,*
   > *political parties, nations*

8. Ask students to raise their hands if they have been in a conflict, either within themselves or with anyone else in their lives (parents, friends, siblings, teachers) in the past month? in the past week? since they got up this morning? Most students will raise their hands.
9. Ask if it is fair to say that conflict is a normal part of life. Write "Conflict is a normal part of life" on the board.
10. Hand out the Personal Conflict Sheet. Ask students to fill in the most recent conflict they have had with at least two of the parties listed. They should write a paragraph for each one. Tell them that they will not have to show this sheet to you, but they will be asked to discuss one of their conflicts with a small group of their peers.
11. When students have finished writing, divide them into groups of four. Ask each

student to take three minutes to describe one of his or her conflicts to the small group. The other three students listen, staying focused on the person speaking. They should use the questions on the bottom of the Personal Conflict Sheet to help the person talk.

12. Bring students back into the large group. Ask three volunteers to share one of their own conflicts with the large group. Try to get one from each of the three categories (with peer, with parent, with teacher).

13. Ask what it was like to share their conflicts with somebody else. Was it comforting or scary to tell someone else a conflict? Ask the students if they noticed anything by doing the exercise. Were other people's conflicts similar to theirs?

14. Summarize that conflict is a normal part of life. Most people in the room, in the school, in the world become involved in conflicts on a regular basis. Also summarize any other insights that resulted from the exercise.

Personal Conflict Sheet

**Describe a recent conflict that you have had with
someone in at least two of these categories.**

1. A conflict with a classmate or friend:

2. A conflict with a parent or guardian:

3. A conflict with a teacher or boss:

Questions to ask when you are listening to someone else's conflict:

Who are the people in the conflict?
When did it start?
How long has it been going on?
What is the conflict about?
Why did it happen?
How does it/did it make you feel?
How does it/did it make the other person feel?
What did you do to try to resolve the conflict?
What would you do differently if this conflict happened again?
Is the conflict resolved, or is it still going on?

Lesson 3.

CONFLICT CAN BE POSITIVE

Purposes:
To teach students that conflict can be positive
To introduce the concept of brainstorming

Materials:
Newsprint and markers, Guidelines for Brainstorming on newsprint

Time:
15 minutes

1. Introduce the concept of *brainstorming* to students. Brainstorming is a technique used to generate a wide range of responses or information from a group. It is especially helpful when people are trying to resolve conflicts. In brainstorming, you call out anything that comes into your mind. Guidelines for brainstorming are:

   - Call out anything that comes to mind.
   - There are no right or wrong answers.
   - Do not judge responses; quantity is more important than quality.
   - You can say the same thing as someone else.
   - You can say things that sound crazy. (This can lead to great ideas.)

2. Practice brainstorming for a minute. Ask students to call out whatever they think of when they hear the word *summer* (or *winter, school, weekends, sisters, parents,* and so on).

3. Write the word *conflict* on newsprint. Ask students to brainstorm whatever they think of when they think of the word *conflict.* Responses might include:

   > *pain, death, friends, fear, guns, anger, solutions, brothers,*
   > *children, war, Hitler, racism, normal, frustration, drugs, gangs,*
   > *violence, peer pressure, compromise, hardheaded people, girls/boys*

4. Once you have about thirty words, stop and ask students whether, if they just walked into the room, they would notice anything unusual about the words on the list. Do they have anything in common? Someone will probably say that most of the words seem negative. This is what you are looking for. If they don't say it, offer it yourself.

5. Ask students, "Does conflict have to be negative?" Ask students to call out anything they think can be positive about conflict. Write these on the board. Students might say:

become closer to people, learn more about the person you are arguing with,
learn new ways to do things, grow as a person, learn to respect people who
are different than you, lead you to get help with something,
lead you to make new friends (after you resolve the conflict),
help you get your feelings out

6. Ask a few students to share with the group a time when something positive happened to them as a result of a conflict.

7. Ask students, "If conflicts can be positive, why do most people only think of them as negative?" Discuss as a group. Possible responses include:

   peer pressure, parental messages, influence of the media,
   kids don't learn any better, fight vs. flight response

8. Close the exercise with a review, saying that conflict can be positive and can provide us with opportunities to grow and to learn. These conflict resolution lessons are designed to help make conflicts positive rather then negative experiences whenever possible.

Lesson 4.

EVERYONE CAN WIN

Purposes:
To teach students that very often people in conflict do better *for themselves*
when they collaborate with each other than when they compete
To introduce the concept of "win-win"

Materials:
Hershey's Kisses™ or some kind of prize

Time:
20 minutes

1. Announce to students that you are going to start off this lesson by playing the Kisses™ game.

2. Ask everyone to stand next to a partner of the same sex and approximate height. (Partners are same sex so that students have a partner who will be able to compete with them.)

3. Ask each person to grab their partner's hand as if they were shaking it.[37] (Optional joke: "Okay, I am going to give you twenty seconds, and I want everybody to kiss their partner as many times as they can.") Explain that this game is called the Kisses™ game because sometimes Hershey's Kisses™ are used as prizes. (You can use Kisses™, M & Ms™, imaginary money, or anything else as a prize.)

4. Tell students to listen well, because very few people figure out and "win" this game. You will give the instructions only once. The basic rules are:

   a. You cannot talk to your partner from this moment until the game is over.
   b. The object of this game is to win. You win by getting as many Kisses™ (M & Ms™, dollars, and so on) **for yourself** as possible.
   c. You get a prize every time you can get the back of your *partner's* hand to touch your hip. Your partner gets a prize every time he or she can get the back of *your* hand to touch *their* hip. You will have twenty seconds to play the game.

5. Demonstrate this with one of the students or a coteacher. To get in the appropriate position, first grab hold of your partner's hand as in a handshake. Then turn slightly away from each other, so that you and your partner are standing shoulder to shoulder about two feet apart, holding hands, and facing in opposite directions. When you are in this position, it will be clear how each person can get the back of the other's hand to touch their hip by pulling it toward them. **Important:** When you demonstrate the game, do it in a competitive mode, so that students see you and your partner struggling against each other to win.

---

[37] I learned this version of this game, also known as Hip-to-Hip, from Jean Sidwell and Sarah Keeney of the New Mexico Center for Dispute Resolution. Another popular version uses a hand position similar to arm wrestling.

6. Start the game immediately after giving the instructions. After about twenty seconds, stop them. Let them laugh it off for a minute and then ask students to be seated.

7. Go around the room and ask each student how many prizes they won. Most pairs will have competed and struggled against one another. A few will have figured out that if they cooperated and let each other win, they would each receive more Kisses™. Whereas most students will report winnings of zero to five prizes, a few will say they won thirty to sixty.

8. Ask a pair that competed to demonstrate how they played the game in front of the class. Comment upon the energy they expend and the small winnings of each person.

9. Ask a pair that collaborated to demonstrate the way they played the game in front of the rest of the class.

10. Discuss the exercise, pointing out that in many conflicts in life, you can win more *for yourself* when you cooperate instead of compete with the person whom you think is your enemy. When two people in conflict cooperate and find a solution that satisfies both of them, this is called a "win-win" solution. Usually people don't get everything that they *want* in a win-win solution, but they get enough of what they *need* to be satisfied. Most people assume that to "win" in a conflict, they have to make the other one "lose." But as in the Kisses™ game, this "win-lose" approach often leads both people to lose (and can leave people feeling angry with one another and unsatisfied with the outcome). Just as conflict resolution tries to help people get the positive out of conflict (as was discussed in the last lesson), it also tries to help them come up with win-win solutions whenever possible.

11. Ask students if they might have competed because they watched you demonstrate the game in a competitive mode. Explain that people often copy the behavior that is "modeled" for them. For this reason, all people—teachers as well as students—have a big responsibility. People follow what we do, and so we need to be a positive influence rather than a negative one. During the game, did any groups notice others that were cooperating and then try to change their strategy?

12. Review the lesson and end.

Lesson 5.

POSITIONS, INTERESTS, AND UNDERLYING NEEDS [38]

Purposes:
To help students practice creating win-win solutions
To introduce the concept of positions, interests, and underlying needs

Materials:
Finding Win-Win Solutions handout for each student,
brainstorming guidelines on newsprint

Time:
25 minutes

1. Tell students that they are now going to practice creating win-win solutions. Hand out the Finding Win-Win Solutions sheet. Once people in a conflict are willing to try to resolve it, they must take two steps to find win-win solutions:

   - Find out what people's interests and underlying needs are.
   - Brainstorm possible win-win solutions.

2. When people are in conflict, they often say what they want or what they are going to do. These are called *positions*. *Interests,* on the other hand, are what people really need. Positions are usually only one of many ways that people can satisfy their interests (meet their needs). As an example, tell the following story:

   Two sisters, lying on their own beds in the room they share, were fighting over whether the shade should be up or down in the room. One would get up and close the shade; the other would get up and open it. Their conflict seemed unresolvable. Their little brother walked in and asked them what was going on. One sister said that the bright sunlight bothered her while she was trying to take a nap. The other sister said she was trying to read a book for homework, and she needed the light from the window to see. Hearing this, the little brother walked over, turned on the lamp near the bed, and closed the shade. Both girls were happy.

3. Diagram this story on newsprint like this, asking the students to fill in the boxes:

	Position	Interest
Sister 1	Shade open	Needed light for reading.
Sister 2	Shade closed	Needed darkness to take a nap.

---

[38] This lesson may be difficult for some middle school students.

4. Now do the first example on the worksheet together with the students.

    Channa's friend Crystal is having some friends over to her house to watch a movie on Halloween night. The movie begins at midnight. Channa really wants to be with her friends, but her parents do not want her out of the house so late. They fear that she will get into trouble.

5. First, ask students what Channa's and her parents' positions are.

    Channa wants to go out to watch the movie at her friend's house.
    Her parents do not want her to go.

6. Explain to students that the best way to identify people's interests is to ask a simple, one-word question: "Why? Why do you want what you say you want?" Ask students: "What is it that Channa and her parents really seem to need and want? What are their interests?" Of course, it is important to ask these questions without being judgmental.

    Channa wants to spend time with her friends, and she might want to see the movie.
    Channa's parents want to make sure that she does not get into trouble.

7. In addition to more obvious interests, people in conflict also have hidden needs. These needs often concern basic emotions like the need to be liked or loved, the need to feel safe and secure, the need to feel in control of one's life, and the need to belong. They are called *underlying needs*. Everybody has these needs. Ask students if they can see any underlying needs that might be a part of this conflict.

    Channa needs to belong and feel part of her group of friends.
    Channa needs to be respected and treated like she can make her own decisions.
    Channa's parents need to feel like they are good parents.

8. Given all of their interests and underlying needs, ask students to brainstorm possible win-win solutions to Channa's conflict with her parents.

    Channa can have the friends over to her house to watch the movie.
    Channa can record the movie and then watch it some other time with her friends.
    Channa and her friends can rent the movie and then watch it some other time.
    Channa can have her friends over to her house earlier in the evening, so that she can
        spend time with them.
    Channa can have Crystal's parents call her parents so they know that she will be safe.

9. Divide students into groups of four or five. Give the groups ten to fifteen minutes to identify the parties' positions, interests, and underlying needs, and then write as many possible win-win solutions to each conflict on the worksheet as they can. Encourage students to follow the brainstorming rules (call out anything that comes to mind, there are no right or wrong answers, do not judge responses, *quantity* is more important than quality, you can say the same thing as someone else, you can say things that sound crazy) when they are trying to make up creative solutions.

10. When students complete the worksheet, bring them back to the large group. Ask whether it was difficult to discover the interests and underlying needs. Do they see how much easier it is to think of win-win solutions once you know peoples' interests and underlying needs? How do you know if a solution is really a win-win solution? Suggest that students strive to apply the win-win approach, either in their own lives or in a conflict that they observe or read about, before the next lesson.

ANSWERS FOR FINDING WIN-WIN SOLUTIONS WORKSHEET

Alejandro and Jason are good friends who live near each other. Both of their houses are only a few blocks from school. Alejandro usually rides his bicycle to school. That way, he can sleep late and still get to school on time. He broke his foot a few months ago, however, and his father had to drive him to school. During that time, he loaned his bike to Jason so that he could ride it to school. Now that Alejandro's foot is better, he wants his bicycle back, but Jason won't give it to him. Jason says that when he walks to school, the other kids tease him. If he rides the bike, they can't do it.

Alejandro's position:
- wants his bike back

Jason's position:
- wants to keep the bike

Alejandro's interests:
- wants to be able to sleep late and still get to school

Jason's interests:
- wants to get to school and not be teased

Alejandro's underlying needs:
- wants to feel he can trust his friend
- wants to feel in control of his life
- wants the safety of the way his life used to be

Jason's underlying needs:
- wants not to be hurt by the other kids
- wants to feel in control of his life

Possible win-win solutions:
Alejandro can give Jason a ride to school on the handlebars of his bicycle.
Alejandro's father can pick up Jason and give them both a ride to school.
Alejandro and Jason can walk together quickly to school so that Jason doesn't get picked on.
Jason can return the bike, and Alejandro can tell him a shortcut to get to school so that he does not go by the other kids.
Alejandro can go with Jason to talk to the kids that tease him.
Alejandro can go with Jason to the assistant principal to complain about the other kids.

Sarah wants to get a job so that she can have more spending money. Her mother does not want her to get a job because she thinks she should devote her energies to her schoolwork.

Sarah's position:
- wants to get a job

Sarah's mother's position:
- does not want Sarah to get a job

Sarah's interests:
- wants more spending money

Sarah's mother's interests:
- wants Sarah to do well in school

Sarah's underlying needs:
- wants to feel like an adult
- wants freedom to make her own decisions

Sarah's mother's underlying needs:
- wants to feel like she has done the right thing to help her daughter to succeed in life

Possible win-win solutions:

Sarah can get a job that allows her to do schoolwork (baby-sitting, working in some types of stores, and so on).

Sarah can find a job that is educational and would help with school (working in a bookstore, working for a college professor, and so on).

Sarah's mother can give her an allowance.

Sarah's mother can give her extra money for working extra hard on schoolwork.

Sarah and her mother can make an arrangement that she can get a job as long as her grades are good. If her grades fall, then she will quit the job.

The mayor wants to close the public library on weekdays because the town doesn't have the money to keep it open. It costs too much to pay the staff. Many parents of young children, however, want it to stay open. They feel it is important for their kids to have access to books during the day.

Parents' position:
- want the library open on weekdays

Mayor's position:
- wants to close the library on weekdays

Parents' interests: Mayor's interests:
- want their kids to have access to books on weekdays

- needs to save the town money

Parents' underlying needs:
- want kids to be prepared for school
- want to feel like good parents

Mayor's underlying needs:
- wants parents to like him (so he can be reelected)

Possible win-win solutions:

The parents can volunteer to staff the library during the week.

The parents can raise money to keep the library open.

A parent can put books from the library in his or her home and let other parents come and take them out.

Finding Win-Win Solutions

Win-Win Solutions: Win-win solutions are solutions that satisfy everyone who is involved in a conflict.

Positions: Positions are what people say they want. They are usually among many ways that they could meet their interests and underlying needs.

Interests: Interests are the reasons people want what they say they want. They are what people feel that they *need*. The best way to find out people's interests is to ask them why they want what they say they want.

Underlying Needs: Underlying needs concern basic emotional needs like the need to be loved, the need to feel safe and secure, the need to feel in control of one's life, the need to belong. Everybody has these needs.

Read the following conflicts and write down the characters' positions, interests, and underlying needs as well as the possible win-win solutions that might satisfy both parties in each conflict.

1. Channa's friend Crystal is having some friends over to her house to watch a movie on Halloween night. The movie begins at midnight. Channa really wants to be with her friends, but her parents do not want her out of the house so late. They fear that she will get into trouble.

Channa's position: **Channa's parents' position:**

Channa's interests: **Channa's parents' interests:**

Channa's underlying needs: **Channa's parents' underlying needs:**

Possible win-win solutions:

2. Alejandro and Jason are good friends who live near each other. Both of their houses are only a few blocks from school. Alejandro usually rides his bicycle to school. That way, he can sleep late and still get to school on time. He broke his foot a few months ago, however, and his father had to drive him to school. During that time, he loaned his bike to Jason so that he could ride it to school. Now that Alejandro's foot is better, he wants his bicycle back, but Jason won't give it to him. Jason says that when he walks to school, the other kids tease him. If he rides the bike, they can't do it.

Alejandro's position: **Jason's position:**

Alejandro's interests: **Jason's interests:**

Alejandro's underlying needs: **Jason's underlying needs:**

Possible win-win solutions:

3. Sarah wants to get a job so that she can have more spending money. Her mother
    does not want her to get a job because she thinks she should devote her energies to
    her schoolwork.

Sarah's position: **Sarah's mother's position:**

Sarah's interests: **Sarah's mother's interests:**

Sarah's underlying needs: **Sarah's mother's underlying needs:**

Possible win-win solutions:

4. The mayor wants to close the public library on weekdays because the town doesn't
    have the money to keep it open. It costs too much to pay the staff. Many parents of
    young children, however, want it to stay open. They feel it is important for their kids
    to have access to books during the day.

Parents' position: **Mayor's position:**

Parents' interests: **Mayor's interests:**

Parents' underlying needs: **Mayor's underlying needs:**

Possible win-win solutions:

Lesson 6.

STYLES OF CONFLICT RESOLUTION

Purposes:
To teach students that there are different styles of conflict resolution
To teach students that they need to choose the right conflict
resolution style for each conflict

Materials:
Conflict Styles Scripts (four copies), Conflict Styles Scenarios handout for each student,
signs for each conflict style

Time:
35 minutes

Note: Before you conduct this exercise, select three students and have them prepare to
act out the Conflict Styles Scripts in front of the class.

1. Ask students to brainstorm ideas in response to the question: "What are the ways—
   not only the good ways—that people use to resolve conflicts?" Write these on the
   board, placing the responses in columns according to whether they are passive,
   aggressive, or collaborative. (Do not place the category headings on the board at this
   point.) Possible responses include:

Passive	Aggressive	Collaborative
ignore it	fight	talk it out
walk away	spread rumors	mediate
run	hurt them	ask a teacher for help
give in	spit	think about their side
	kick	win–win solutions
	pass notes about them	

2. Place the category headings above the columns and explain that people approach the
   resolution of conflicts in three general ways: passively, aggressively, or collaboratively.
   When using the *passive* approach, people give in or withdraw from the conflict and
   from those with whom they are in conflict. People usually forgo their immediate and
   sometimes their long-term needs when they use the passive style. Key phrase: My
   immediate needs are *less* important than your needs. When using the *aggressive*
   approach, people take forceful action to deal with a conflict and with those with
   whom they are in conflict. The aggressive approach usually means people try to meet
   their immediate needs, even at the expense of the other party's needs and often to
   the detriment of their relationship. Key phrase: My immediate needs are *more* important then your needs. In the *collaborative* approach, people seek first and foremost to
   understand the party with whom they are in conflict. The collaborative approach
   means that people try to meet their needs, but they also try to meet the needs of the

other person. The collaborative approach leads to win-win resolutions. Key phrase: Your needs and my needs are *both* important.

3. Read the introduction to the Conflict Styles Scripts to students, and then ask the previously selected students to act out the scripts in front of the group. After each script, ask how students think the characters feel. Do they think the conflict is resolved?

4. After students get a chance to react to the scripts informally, ask them which of the three styles they are most comfortable with (or use most often). Explain that there is no right or wrong answer. Hang the conflict style signs up at different corners in the classroom and ask students to go and stand where they are most comfortable.

5. Ask students which style they think is best. Encourage friendly debate. Given the setting, many people will say collaboration is the best. Then offer this scenario:

   You are walking down an unfamiliar street at night. You are all alone. Suddenly, you see the shadows of four large people across the road. They start to come over to you saying that they want your hat.

6. Ask students to stand under the style that they think is best for this situation (passive). After everyone gets to where they want to be, have them discuss why they chose what they did. Now offer this senario:

   You are walking and talking with a friend who has many personal problems. All of a sudden, he walks out on the nearby railroad tracks and says he wants to end his life. You see that a train will be coming in one minute.

7. Again tell students to stand under the style that they think is best for this situation (aggressive). After everyone gets to where they want to be, have them discuss why they chose what they did.

8. Explain that there is no one right way to resolve all conflicts. The best conflict resolvers pick the style that is most appropriate for each conflict. Too often, however, students use collaboration the least. Although collaboration is not always the best style, schools—and the world—would be much better places to live and learn if we collaborated more often.

9. Tell students that you want them to try each style. Divide them into groups of three and hand out the Conflict Styles Scenarios to each student. (These directions are difficult so you will have to walk students through them.)

10. Have students count off by three in each group so that each group has a 1, a 2, and a 3. Direct students to read the scenarios one at a time and respond as the students in the examples might. For Scenario A, student 1 uses the passive approach, student 2 uses the aggressive approach, and student 3 uses the collaborative approach. Group members should help each other respond in the appropriate manner. For Scenario B, the students switch styles. Student 2 is passive, 3 is aggressive, and 1 is collaborative. Finally, for the last scenario, each student switches again: 3 is passive, 1 is aggressive, and 2 is collaborative.

11. When you are finished, have students come back into the large group. Ask them for their comments about the exercise. How did they like trying a new style? Review that there are different styles of conflict resolution and that it is best to choose a style to suit each conflict. Explain that for most people, collaboration is the hardest one, because it requires the most skill and patience. Advise students that they will learn and practice some of these skills in the remaining lessons.

POSSIBLE RESPONSES FOR CONFLICT STYLES SCENARIOS

Scenario A: An acquaintance of yours is always borrowing your Spanish book and not returning it. Last night when you were about to study for a test, your book was not in your book bag. You think your acquaintance probably took it and forgot to put it back.

Student 1	**Passive:** "Hey, how did you like my Spanish book? Is it helping you?"
Student 2	**Aggressive:** "You jerk! You stole my book and I couldn't study for my test!"
Student 3	**Collaborative:** "Last night I couldn't find my Spanish book and I was really upset. I know you sometimes borrow it. Do you know where it is?"

Scenario B: A student on your team is making rude comments about a friend of yours. It is beginning to bother you, although no one else on the team has said anything.

Student 2	**Passive:** Leaves the room whenever the person is making the rude comments.
Student 3	**Aggressive:** "Hey, stop calling my friend names or my fist will have to keep your mouth shut!"
Student 1	**Collaborative:** "Could you stop calling my friend names? It really is starting to bother me. Why are you doing it? Are you upset with him about something?"

Scenario C: One of your best friends is always late. This morning you planned to meet her on the way to school, and you had to wait an extra fifteen minutes before she showed up. This made you mad.

Student 3	**Passive:** "I am glad you made it. I was worried about you."
Student 1	**Aggressive:** "You are always late. I wish you would think about someone else besides yourself."
Student 2	**Collaborative:** "I am really upset that I had to wait for you. Did anything happen this morning? Is there a reason why you seem to be late so often? I'd like to work this out so I don't have to wait for you like this."

Conflict Styles Scripts

Background

John and Maria are close friends, but not boyfriend and girlfriend. Maria often tells John things about her personal life, including stories about what happens when she spends time with other boys in the school.

Maria is mad at John because she told him something about a boy named Will, and John went and told other people. Last night, Will called Maria and was very upset. Will said that he never wanted to speak with Maria again.

A. Passive

Maria gets to history class early and her friend Adam is there.

Maria: Boy, am I mad. John went and told everyone what I told him about Will. I can't believe he did that! Now Will won't speak to me.
Adam: Have you spoken to John about this?
Maria: A lot of good that would do!

Just then John comes into class.

John: How's it going?
Maria: *(just looks away)*
John: What's the matter?
Maria: Nothing.
John: Okay. *(He rolls his eyes, shrugs, and goes to his seat.)*

B. Aggressive

When John comes into history class, Maria confronts him.

Maria: John, are you stupid! Are you trying to ruin my relationship with Will? Why did you tell Will what I told you? I can't believe you can be so dense.
John: Hey, I didn't tell Will anything. You are crazy! I don't need you coming up to me and acting like a jerk.

C. Collaborative

When John comes into history class, Maria asks him if he can step outside to talk for a minute.

Maria: Hey, John. Can you step outside of class and talk to me for a minute?
John: Yeah, sure. *(They move outside.)*
Maria: John, Will called me up last night and told me he didn't want to speak to me anymore. He said everybody knows what happened last week. You are one of the only people that I told. Did you tell anyone?

John: Well, I don't know.

Maria: What do you mean, "you don't know?"

John: Well. . . . . I might have mentioned it to Tiara. But I assumed you had already told her. You tell her everything.

Maria: Oh, no. Tiara can't keep a secret. Now what am I going to do? I am really upset with you, but I can't talk now. I've got to find her . . . *(runs off to find Tiara)*.

John: *(calling after her)* Hey, I'm sorry.

From *Students Resolving Conflict: Peer Mediation in Schools*, published by GoodYearBooks. Copyright © 1995 Richard Cohen.

Conflict Styles Scenarios

Passive: "My immediate needs are less important than your needs."
When you take the passive approach you withdraw from the people in conflict. You forgo your immediate and sometimes your long-term needs.
You ignore or avoid the person or the subject, run away, pretend the problem doesn't exist, give in.

Aggressive: "My immediate needs are more important than your needs."
When you take the aggressive approach you take forceful action to deal with a conflict and with the people in conflict. You try to meet your immediate needs, often at the expense of the other party's needs and often to the detriment of your relationship with him or her.
You fight, take charge, dominate, control.

Collaborative: "Your needs and my needs are both important."
When you take the collaborative approach you first and foremost try to understand the other party. Then you attempt to meet his or her needs as well as your own.
You talk, work together, communicate, get help, go to a mediator.

Scenario A:

An acquaintance of yours is always borrowing your Spanish book and not returning it. Last night when you were about to study for a test, your book was not in your book bag. You think your acquaintance probably took it and forgot to put it back.

Scenario B:

A student on your team is making rude comments about a friend of yours. It is beginning to bother you, although no one else on the team has said anything.

Scenario C:

One of your best friends is always late. This morning you planned to meet her on the way to school, and you had to wait an extra fifteen minutes before she showed up. This made you mad.

Lesson 7.

THE PROS AND CONS OF FIGHTING

Purpose:
To teach students that fighting and violence are usually not
effective approaches to conflict resolution

Materials:
Newsprint and markers

Time:
20 minutes

1. Ask students which of the three conflict resolution styles—passive, aggressive, collaborative—they think is most popular among their peers. Their response will often be aggressive.

2. Invite students to look at the pros and cons of fighting and aggression. Put the word *Fighting* in the middle of the board, with a + on one side and a - on the other.

3. Ask students to brainstorm first the positives of fighting, and then the negatives. Write their responses on the board. Responses might include:

Fighting

Positive +	Negative -
Get a good reputation for being tough	Get hurt
Won't get picked on anymore	Get killed
Release energy	Get a bad reputation
Get rid of aggressive feelings	Look stupid
End the conflict	Get suspended
	Parents are mad
	Police get involved
	Miss school
	Won't end the conflict
	Could spread to bigger fight
	Have to go to hospital

4. Be sure not to judge students' positive ideas about fighting immediately. Young people are used to hearing adults put down fighting, and they will turn off if you do that right away. Guide students to think for themselves and reach their own conclusions.

5. Point out what hopefully will be obvious: that there appear to be many more negatives to fighting than positives. Though it may be important when we are in a conflict to express ourselves and try to get what we want, does fighting seem like a very effective way to do this?

6. Three other points can be made about fighting:

    - Fighting is usually positive only if you win.
    - Even if you do win, often fighting does not end the conflict. The loser wants to get revenge and so the winner has to "watch their back." The loser might even get his or her friends involved.
    - Some people think "I want to take matters into my own hands. I don't need other people involved. I am going to fight him or her." But fighting almost always leads other people—teachers, principals, parents, police—to become involved.

7. Engage students in a general discussion about fighting. Why do they think it is so popular among their peers? Do they see fighting as a problem at school? Is it easier to fight than to talk things out? Do many of their peers avoid conflicts, but they just don't hear about those conflicts?

8. Conclude by asking students if they have learned anything by looking at fighting in this way. Has it changed or challenged their ideas at all? Will they be as quick to fight in the future?

Lesson 8.

CONFLICT ESCALATION*

Purpose:

To teach students that the level of tension in a conflict increases and decreases according to how people communicate with each other

Materials:

Escalation Dialogue: *The Messy Apartment,* newsprint and markers

Time:

20 minutes

Note: Before you conduct this exercise, select two students and have them prepare to read the Escalation Dialogue: *The Messy Apartment.*

1. Review the styles of conflict from a previous lesson. Explain that the most important skills involved in conflict resolution, and especially collaboration, are communication skills. These skills enable people to relate to one another effectively. It is very hard to communicate effectively with someone when you are in conflict with him or her. And if you do it poorly, it can increase the tension and make your conflict worse. Let's look at an example.

2. Ask the two students to act out the Escalation Dialogue: *The Messy Apartment.*

3. Afterward, ask students if they think Jean and Sam's conflict was more resolved or less resolved after their discussion. Why?

4. Draw a picture of stairs on the board. Explain that the picture represents the level of tension in Jean and Sam's conflict. The level of tension went up in their conflict, and so these stairs also go up. When the level of tension rises in a conflict, this is called *escalation.*

5. Ask students, "What did Jean or Sam do or say that made the conflict escalate? What raised the tension in their conflict?" You might have to read the story again. List their responses on the escalator. They might include:

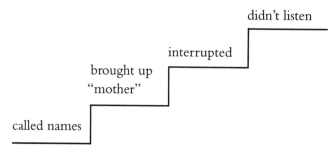

(also threatened, judged, blamed, and so on)

---

*This lesson is based on the work of William Kreidler.

6. Ask how students in your school tend to escalate conflicts. Students may say: by getting friends involved, bringing up mother, ignoring someone, spreading rumors.

7. Starting from the top edge of the escalation diagram, draw the escalator going down. Explain that effective communication can make the escalator go down—it can "de-escalate" a conflict and make tension decrease. Ask students, "What could Jean or Sam have done to make the escalator go down?" Students might say:

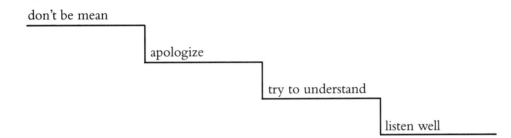

don't be mean

apologize

try to understand

listen well

(also be silent, don't interrupt, don't blame, ask each other what they want, acknowledge their own and each other's feelings, and so on)

8. Write *Fouls* on top of a piece of newsprint. Explain that just as athletes are prohibited from doing certain things in sporting events, there are things that can and should be prohibited from constructive communication. Ask students to call out anything from the list they just generated that they would like to ban from the way they speak to each other. When someone calls something out, check with the rest of the group to see if everyone is willing to try not to do that. If all agree, write it on the foul sheet. Leave the Fouls up whenever you meet and encourage students to watch for fouls in communication.

9. Review the lesson. Ask students to think of one thing that they can do to de-escalate the next conflict that they become involved in.

Escalation Dialogue:
The Messy Apartment

Jean and Sam are college roommates. It is Sunday morning, and they are encountering each other for the first time in days.

Jean (*enters the room, yelling*): Do you know what you have done? I can't believe that you've done it again!

Sam: What do you mean "done it again?" Done what?

Jean: You have no idea?

Sam: No. I have no idea. You're always accusing me of doing something. Why don't you stop whining and tell me what the problem is.

Jean: You've left the apartment looking like a garbage dump, and I have a date coming over here in an hour. Now I have to clean up your mess again! How many times have . . . .

Sam: Hey, back off, Jean. I did clean up a little yesterday, but I have been working ten hours a day to get this paper done. Sometimes you have to give a little. I didn't know you were having someone over. And besides, this place can't always be like your mother's house. Both of us live here . . . you still aren't used to that.

Jean: You are the one who needs to get used to it. Don't you realize that I might want to cook something, or have friends over, or whatever? Roommates are supposed to respect each other's needs. But your stuff is everywhere. You can't be so lazy . . . .

Sam: What, like as lazy as you!? When is the last time you got to class on time? You are the only person I know who can sleep for an entire day. Now, that is lazy!

Jean: Hey. You know that I am working nights now. And stop changing the subject. The problem is, you live like a pig!

Sam: Relax or this "pig" won't give you the rent next month!

Lesson 9.

I MESSAGES: SPEAKING TO PROMOTE COLLABORATION

Purpose:

To teach students how to express their needs in a way that invites collaboration and does not make the other person defensive

Materials:

I Message formula written on newsprint, I Message Scripts for each student, I Message Worksheet for each student, newsprint and markers

Time:

35 minutes

1. Explain that students are now going to learn one way to express their needs to someone without making a conflict escalate. This method encourages the other person to really listen to what the student needs. This technique is called an *I Message*.

2. Select two students to read the I Message Scripts. Have them read the first script. After they are finished, ask students: "How do you think Emerson feels? How do you think Ngoc feels? Do you think their conflict is closer to being resolved after their discussion? Why or why not?"

3. Have the same students read the second script. Ask the same questions: "How do you think Emerson feels? How do you think Ngoc feels? Do you think their conflict is closer to being resolved after their discussion? Why or why not?"

4. Ask students what differences they noticed between the two skits in the way the characters spoke to each other, in their body language, in their tone of voice, in the words and expressions that they used.

5. Write *You* and *I* on the board. Explain that one of the major differences between the two scripts is that in the first one, the characters used many "You Messages." In the second one, they used many "I Messages." Hand out the scripts to each student.

You Messages blame the other person. This makes them feel attacked, and as a result, they often counterattack when they get their chance to speak. The conflict escalates (goes up the escalator), and the parties are left feeling angry and hurt. They might even want to fight.

I Messages, on the other hand, express the speaker's needs and feelings without attacking. Although it can still be uncomfortable to hear an I Message, the listener doesn't feel as defensive. As a result, the listener can say how he or she feels in response. I Messages can make it easier for people to work together—to collaborate—to solve a conflict.

Note: With younger students, you might read the stories over again and have them raise their hands or make an X on the board every time they hear either a *you* or an *I*. (There are sixteen *you*'s and four *I*'s in script 1; three *you*'s and fourteen *I*'s in 2.)

6. Have students pick out one inflammatory You Message and one I Message from the scripts. Write them on the board. Ask students how they would feel if someone said these things to them. Which would make them defensive and aggressive and which would make them want to collaborate to work out the conflict?

7. Write the I Message formula on the board:

A. I feel................ (state a feeling)
B. When you............... (state the behavior of the other person)
C. Because............... (state the effect that behavior has upon you)

Explain the formula to students. Stress that even with the formula, it is easy to make the mistake of turning an I Message back into a You Message.

A. I feel . . . (state a feeling)

This is where students say how they are feeling. It is very important that they respond with a feeling (sad, frustrated, happy, lonely, frightened, jealous, excited, hurt, angry) and *not* a thought. When people add the words *like* or *that* after the "I feel" ("I feel *like* you were wrong to . . . ."; "I feel *that* friends should not . . ."), it is a sign that they are expressing a thought rather than a feeling.

B. When you . . . (state the behavior of the other person)

Students should state specifically what the other person has done, not their interpretation of the person's behavior. (". . . when you took my hat while I was talking to Leslie," rather than ". . . when you embarrassed me in front of Leslie," or worse, ". . . when you acted like a jerk in front of Leslie.")

C. Because . . . (state the effect that the behavior has upon you)

Students should state the specific effect that the other person's behavior has had upon them. ("I felt mad when you took my hat while I was talking to Leslie, because *our conversation stopped and I don't know when I will get a chance to speak with her like that again.*) It is easy to turn the I Message back into a You Message at this point. ("I felt mad when you took my hat while I was talking to Leslie, because *you don't know how to act in front of girls.*)

Be sure to explain that the formula is just a guide to teach students how to speak in I Messages. Once they become comfortable with them, they don't have to follow the formula exactly; they can make I Messages in their own way.

8. Divide the group into pairs and hand out the I Message Worksheet. Have students help each other fill in an I Message for each example.

9. Come back together in a group and go over the worksheet. More than one student can give their I Messages for each example. Here are some sample responses:

■ Your teacher is always calling on you to answer questions. She never seems to call on anyone else as much as she calls on you.

I feel	*embarrassed*
When you	*call on me a lot*
Because	*the other kids might think I am the "teacher's pet"*

- This kid you know in school told you that one of your best friends is spreading rumors about you. You see your best friend in the hall.

I feel	*hurt*
When you	*spread rumors about me*
Because	*it makes me feel like I can't trust you anymore*

- Your sister is always watching what she wants on the television. Today, she came into the room while you were watching something, and she turned the channel without asking you.

I feel	*angry*
When you	*change the channel without asking me*
Because	*I miss the show that I want to watch*

- Your mother got you exactly what you wanted for your birthday.

I feel	*loved*
When you	*get me what I want for my birthday*
Because	*it shows me that you listen to me*

10. Ask for students' impressions of I Messages. Do they think they might help in a conflict? What was difficult about making them? Is there anyone in their lives right now to whom they would like to give an I Message?

11. End the lesson by explaining that there are no guarantees with I Messages. People still might not do what you want them to do, even when you use I Messages. But because they open the way for collaboration, they can help you resolve conflicts more effectively.

To extend the lesson:

Divide the group into two lines facing one another (sometimes referred to as "hassle lines"). The people in one line are the A's, those in the other are the B's. Provide students with a scenario that they can act out twice: once using You Messages, and once using I Messages. Ask students to freeze in the middle of each enactment and have them observe their body language, facial expressions, proximity to each other, and so on. Make up your own scenarios, or use the following examples:

- Person B just learned that person A wrote something negative about him or her on the bathroom wall.
- Person B was playing with his or her food and spilled soda all over person A's lap.

I Message Scripts

Background

Emerson was talking to a girl named Leslie in a crowd of people. All of a sudden, Ngoc★ came up and grabbed his hat as a joke. They meet up again twenty minutes later in their next class.

Script 1

Emerson: Where do you come off acting like that, man? What are you, stupid? I was talking to Leslie, and then you have to come up and grab my hat. I had been trying to talk with her this whole year. You blew it for me. Don't you have eyes? It's no wonder you don't have a girlfriend: you don't know anything about women! I wish you would just stay out of my business.

Ngoc: What is your problem? I was just fooling around. You take things too seriously. You expect the world to stop when you are talking to some girl. If you were more relaxed about things, maybe she would like you better. You are the one that went crazy in front of her! Maybe that will teach you a lesson!

Script 2

Emerson: Hey, Ngoc. I feel really angry by what happened before. I have been trying to speak with Leslie for the whole year, and today, when I finally get her attention, you took my hat, and it distracted me. Now I'm afraid that she might think I am a fool. I need you to back me up in those situations.

Ngoc: Oh, I didn't realize. I'm sorry if I messed up. I was just playing around, like always. Sometimes I need to think about what I am doing more. I won't do it again, Emerson. Is there anything I can do to help you talk to her again?

★pronounced "knock"

I Message Worksheet

Formula

I feel _____ *(state your emotion)* _____

When you _____ *(state the specific behavior)* _____

Because _____ *(state the effect the behavior has on your life)* _____

Complete the following examples:

1. Your teacher is always calling on you to answer questions. She never seems to call on anyone else as much as she calls on you.

I feel _____

When you _____

Because _____

2. This kid you know in school told you that one of your best friends is spreading rumors about you. You see your friend in the hall.

I feel _____

When you _____

Because _____

3. Your sister is always watching what she wants on the television. Today she came into the room while you were watching something, and she turned the channel without asking you.

I feel _____

When you _____

Because _____

4. Your mother got you exactly what you wanted for your birthday.

I feel _____

When you _____

Because _____

Lesson 10.

ACTIVE LISTENING I:
LISTENING TO PROMOTE COLLABORATION

Purpose:
To teach students to listen in a way that encourages and supports
the speaker and that invites collaboration

Materials:
Active Listening Goals on newsprint, newsprint and markers

Time:
20 minutes

1. Review I Messages and explain that communication is a "two-way street." In addition to expressing our own needs, we need to be able to listen to the other person's needs. Only in this way can we collaborate in resolving our conflicts. People often think of listening as a passive activity. The listener sits back and lets the words of the other person come to him or her. But *active listening* is very different. In active listening the listener uses all his or her available attention and energy to accomplish two goals. Write the goals on newsprint:

   a. To truly understand what the speaker is communicating.
   b. To make the speaker feel understood.

2. Explain that to listen actively, try to stand in the speaker's shoes and feel how he or she might feel. Do not give opinions, or judge the other person's actions, unless asked to do so.

3. Tell the students that you would like to demonstrate active listening for them. Ask for a volunteer to come up and talk to you so that you can demonstrate. (Choose someone who can talk comfortably in front of the group.) Have that student sit across from you. Provide him or her with an easy (i.e., not very revealing) topic to talk about: what they did over the weekend, the best thing they did last summer, what they want life to be like in ten years, and so on.

4. Ask the student to begin talking. As he or she is talking, demonstrate *poor* listening skills: look away, fidget, interrupt, talk about yourself, slouch in your chair, say hello to others, and so on.

5. After two minutes, stop and ask students what they observed. They will point out all the things you did incorrectly. Then ask students what one should do when actively listening, and list these on the board. Some possibilities include:

   make eye contact (if culturally appropriate), say "uh-huh" or "yes,"
   summarize/paraphrase, encourage other person to speak, sit up straight,
   ask questions, sit in an open posture, smile, nod your head, don't judge speaker

6. Divide the students into pairs. Have them decide who is going to speak first and who is going to listen. Assign an easy topic to speakers about which they will have a good deal to say. (One example is what students would do if they won ten million dollars.) Ask the speakers to speak, and ask the listeners to listen *poorly* until you tell them to stop.

7. Stop the students after one minute. Ask the speakers how it felt to be listened to in that way. Did they want to continue talking? Do people ever listen to them that way in real life? Do teachers, friends, parents, or siblings listen like this sometimes? Have them share a few examples.

8. Have the students try it again, with the same person speaking about the same topic, but this time ask the listeners to listen *actively*.

9. Stop the students after a few minutes and ask for their impressions. How did it feel to be listened to in this way? Did they want to continue talking? Stress that being listened to creates an almost palpable feeling in the speaker; he or she feels connected to the listener and wants to continue talking. Active listening is a simple but wonderful gift that we can give to someone else.

10. Next, write the word *Summarizing* on the board. Ask students what *summarizing* means (repeating things back in a shorter or condensed form). Tell students that you are now going to relate a short story about your life. When you are finished, you are going to ask a few volunteers to summarize. Tell students a story, ideally a real incident from your life that you have some feelings about. For example:

This morning I got up and let my dog out in the backyard like I always do before I leave for school. When I went to call her in, however, she wasn't there. I was late for school, and so I began running around my block, looking in other people's yards for my dog. Her name, by the way, is Lucy. I was calling her, and it was so early—I have to leave my house at 5:30 A.M. to get to school on time—that I was afraid I would wake people up. I didn't see her anywhere. Finally, I went back to my house, and she was sitting right on the steps waiting for me! I don't know what I would have done if she wasn't there.

11. Ask for volunteers to summarize your story. Make the point that they don't have to say everything in the summary, only the important points.

12. Have the students go back into their pairs and switch roles. The speakers are now listeners, and the listeners are now speakers. Repeat step 6 first. The speakers talk about the same topic, and the listeners listen *poorly*.

13. After briefly discussing the poor example, ask the pairs to do it one more time, but this time using active listening. In addition, tell the listeners that after a few minutes, you are going to ask them to summarize to the speakers what they said.

14. After two to three minutes of listening, ask the listeners to summarize back to the speakers. Give them a minute or so to do this. Then ask how it felt (to the speaker and to the listener) to summarize. What was difficult about summarizing? What was easy about it?

15. Review the lesson. Ask the students to relate one thing that they learned about listening. Explain that as with I Messages, sometimes active listening can feel forced and unnatural at first. But with practice, active listening will become more comfortable. Encourage students to try it whenever possible.

Lesson 11.

ACTIVE LISTENING II: LISTENING FOR FEELINGS

Purpose:
To teach students to listen to peoples' feelings as well as to
the content of what they say

Materials:
Newsprint and markers

Time:
25 minutes

1. Review the basics of active listening. Then explain that there is another important aspect of listening: *listening for feelings.* Make these points:

   - **Everybody has feelings.** Every person in the world is feeling something at all times. In fact, each student in the room is feeling something, or perhaps many things, right now: excitement, sadness, boredom, loneliness, calmness, anger, interest. ·

   - **There isn't a right or wrong way to feel.** We cannot say that there is a "right" way to feel about anything. Everyone is different, and we have our own, unique reactions to things.

   - **When people know how you feel, it helps them understand you better.** When I know how you feel, I am better able to understand why you behave a certain way. I can say, "Oh, you are upset about doing poorly on your test; that is probably why you just walked out of class and didn't say good-bye to me."

   - **People rarely say how they are feeling directly.** It is uncommon for people to walk up to one another and say: "I feel sad today," or "I am really enthusiastic right now!" If we want to know how someone is feeling, most of the time we either have to guess, or we have to ask them.

2. Although people usually don't say directly how they are feeling, they often tell us in indirect ways. Ask students how they can tell the way someone is feeling. List answers on the board. Possible responses include:

   *facial expression, tone of voice, body language, what they say,
   the way they dress, how they behave, what they don't say, the words
   they use, when they are silent*

3. Explain that students are now going to practice guessing how people are feeling. This is part of listening for feelings, and it is something they can do whenever they are actively listening to someone. First, have students brainstorm a list of at least twenty-five feelings and put the list on the board:

    mad, jealous, happy, frightened, proud, depressed, lonely, in love, ecstatic, angry, furious, hurt, bored, irritated, anxious, upset, goofy, excited, stressed out, disappointed, confused, appreciated, frustrated, guilty, rejected, content

4. Explain that when listening for feelings, be careful not to appear to be *telling* people how they feel. When you tell people how they feel, they can become defensive and less trusting. It is better to guess how people feel in the form of a question. "Are you feeling confused?" is better than "You are confused."

5. Divide students into groups of four. One at a time, each student should pick one of the feelings from the board and act it out. They can talk, but they should not say the feelings directly ("I can't believe that someone who calls themselves my friend would be so mean to me!"). The person to each actor's right tries to guess the feeling. Each group should go around the circle twice, so that everyone can act out and guess two feelings.

6. Finally, tell students you are now going to put all that they have learned about active listening together. Review the basics of active listening (eye contact, open posture, don't interrupt, nod your head, summarize, and so on). Then divide the groups of four into groups of only two. Students should decide who is person A and who is person B in their groups.

7. Explain the following process. Person A will talk for three minutes. Then person B will summarize what person A said for two minutes. Then person A will tell person B how accurate his or her summary was and correct any misunderstandings. Finally, person B will summarize one last time. Ask students to do the best active listening that they can. To make the exercise more realistic and full of feeling, assign a personal topic for the speakers to discuss. An excellent topic for students to discuss is their relationships with their parents, but this should only be used if you have developed an appropriate level of trust and safety in the group. Alternative topics include relationships with siblings or what it is like to be an only child, experience in school so far this year, or opinions about controversial topics like gun control, euthanasia, and school-specific issues. (See step 7a below.)

7a. In a different approach, divide students into two groups according to their difference of opinion about an issue of importance to them. (There should/should not be metal detectors in school; there should/should not be grades in school; there should/should not be school over the summer.) Then have them do step 7 again. This tests their ability to listen and summarize without giving their own opinions. At the end of the exercise, ask students if doing this changed their opinions about the issue. If so, why?

8. After students do this process once, ask for their impressions: Was it hard to do? Were they able to identify the feelings? How did the speaker feel to be listened to in this way? Then have the students switch roles and do the exercise again.

9. Conclude by asking students to thank their partners for speaking so honestly with them. Ask students how they think they might use this process at home and in school. Is there anyone whom they wish would listen to them like this? Is there anyone whom they want to try to listen to like this? A few students can share examples.

Lesson 12.

THE SIX BASIC STEPS OF CONFLICT RESOLUTION

Purpose:
To teach students a process they can use to resolve their own
conflicts inside and outside of the classroom

Materials:
Poster with the Conflict Resolution Steps on it, a Conflict Solver Worksheet for
each student, Conflict Solver Role-Plays for each student

Time:
25 minutes

1. Introduce the conflict solver process that students can use to resolve their own conflicts. The process builds upon what students have learned thus far and requires that
they apply their new skills and knowledge. Go over each stage of the process:

1. Agree to solve the conflict.
Students should ask the person they are in conflict with if he or she wants to solve it.
The process will only work if both students want to solve the conflict. If they agree, students
should get a Conflict Solver Worksheet.

2. Explain the conflict.
One at a time, students use I Messages and explain their concerns to each other.
When one student is finished speaking, the other summarizes the story as best he or
she can. (If there is a problem deciding who goes first, start with the person whose
birthday comes first in the calendar year.) After both students are finished, they
should find each other's interests and underlying needs and write them on the
Conflict Solver sheet.

3. Brainstorm possible solutions.
Either one at a time, or together if possible, students brainstorm as many solutions to
the problem as they can come up with. They should write the potential solutions on
the Conflict Solver sheet. *Students should not judge solutions at this point.*

4. Choose a solution.
Together, students should discuss the positives and the negatives of each possible solution. After they have done this, they should choose the best one (or try to come up
with some better ones). It is also helpful to choose a time in the next few days when
they will evaluate how well the solution is working.

5. Do the solution.
Students implement the solution that they choose.

6. Evaluate the solution.

Students meet and talk about whether the solution is working and if they are both satisfied. If it is, then they have truly solved the conflict. If it is not, then they should go back to step 1 and start again.

2. Stress these three rules for the process:

   - Students have to follow the class contract created in Lesson 1 when they are solving conflicts (no put-downs, interrupting, and so on).
   - Students should not try this when they are really angry. They should wait until they have calmed down.
   - It is okay to ask for help whenever they need it. (This is what mediators do!)

3. After you have discussed this process, you will want students to practice it. There are two options for this:

   Option One: If there are students who have conflicts with each other in the room, ask them (in private) whether they would be willing to use the process in front of the group. If they are, the rest of the group observes and helps them.

   Option Two: Have students divide into groups of four. Two students act the part of one person in conflict, and the other two act the part of the second person. Students can either:
   a. Make up a conflict together.
   b. Use a conflict from one of their lives. The student with the conflict explains the situation to the group members. Then, if possible, the student with the conflict acts the part of the *other* party.
   c. Use one of the role-plays on the Conflict Solver Role-Play handout. (Students should only see their characters' descriptions, *not* both characters' descriptions.)

   If you have time, you can do both option one and option two.

4. Ask students what the hardest part about doing this was. Do they think this will work for their own conflicts? What will get in the way? How can they overcome those obstacles?

5. Make it clear to students that as with all of this work, it helps to follow the steps exactly at first. Later, they can be more flexible.

6. Tell students that what mediators do is help people go through the conflict resolution process when they can't do it on their own.

To extend the lesson:

Have four students act out one of the case transcripts in this book in front of the class.

Conflict Solver Worksheet

Six Steps to Conflict Resolution

1. **Agree to solve the conflict.** Ask the other person if he or she wants to solve the problem with you. *It will only work if you both want to solve the conflict.*

2. **Explain the conflict.** First one person tells his or her story using I Messages, and the other person summarizes. Then the second person tells his or her story using I Messages, and the first person summarizes. After you both have spoken, try to write all of your positions, interests, and underlying needs on this worksheet.

3. **Brainstorm possible solutions.** Brainstorm together as many solutions to the conflict as you can come up with and write them on this worksheet. *Do not judge solutions at this point.*

4. **Choose a solution.** Together, discuss the positives and the negatives of each possible solution. Then choose the best one—or try to come up with a better solution. Also establish a time during the next few days to meet and talk about whether the solution is working.

5. **Do the solution.** Try out the solution that you think is best.

6. **Evaluate the solution.** Meet to talk about whether the solution is working in a way that you both like. If it is, congratulate yourselves! If it is not, then go back to step 1 and start again. If you can't find a solution no matter how hard you try, then ask the teacher or a peer mediator for help.

Remember:

- Follow the class contract (no put-downs, interruptions, and so on).
- Do not do this when you are very angry at the other person or he or she is angry at you; wait until *after* you have calmed down a little.
- It is okay to ask for help.

Person 1's position: Person 2's position:

Person 1's interests: Person 2's interests:

Person 1's underlying needs: Person 2's underlying needs:

Possible win-win solutions:

Conflict Solver Role-Plays

Note: The students who are acting in these role-plays should only see their own characters' descriptions, not both descriptions. Also, they should not read these when they are acting in the role-play. Instead, they should use them as a guide. Students should play the characters in their own ways and using their own words.

Role-Play 1
Ruth Yamamoto

I have been friends with Suzie on and off for many years. Lately things have not been very good between us. I haven't talked to her for over two months. I used to really like her, though.

Recently my friends have been saying that Suzie and my boyfriend, Carey, have been spending a lot of time together. My friends say that they see them walking to school together, eating lunch together, and things like that. I don't eat lunch at the same time as Carey.

I tried to talk with Carey about this but he denies that anything is going on between Suzie and him. He says they are just friends.

Today between classes I saw Suzie and Carey talking in the halls. They didn't see me and so I spied on them for a few minutes until they parted. Then I went up to Suzie. I was really mad and I started yelling at her. People started to crowd around and I started to feel embarrassed, so I went to class.

I want her to back off and leave Carey alone. I don't think I could ever be her friend again.

Role-Play 1
Suzie Blake

I have been friends with Ruth on and off for many years. Lately things have not been very good between us, and I haven't talked to her for over two months. I used to really like her, though.

Recently I have been spending a lot of time with this guy Carey. He is going steady with Ruth, and I like him too, but only as a friend. That is the main reason why I haven't been spending time with Ruth lately; I didn't want to upset her.

Carey once said that he likes me more than Ruth. He said that I am more fun to be with. But I have told him that I just want to be friends.

Today Ruth came up to me in the halls and suddenly started yelling at me. She was really mad and accused me of "stealing" Carey. I was shocked and didn't really know what to say. When the bell rang for class, she just left.

Role-Play 2
Willie James

I am not very good at sports, but I like to play anyway. I am usually one of the last ones picked for teams, and sometimes the other guys tease me.

Paul is one of my friends. He is better at sports than me. We are in many of the same classes and we joke around a lot.

I got new sneakers recently. Yesterday when I was playing football, this guy Ashok stepped on them. I got really mad at first, but I realized it was a mistake and Ashok said that he was sorry.

Soon, however, the rest of the guys started stepping on my sneakers and laughing and saying "Ooops!" I didn't know what to do. I was mad but I was also scared. I was especially mad at Paul, because he was doing it too! My sneakers are now all full of mud. Later when I was in science class, Paul stepped out of the room for a minute. I took his pen off of his desk—it is a fancy pen with different inks—and stepped on it and crushed it. "Ooops!"

When Paul came back to class and saw that his pen was busted, he had a fit. This guy Glenn pointed out that I did it. (He must have seen.) Now Paul is threatening me. He said he would get me.

Role-Play 2
Paul Shapiro

Willie and I are friends. We are in many of the same classes together and we joke around a lot. He is not very good at sports, and some of the other guys tease him, but I like him.

I stepped out of science class today for a minute. When I got back, my pen was busted. I really liked this pen because I like to draw and the pen has four different colored inks in it. It looked like someone had stepped on it. I got really mad. Glenn, another kid in class, said that Willie did it. I was so angry that I just went over and started threatening Willie.

Earlier today everyone was stepping on Willie's new sneakers during recess. I did it also, but I don't know why. I felt badly afterwards. This may be why Willie was angry with me.

He shouldn't have busted my pen, though. I am so angry. He should buy me a new one. It cost about twenty dollars. It was a gift from my aunt.

CHAPTER 11

Program Forms

The following forms are those most commonly used by peer mediation programs. Feel free to modify them to meet your needs.

Implementation Timeline

Use this timeline as an implementation reference. As the timeline illustrates, implementing a peer mediation program successfully often requires many months of planning. Phase I: Securing Support and Program Development, for example, can take place during the school year prior to the year in which you implement the mediation program.

Bear in mind that this is only a guide; schools implement peer mediation programs in various ways. Some schools choose coordinators as soon as they discover this idea, while others wait until after the staff has been trained to select a coordinator. Because all program initiators face unique circumstances, the implementation process looks different in every school.

Phase I: Securing Support and Program Development

Approach the school administration to gauge interest	Week 1
Administer Needs Assessment Questionnaire for Teachers	Weeks 1–3
Present peer mediation concept at a staff meeting	Weeks 2–3
Present peer mediation to groups of students	Weeks 3–5
Form an advisory committee	Weeks 3–5
Meet with advisory committee and determine preliminary program design and funding needs	Weeks 5–10
Begin discussions with potential training sources	Weeks 5–10
Secure necessary funding through grant writing, the school department, state agencies, local business, etc.	Weeks 10+
Hold regular meetings with advisory committee to formulate policies re: confidentiality, voluntariness, issues that are appropriate for mediation, training, scheduling, curricular components, and program evaluation	Weeks 10+

Phase II begins after minimum funding is secured.

Phase II: Program Implementation

A. Pretraining	
Select a peer mediation coordinator	Weeks 1–2
Conduct optional staff training	Week 3
Decide upon dates for student training (with approval of administration and teachers)	Week 3
Seek nominations for trainees	Week 4
Organize training logistics (site, transportation, food, press)	Weeks 4–7
Interview nominees	Week 5
Select trainees	Week 6
Inform trainees (as well as their parents and teachers) of their selection	Week 6

B. Training

Provide training for training assistants (optional)	Week 7
Develop master schedule of mediators' availability	Weeks 7–10
Train student mediators	Weeks 8–9
Have student mediators get permission from their teachers to mediate during class	Week 10
Begin outreach campaign to student body using the mediators	Weeks 10–11

C. Casework and Program Maintenance

Mediate cases	Weeks 10+
Follow up on cases	Weeks 10+
Continue outreach and promotion	Weeks 10+
Maintain case records	Weeks 10+
Conduct regular meetings with mediators	Weeks 11+
Continue ongoing program design	Weeks 12+
Conduct evaluation of program	Final two months of year
Plan for the following year	Final two months of year
Plan possible outreach and expansion of program into other schools within your system	Final two months of year

Needs Assessment Questionnaire for Teachers

Dear Teachers:

We are considering implementing a school-based peer mediation program similar to the one described in the attached brochure. The mediation program will train students and a small group of teachers to help their peers resolve interpersonal conflicts. School mediation programs appear to be responsible for reducing suspension rates, improving school climates, and increasing student self-esteem in thousands of schools across the country.

We need your input and advice. Please fill out this brief, confidential questionnaire and return it to _____ by _____. Thank you.

1. How much class time do you spend dealing with conflicts between students?
   A. Less than 10 percent   C. 25 to 50 percent
   B. 10 to 25 percent   D. More than 50 percent

2. How do you usually deal with conflicts between students?
   A. Refer to department head   E. Act as a mediator between students
   B. Refer to principal   F. Give detention
   C. Ignore them   G. Other:_____
   D. Let students work it out themselves

3. How effective are the methods you currently use to resolve conflicts between students, especially in terms of preventing the reoccurrence of conflict? (Circle one.)

   1   2   3   4   5   6   7   8   9   10
   Not effective   **Very effective**

4. How effective are the methods those in charge of discipline currently use to resolve conflicts between students, especially in terms of preventing the reoccurrence of conflict? (Circle one.)

   1   2   3   4   5   6   7   8   9   10
   Not effective   **Very effective**

5. What do most of the conflicts that you observe between students concern?
   A. Gossiping/Rumors   E. Cutting in line
   B. Boyfriend/Girlfriend difficulties   F. Cliques/Gangs
   C. Name-calling   G. Racial tension
   D. Poor sportsmanship   H. Other:_____

6. Where do most conflicts occur?
   A. In the hall
   B. In the classroom
   C. In the lunchroom
   D. In the gym
   E. Other:_____

7. When do most conflicts occur?
   A. Before school
   B. During classes
   C. During lunch
   D. After school
   E. Between classes
   F. Other:_____

8. Please check whether you agree, disagree, or don't know for the following statements:

	agree	disagree	don't know
I think peer mediation is a good idea.			
I think this program can work at our school.			
I would feel comfortable referring students to the peer mediation program.			

9. Any other comments or suggestions?

10. If you are interested in participating in a conflict resolution/mediation training for teachers, *please print* your name here:

★★★★Note: _____ will be making
a brief presentation and answering questions about peer mediation
at the staff meeting on _____★★★★

Thank you

Peer Mediation Program Coordinator Job Description

The peer mediation coordinator must be based in the school; have anywhere from one to six hours during each school day to devote exclusively to peer mediation (varies with program design); *not* be a school disciplinarian. In addition, the coordinator ideally

- has excellent communication skills;
- has a demonstrable ability to win students' trust;
- is self-motivated and able to work independently;
- is well liked by school staff.

The responsibilities of the peer mediation coordinator include:

Program Design
- identifying potential sources of financial support
- creating and overseeing an advisory council
- overseeing all aspects of program design
- designing the referral process and related forms

Outreach and Publicity
- coordinating in-school publicity and education of both staff and students
- maintaining positive relations with administrators, disciplinarians, and teachers
- maintaining relations with parents and the community
- keeping the school and community updated on the program's progress

Training
- overseeing selection of trainees
- coordinating all aspects of the training, including locating trainers, arranging for the training site, obtaining parental permission, and providing refreshments
- training mediators themselves if they are able

Casework
- coordinating mediator availability
- taking referrals
- explaining mediation to parties and encouraging them to try mediation
- determining when an intervention other than peer mediation is necessary
- scheduling mediation sessions
- locating appropriate mediators for each session
- mediating cases when necessary
- supervising mediation sessions
- helping mediators improve their skills
- following up on all cases

Program Maintenance
- keeping records
- recruiting new mediators
- facilitating regular meetings with mediators
- coordinating program evaluation

Student Nomination Form

Dear Teachers:

We are seeking nominations to assist us in selecting approximately eighteen students to be peer mediators. We want to assemble a diverse group of students who represent all grades, racial and ethnic backgrounds, cliques, and so on in the school. We are not seeking only high achievers; we are also interested in including students who might not be living up to their leadership potential. Other qualities that nominees might possess include:

Respect of their peers   Commitment

Communication skills   Empathy

Responsibility   Sense of fairness

Confidence   Concern for others

Once selected, students will participate in a twenty-hour mediation training. The dates and times for the training are:

       October 18–12:00 to 5:00 (In-service day)
       October 20–8:00 to 2:00
       October 21–9:00 to 4:00 (Saturday)
       October 24–12:00 to 2:00

Students who complete the training will serve their peers by mediating interpersonal conflicts. As discussed at the recent staff meeting, we will not pull students from your class to mediate unless you give us permission to do so. Student mediators will be required to make up any work that they miss while mediating.

Thank you for your time and support,

_____

PLEASE RETURN TO_____ **BY** _____.

Nominee 1: _____ Grade: _____ Homeroom: _____

Nominee 2: _____ Grade: _____ Homeroom: _____

Nominee 3: _____ Grade: _____ Homeroom: _____

Nominee 4: _____ Grade: _____ Homeroom: _____

Peer Mediator Interview Guidelines

Conducting individual interviews with nominees helps you select appropriate students to train as mediators. You want to determine each candidate's interest, commitment, and ability. Coordinators, student mediators, advisory council members, or any combination of the three can conduct these interviews. The following is a sample agenda:

A. Welcome the student.

B. Describe the program and the commitment involved:

- Describe the responsibilities of the mediator and how the program will work.
- Training will be held on _____.
- Review the Peer Mediator Contract. If selected, the student must sign a contract with the program which requires that he or she
    come to every training session;
    be willing to mediate during school;
    make up any work missed while mediating;
    occasionally give time before or after school to the program.
- Ask if the student has any questions.

C. Review nominee's written application (if one was used).

D. Ask student to respond to a series of questions that might include:

- What does mediation mean to you?
- Why do you think you would make a good mediator?
- Do people come to you with problems? What kinds of problems? What do you do?
- If two students were fighting over a rumor, what are some ways you could help them resolve the situation?
- What does it mean to be a good listener?
- Do you know what confidentiality is? Do you think that you could keep things confidential?
- Would you be willing to come to mediation if you were in a conflict?
- Do you speak any other language besides English?

E. Answer any final questions the nominee might have about peer mediation.

F. Thank him or her for participating in the interview process and indicate when you will make your final selection.

Parent Permission Letter

Dear Mr./Ms._____:

We are pleased to inform you that your child, _____ , has been selected by the _____ School Mediation Program to be trained as a peer mediator.

Mediation is a form of conflict resolution in which trained students, under adult supervision, help their peers talk out and resolve interpersonal conflicts. Student mediators do not take sides or make decisions for their peers; instead, they help them create their own resolutions to conflicts. Peer mediation is a safe, effective program that has been implemented in thousands of schools across the United States.

In their training, students will learn important life-skills—active listening, negotiation, problem solving—that will benefit them personally and academically. Experience as a peer mediator has also been shown to increase students' self-esteem and self-confidence.

The peer mediation training will be conducted by _____
_____ , on _____.
Students who participate in the training will miss some classes, and they will be responsible for making up their schoolwork. When the training is complete, students will mediate conflicts between their peers for the remainder of the school year. We will make every attempt to schedule mediation sessions so that they do not interfere with academics.

We hope you will consider giving _____ permission to participate in this excellent program and sign the permission slip below. Teachers and students recommended your child because they thought he or she could be a leader in the school.

Congratulations to you and to your child for being selected. Feel free to call us if you have any questions or concerns.

Sincerely,

_____

I, _____ , give my child, _____ ,
permission to participate in the peer mediation training.

Signed:_____

Teacher Permission to Mediate Form

Dear Teachers:

As you are probably aware, _____ was recently trained to be a peer mediator. Our school peer mediation program is now ready and excited to begin mediating. Although we will be making every effort to schedule mediation sessions so that they do not interfere with academics, occasionally we will have to pull students out of class to mediate. Please indicate below whether it is currently okay for this student to mediate occasionally during your class. We will check back with you regularly to update this information. Of course, students will be required to make up any work that they miss.

Signature	Subject	Period	Room	YES or NO	Teacher
Teacher 1:					
Teacher 2:					
Teacher 3:					
Teacher 4:					
Teacher 5:					
Teacher 6:					
Teacher 7:					

Comments (please put your name next to comments):

Feel free to contact us if you have any questions or concerns.
Sincerely,

Peer Mediator Contract with Program

I, _____ , agree to participate in a twenty-hour training course in mediation. I will attend all of the training sessions, arriving on time and ready to learn. After completion of the training, I agree to serve as a peer mediator for at least one year and ideally for as long as I am a student at the _____ School. I will devote a minimum of three hours each month to the peer mediation program.

I agree to arrive at all mediation sessions on time. I will let my teachers know if I must miss a class to mediate, and I will make up any work that I miss.

I understand that as a peer mediator, I will have a responsible position in the school. I will strive to live up to this responsibility. I agree to resolve my own conflicts peacefully whenever possible, and if I am having a problem with someone that I cannot resolve on my own, I will seek assistance from the mediation coordinator. I further agree to abide by the disciplinary code of the mediation program.

_____   _____
Signature   Date

Peer Mediator Oath

As a peer mediator, I, _____ , promise to help the students of the _____ School settle their differences peacefully.

I understand the importance of confidentiality, and I promise to keep everything that I learn in mediation sessions confidential.

I understand that I will be a leader in the school. I will act in a way that is worthy of this responsibility.

Finally, I will always try to improve my skills and become a better mediator.

Peer Mediation Referral Form

Date: _____ Time: _____
Referred by: _____

1. **Names and schedules of students in conflict.** *(Fill in as much as you can and include teachers' names and room numbers.)*

Student 1: _____ Grade: _____ Home Room: _____
Period 1:   Period 3:   Period 5:   Period 7:

Period 2:   Period 4:   Period 6:   Period 8:

Student 2: _____ Grade: _____ Home Room: _____
Period 1:   Period 3:   Period 5:   Period 7:

Period 2:   Period 4:   Period 6:   Period 8:

Student 3: _____ Grade: _____ Home Room: _____
Period 1:   Period 3:   Period 5:   Period 7:

Period 2:   Period 4:   Period 6:   Period 8:

Other students involved:

2. **What is the conflict about?** *(Circle as many as you need.)*
   Rumors   Name-calling   Gangs   Boy/Girlfriend   Stealing
   Threats   Friendship   Teasing   Prejudice   Fighting
   Other (describe briefly):

3. **When did the conflict occur?**

4. **Do the students know that you are referring them to peer mediation?**
   ☐ Yes   ☐ No

5. **When should this conflict be mediated?** *(Check one.)*
   ☐ Whenever you get a chance   ☐ As soon as possible   ☐ Today/Urgent!

   Please return this to _____ or drop it in the referral box outside the Mediation Center.

Thank You!

Case Summary Form

Case # _____

Student 1: _____ Grade: _____ Home Room:____
Student 2: _____ Grade: _____ Home Room:____
Student 3: _____ Grade: _____ Home Room:____
Student 4: _____ Grade: _____ Home Room:____

Referred by: *(Check one.)*

Student:
- ☐ Self-referred
- ☐ Other party
- ☐ Mediator
- ☐ Friend
- ☐ Observer
- ☐ Other:

Adult:
- ☐ Disciplinarian
- ☐ Teacher
- ☐ Counselor
- ☐ Principal
- ☐ Staff
- ☐ Other:

Cause of dispute:

A mediation session was held on: _____
Mediated by: _____
Supervised by: _____

Outcome:
- ☐ Written agreement
- ☐ Verbal agreement
- ☐ No agreement

- ☐ Resolved prior to session
- ☐ Referred to disciplinarian
- ☐ Other:

No session: *(Please explain why.)*

Parties referred to:

Race of parties:

Party 1: ☐ Cauc. ☐ Afri. Amer. ☐ Asian ☐ Hispanic ☐ Nat. Amer. ☐ Other

Party 2: ☐ Cauc. ☐ Afri. Amer. ☐ Asian ☐ Hispanic ☐ Nat. Amer. ☐ Other

Party 3: ☐ Cauc. ☐ Afri. Amer. ☐ Asian ☐ Hispanic ☐ Nat. Amer. ☐ Other

Party 4: ☐ Cauc. ☐ Afri. Amer. ☐ Asian ☐ Hispanic ☐ Nat. Amer. ☐ Other

Sex of parties:

Party 1:	☐ Male	☐ Female
Party 2:	☐ Male	☐ Female
Party 3:	☐ Male	☐ Female
Party 4:	☐ Male	☐ Female

Grade of parties:

Party 1:

Party 2:

Party 3:

Party 4:

Follow-up contact:

1. Date: _____ Place: _____

Is the agreement still working?　　☐ Yes　　☐ No

Comments:

2. Date: _____ Place: _____

Is the agreement still working?　　☐ Yes　　☐ No

Comments:

Peer Mediation Agreement Form

Parties: _____

_____

    We have participated in a mediation session on _____ , and we voluntarily agree to the following:

    We believe that this is a fair agreement. If for any reason we are having problems that we can't resolve on our own, we agree to come back to mediation to get help.

Signed:

Party _____ Date:_____

Party _____ Date:_____

Mediator _____ Date:_____

Mediator _____ Date:_____

Post-mediation Session Questionnaire

For program only: Case # _____ *Party #* _____

Your name: _____ Date: _____

  Please answer these questions honestly. Check the boxes that represents the best answers.

1. I am a:
    ☐ Student
    ☐ Teacher
    ☐ Administrator
    ☐ Parent
    ☐ Other:

2. Have you ever been to mediation before?   ☐ Yes ☐ No

3. Do you think that the mediators:
    a. Knew what they were doing?   ☐ Yes ☐ No
    b. Listened to you?   ☐ Yes ☐ No
    c. Understood your feelings?   ☐ Yes ☐ No
    d. Acted fairly?   ☐ Yes ☐ No
    e. Helped you?   ☐ Yes ☐ No

4. How would you describe your relationship with the other person before this situation? (Check as many as you like.)
    ☐ Friends
    ☐ Acquaintances
    ☐ Classmates
    ☐ Strangers
    ☐ Relatives
    ☐ Enemies
    ☐ Boyfriend/Girlfriend
    ☐ Other:

5. How did you feel toward the other person when you came into the mediation session? (Check as many as you like.)
    ☐ Angry
    ☐ Scared
    ☐ Worried
    ☐ Frustrated
    ☐ Didn't care

☐ Revengeful

☐ Hurt

☐ Other:

6. Did the mediation session change your feelings toward the other person?

☐ Yes, for the better

☐ No, not at all

☐ Yes, for the worse

Please explain:

7. Did you reach an agreement with the other person? ☐ Yes ☐ No

If you didn't reach an agreement, skip to question 11.

8. Are you satisfied with your agreement? ☐ Yes ☐ No

9. Do you think the other person will follow the agreement?

☐ Yes

☐ Not sure, but probably

☐ Not sure, but probably not

☐ No

10. Will you follow this agreement?

☐ Yes

☐ Not sure, but probably

☐ Depends if the other party does

☐ Not sure, but probably not

☐ No

11. If no agreement was reached, why do you think this happened?

12. Would you come to mediation again? ☐ Yes ☐ No

13. What do you think of mediation in general?

14. Would you like to be a mediator in the future? ☐ Yes ☐ No

Mediator Post-session Self-Evaluation

Mediator's name: _____

For each of the following, put a check in the box according to whether you did the following very well, just okay, or poorly and you need improvement.

	very well	okay	poorly
Welcomed the parties			
Said the opening statement			
Made the parties feel comfortable			
Asked questions			
Actively listened			
Ended with each party before I heard from the next one			
Took notes			
Kept control of the session			
Found the real issues			
Stayed neutral and didn't take sides			
Worked together with my co-mediator			
Helped parties think how *they* could resolve the situation			
Avoided making suggestions			
Understood when to call for private sessions			
Knew how to use private sessions			
Wrote the agreement			
Knew what to say at the end of the mediation			
Gave feedback to my co-mediator			
Accepted feedback from my co-mediator			

The things I did best in this session were:

The things I will do differently next time I mediate are:

Sample Codes of Discipline

The following are excerpted from the student handbooks or disciplinary codes of three different schools.

Example 1: High School Disciplinary Code

Rule 7: No Fighting

Offense 1: The student(s) will be suspended immediately and a hearing will be arranged as soon as possible with the students' parent(s) or guardian(s) and the house master. The student(s) will lose "Open Campus" privileges and/or have other restrictions placed on their unscheduled time for five weeks. Joint or group counseling or attending a mediation session will be mandatory.

Brookline High School, Brookline, MA

Example 2: High School Student Handbook

Project Peace—Student Mediation

Project Peace provides students with a way to reach an agreement in an effort to help resolve a dispute, settle an argument, or end a conflict. It allows students to reach the agreement they want rather than settle for an agreement decided by somebody else, like a teacher or administrator. Specially trained students and teachers—called mediators—meet with those in conflict during the school day to help them work out a solution. Participation in mediation is voluntary and confidential. At a designated time and place, mediators will meet the disputants, listen impartially to both sides of the problem, focus on the key issues, and help the individuals in conflict *arrive at their own solution* to their problem. Mediators will not be judges or disciplinarians: they will not tell disputants what to do or how to solve their problems. An agreement, once reached, must be acceptable to both parties.

Students may request mediation by contacting Esther Sipperstein (Peer Mediation Coordinator), Jean Krupowicz (Vice-Principal), or by completing a referral form available in all school offices.

Promote Peace—Solve your problems with Project Peace!

Whitman-Hanson Regional High School, Whitman, MA

Example 3: Middle School Student Handbook

Students and staff will now be able to resolve disputes in an atmosphere that is non-coercive, nonjudgmental, and nonpunitive. The disputants (student and student or students and staff) voluntarily attend mediation sessions and with the help of trained student and staff mediators, work to reach a mutually agreed upon resolution that will prevent the conflict from reoccurring. More information is available by contacting Shalita Akeebah, Peer Mediation Coordinator, in room 17.

Martin Luther King Middle School, Dorchester, MA

Appendices

Legal Considerations of Peer Mediation Programs[39]

Because legal issues represent an important area of school administration, administrators and coordinators sometimes raise concerns about the legal implications of operating a peer mediation program. Educators wonder whether their school can be sued if its mediation program is somehow involved in an incident during which a student is injured.

This appendix attempts to address this concern, providing both a general overview of legal principles relevant to peer mediation, and an analysis of how these legal principles might apply to the design, implementation, and maintenance of peer mediation programs.

It is important to note at the outset that the author is aware of no legal problems involving peer mediation programs. Athough it is always possible that a school could be sued for actions related to its peer mediation program, this is not probable. In fact, a well-run mediation program may actually reduce a school's susceptibility to legal liability.

To understand why this is so, we must first take a look at the law of torts.

THE LAW OF TORTS

The law of torts provides an injured person with the right to sue someone else to obtain compensation. For example, if a student by the name of Jason O'Malley is injured on the Chaney Middle School playground, the law of torts enables him (and his parents) to sue the school.

In any tort lawsuit, two different questions arise. The first is whether the legal system will recognize such a lawsuit: will the courts even allow Jason and his parents to sue the school? This is a matter of public policy. The second question concerns whether the lawsuit, if recognized by the courts, will ultimately succeed. This is determined by referring to the legal concept known as *negligence*. We will discuss these two questions separately.

PUBLIC POLICY AND SCHOOL IMMUNITY

The law of torts attempts to balance the societal burdens resulting from legal liability against the societal benefits to be derived from it. In our example, the law must balance the social burden of exposing schools like Chaney to financial liability against the benefit derived from allowing students like Jason to seek compensation. In this example, the O'Malleys would probably be allowed to sue because public policy has determined that the benefits outweigh the burdens. This does not mean that the student will necessarily triumph in court; that will depend on what exactly happened on the playground.

---

[39] This appendix is based on work by Richard McNulty, a student at Harvard Law School in Cambridge, Massachusetts.

In some situations, however, public policy precludes an injured party from bringing a lawsuit against a school. In these cases, schools are granted immunity. As an example, courts have refused to subject schools and teachers to legal liability for educational malpractice. Despite numerous attempts, judges generally refuse to listen to parental claims that a school "did not educate my child properly."[40] The public policy reasons behind this refusal include the difficulty of defining a proper standard of educational effectiveness, the burden that such suits would impose on public school systems' limited resources, the potential burden on the courts, and the uncertainty in determining compensation for the injury.

Will public policy grant immunity to schools for problems that occur in the context of peer mediation? To some extent, this is likely. One reason is that it is generally agreed that peer mediation teaches young people a unique and important set of life-skills. In addition, there is a growing consensus that society cannot ignore the violence that plagues schools. Federal, state, and local governments across the country support the establishment of peer mediation programs.[41] Such public policy considerations make it reasonable to believe that peer mediation programs may be immune from lawsuits to some extent. If school violence continues to escalate, liability may even be imposed upon schools that fail to implement violence prevention measures such as peer mediation.

Many school disciplinary policies are already immune to legal action, and this immunity would likely apply to mediation programs as well. Variations in state laws, school-board policies, and peer mediation practices, however, make it impossible to generalize regarding the scope of immunity. In some states, schools are immune as long as the administration shows a minimum amount of care in the development and application of disciplinary procedures. Other states hold schools to a stricter level of scrutiny. Specific questions regarding potential legal liability should be addressed to your school attorney as much of the law in this area is subject to interpretation.

To the degree that a peer mediation program is not immune to lawsuits, students injured in the context of peer mediation programs may be able to sue their school. This brings us to the second question: If the courts allow a lawsuit, will such a suit succeed? This is a question of negligence.[42]

NEGLIGENCE AND THE RULE OF REASONABLE CONDUCT

Negligence is an example of a tort—a situation where an injured person sues someone else to obtain compensation—and it involves injuries that are neither expected nor intended. If a negligence lawsuit is to succeed, four factors must be present:

---

[40] An exception to this general rule is the administration of special education programs.

[41] The Safe Schools Act, for example, is a piece of federal legislation introduced by President Clinton that attempts to deal with school violence. Peer mediation is specifically mentioned in this act as one creative approach to violence prevention that the law intends to encourage.

[42] Since the author believes that there have been no lawsuits involving peer mediation programs, this analysis is purely speculative. If a lawsuit were to arise, schools would have a variety of defenses, including, in many states, immunity. A specific analysis of these defenses is beyond the scope of this appendix.

1. A duty or obligation, recognized by law, requiring an institution or individual to conform to a certain standard of conduct for the protection of others against foreseeable, unreasonable risks
2. A failure to conform to the standard required
3. A reasonably close causal connection between the failure to conform to the standard required and the resulting injury
4. An actual loss or injury to a third party

Returning to the playground example, let's say the O'Malleys claim that the Chaney School was negligent because when Jason was injured, only one teacher was supervising a playground of almost two hundred students, including students known to be troublesome. The O'Malleys would be able to prove the school's negligence if they could show that

1. the school had a legal duty to supervise the students;
2. the school failed to reasonably supervise the students;
3. their son Jason's accident was reasonably related to the lack of supervision;
4. Jason was injured in the accident.

Institutions may be found negligent when they fail to abide by what lawyers refer to as the "standard of reasonable conduct in the face of apparent risks." One challenge in negligence lawsuits, however, is that there are no concrete rules for determining what constitutes "reasonable conduct." Under some circumstances, one teacher on a playground of two hundred might constitute "reasonable" care. Under others, even ten teachers would be insufficient. It would be up to a jury to determine if the Chaney School's conduct was reasonable given the apparent risks.

Analogously, there are no concrete rules for determining what constitutes "reasonable conduct" in the context of peer mediation. We can, however, consider how three legal duties that exist in schools should guide the design, implementation, and maintenance of a mediation program. These duties are

1. the duty to reasonably supervise,
2. the duty to use reasonable care in selection, retention, and training,
3. the duty to act reasonably to prevent harm.

Consideration of these issues, from both a legal and a nonlegal perspective, will enable coordinators to do their jobs most effectively.

APPLYING THE LAW TO SCHOOL-BASED PEER MEDIATION

The Duty to Reasonably Supervise

All schools have a legal duty to supervise student activity. This supervision need not be constant, however. What constitutes reasonable supervision will depend on the activity in which students are engaged, the age of the students, the reason for and the duration of the lack of supervision, and the ability of the school to anticipate problems deriving from the lack of supervision.

Whenever schools (and therefore peer mediation programs) are not immune from negligence liability, the duty to supervise properly is usually the responsibility of the mediation coordinator. Applying the general rule of negligence, the degree of supervision should be determined by standards of reasonable conduct in light of the apparent risks. *These standards will often parallel common sense.* When supervising cases, important factors to consider include the type of conflict being mediated, the previous history of the students involved, and the experience of the student mediators.

Many peer mediation cases—simple disputes involving teasing, returning borrowed property, gossip—do not require a great deal of supervision. On the other hand, sometimes a mediation session is held to resolve a recent fight between students who are considered to be volatile. Because further violence is foreseeable in this scenario, the duty to supervise increases. If your mediators are relatively inexperienced, the duty to supervise increases further. Given these circumstances, the coordinator should be present in the room during such a session.[43] Whenever the propensity for injury increases, so does the school's duty to provide adequate supervision.

The duty to supervise applies not only during the mediation session, but also to the entire process of mediation, including when students are on their way to mediation, when they wait outside the mediation room for a session to begin, and when they return to class after a session ends. Again, this does not mean that constant supervision is required. If you develop procedures that reasonably address the potential for problems throughout the mediation process, and if you ensure that these procedures are in place, you should have no problems.

The Duty to Use Reasonable Care in Selection, Retention, and Training

Schools also have a duty to use reasonable care in the selection, retention, and training of teachers and staff. This applies primarily to the peer mediation coordinator. Again, invoke the standards of reasonable conduct in light of the apparent risks when selecting and training your coordinator. Consider the types of conflict you expect your peer mediation program to handle. Given your school population, you might decide that advanced training for the coordinator in prejudice reduction, crisis intervention, or gang relations is warranted.

An argument could also be made to apply the same legal duty to the selection, retention, and training of peer mediators. This argument would most likely fail as to the selection of mediators because of the inherent difficulty in defining a proper standard for the evaluation of peer mediators (especially given the advantages of having a diverse mediation team). But it is wise to use "reasonable care" in the retention and training of student mediators as well.

The Duty to Act Reasonably to Prevent Harm

Whenever a school is specifically aware of a student's propensity to do harm, it has a duty to take reasonable steps to prevent the student from doing so. In peer mediation, a

---

[43] This assumes that an experienced adult coordinator would enhance the mediation process by monitoring hostility levels and intervening if necessary. An argument can be made, however, that the presence of an adult actually hinders the mediation process. Such an argument might succeed in court if the jury could be convinced that, given the circumstances, it was reasonable to mediate the case without adult supervision.

student's "propensity" to do harm is usually discovered in the form of threats made against oneself or others. Threats are not uncommon in peer mediation sessions. Experienced coordinators and mediators become adept at determining when a threat crosses the threshold of danger that necessitates action beyond the scope of mediation. When this threshold is crossed, schools may have a legal duty to warn the individuals at risk, their parents, and the proper legal authorities.

While coordinators evaluate threats primarily on instinct, a number of factors can help determine the level of danger associated with a threat. These include the specificity of the threat, its potential severity for harm, whether the threat is directed at an identifiable victim, whether the victim is aware of the threat, and the imminence of danger. Given the right combination of these factors, it is likely that a mediation coordinator would incur a legal duty to warn the proper people.[44] The coordinator's actions would then have to meet the standard of reasonable care. Whenever this situation arises, it is in the school's and the coordinator's best interests to document the events thoroughly.

CONFIDENTIALITY AND SCHOOL SAFETY

The last duty, the duty to act reasonably to prevent harm, leads to the final focus of this appendix, and a subject that is fundamental to peer mediation: confidentiality. The duty to warn will often conflict with the notion of confidentiality. In fact, many states have laws that *require* mediators to keep certain information confidential. The scope of confidentiality normally applies to pre-mediation screening interviews, the mediation session itself, post-mediation discussions among mediators and supervisors, and all records associated with the mediation. Because confidentiality laws vary tremendously from state to state, however, it is impossible to define the parameters of confidentiality in any general sense. Furthermore, peer mediation implicates different public policy considerations than nonschool mediation, and it is unclear whether state confidentiality laws fully apply to school-based peer mediation programs.

School mediation programs must balance the need to maintain confidentiality (and protect the integrity of their program) with the necessity of sharing certain information with outside authorities. This is not always easy. A consideration of the relevant legal issues can help you develop a sound policy in this regard.

One of the primary purposes of peer mediation is to address school safety concerns. To the extent that breaking confidentiality would undermine the integrity and effectiveness of a program, confidentiality should be protected. But whenever this policy directly implicates other safety concerns—whenever keeping something confidential might lead to personal injury—then confidentiality may need to be breached so as to address those concerns.

In some jurisdictions, specified professionals, and sometimes anyone, have a legal duty to report certain crimes even if no one has requested the information. Most states require individuals to report felonies and gunshot wounds, for instance, and all fifty states

---

[44] This school-based duty to warn is similar to the duty to warn that some states impose on other professionals. For example, a number of states require that when a psychologist determines, or should determine pursuant to the standards of the profession, that a patient presents a serious danger of violence to another, the psychologist incurs an obligation to use reasonable care to protect the intended victim from such danger.

have laws requiring designated professionals (including teachers and social workers) to report child abuse and neglect. Thus, depending on the state and the professional capacity of the mediation coordinator, he or she may have a legal duty to report suspected child abuse to the proper authorities, even if such a report would breach confidentiality.

A mediation coordinator's experience and unique relationship with the students involved in mediation may also implicate other legal duties. For example, in many states, the unique relationship between school counselors and students yields a duty on the counselors' behalf to inform parents when they have knowledge of a student's suicidal statements. This same duty might well apply to the mediation coordinator who is privy to similar information.

Unless a specific legal issue has been addressed by state law (such as child abuse or student suicide), it is difficult to determine the proper balance between confidentiality and school safety concerns. For mediation coordinators who wonder how to proceed when they suspect or know of student involvement with drugs, weapons, or other criminal acts, the law provides no easy answers. Legal duties to report danger and the limits of confidentiality vary from state to state, and often the best the law can do is provide the general rule of negligence: Where a duty exists, one must act reasonably in the face of apparent risks.

When the law fails to provide specific guidance, the creativity of a mediation coordinator plays an invaluable role. Coordinators can persuade students to approach authorities on their own. When this is not possible, coordinators may still be able to advise the proper people discreetly without threatening the integrity of their program. Thankfully, the law, common sense, and the dictates of compassionate action are usually in alignment. Once they have familiarized themselves with the issues, coordinators' instincts will usually lead them to do the right thing.

THE ROLE OF THE LAW IN YOUR MEDIATION PROGRAM

Legal considerations, in and of themselves, are not sufficient to define the appropriate guidelines for a peer mediation program. The law does, however, encourage the development of these programs, and it does provide an impetus for program designers to consider delicate situations in advance. By examining these issues, guidelines and procedures can be designed that most effectively address concerns about school safety. After your program is operational, continue to evaluate and review specific problems.

To summarize, a sound mediation program should provide

- adult supervision when student safety is an immediate concern,
- reasonable care in the training and evaluation of mediation coordinators and student mediators,
- reasonable efforts to prevent harm,
- well-defined and properly communicated policies that balance confidentiality issues and safety concerns.

APPENDIX B

Suggestions for Grant Writing

It is often necessary to write grant proposals to secure funding for a peer mediation program. Before beginning to work on a proposal, first determine whether there is someone within your school system whose job it is to write such proposals. Many schools have grant writers who can provide invaluable assistance, directing you to likely sources of funding and sometimes even writing the grant proposal for you.

This book contains more than enough material to serve as the core of a grant proposal. The following suggestions, organized according to the sections of a typical grant proposal, will help you use the information in this book for your proposal:

- **Statement of Need.** This section explains why *your school in particular* needs a peer mediation program. Include data like the suspension and detention rate, interest in conflict resolution among staff and students, recent incidents of schoolwide conflict and tension. Refer to the information in the Introduction and first part of this book.
- **Program Summary.** A generic program summary can be found in Chapter 3 in the sections on the Peer Mediation Program and the Peer Mediation Process.
- **Program Goals.** The list of potential benefits attributed to peer mediation programs, found in Chapter 3, can help you determine the goals of your program. See also the section on Program Evaluation in Chapter 5.
- **Implementation Timeline.** See Chapter 11 for an implementation timeline that can be modified to meet your needs.
- **Budget.** You will have to determine this on your own. Refer to Chapter 5 (especially the section on funding) for some guidelines. Also speak with sources of training and program evaluation to determine potential costs.

APPENDIX C

Private Sessions

Private sessions are the separate, individual meetings that mediators hold with parties during a mediation session.[45] In their most common form, one party (or group of parties) is asked to meet with the mediators while the other party or parties wait outside the room. Each party is given the opportunity to meet with the mediators when private sessions are called. In almost all applications of mediation in the adult world—labor, divorce, environmental, family, international—mediators take some form of private session.

There has been some debate in the young peer mediation field concerning the use of private sessions. In fact, whether or not student mediators are encouraged to take private sessions is one of the biggest structural difference between mediation models. In many peer mediation programs, private sessions are taken as a matter of course. Students in these programs would feel uncomfortable if they did *not* take private sessions. In other programs, mediators never take private sessions, and the entire process is conducted in a joint session. These latter student mediators never consider the possibility of private sessions.

Consider this summary of the cases for and against private sessions:

- **Against the Use of Private Sessions.** The goal of mediation is to help parties *work together* to resolve their differences. Private sessions are destructive to this process in that by separating parties, they encourage the mediator to do work that the parties themselves ought to do.
- **For the Use of Private Sessions.** Mediation is necessary exactly because the parties cannot negotiate effectively on their own. Private sessions only acknowledge this fact. It is naive—and results in unsound agreements—to assume that what can be learned in a joint session is enough to resolve all disputes.

Below is a detailed list of the strengths and weaknesses of private sessions as a tool in school-based disputes.

Potential Strengths of Private Sessions

- They provide the parties with physical and psychological space in which they can safely reflect upon their situation.
- They enable student parties to develop a deeper level of trust in the mediators and in the process.
- They enable mediators to ask questions that might be too sensitive to ask when the other parties are present.
- They enable a student party to say things that he or she might not feel comfortable saying in front of the other party. This provides mediators and ultimately the parties themselves with a more accurate understanding of the dispute and leads to a more comprehensive resolution.

---

[45] Private sessions are sometimes referred to as *caucuses* or *individual sessions*.

- They enable mediators to transmit information between parties in a manner most conducive to mutual understanding.
- They enable mediators to explore discrepancies between the parties' public positions and private realities.
- They provide mediators with a tool to balance the power between parties.
- They give mediators an option if they are stuck and need time to collect themselves and strategize.
- They enable mediators to talk to one another (and to their coordinator) without the parties present (in the breaks between private meetings).

Potential Limitations of Private Sessions

- They are simply unnecessary in many student disputes. They waste time and focus mediators and parties in the wrong direction.
- They create an option that mediators rely too heavily upon when tensions are high. Parties need the mediators to guide them through difficult negotiations *together* rather than separately.
- They increase the complexity of the mediators' work, especially in transmitting information, and student mediators might have difficulty handling this.
- They require a separate waiting area and so are more logistically demanding of a program.
- Student mediators might be unable to handle the sensitive issues (suicide, abuse, strong feelings) that surface in private sessions.
- They increase the time needed for mediation sessions.
- If done incorrectly, private sessions might foster distrust between the parties and toward the mediators.

In the end, neither blanket rejection nor wholesale incorporation of private sessions is appropriate for peer mediation. Many student disputes do not require private sessions. The issues in these disputes are straightforward, and student parties have nothing to say in private that they cannot or will not say in the joint session. But some parties benefit greatly from the use of private sessions. If conducted properly, there is little to lose and potentially much to be gained in holding private sessions.

Peer mediation has the greatest potential effectiveness when mediators have the option of using private sessions. Student mediators (in grades six through twelve) should be trained to use them whenever they feel they are necessary.

APPENDIX D

Implementing Peer Mediation Programs in Many Schools Simultaneously

Although this book has focused on implementing a peer mediation program in a single school, school mediation programs can also be implemented on a systemwide, county-wide, or even statewide basis. Implementing programs in many schools simultaneously has a number of potential advantages, including:

- An economy of scale can potentially save time, money, and human resources. Schools can raise funds together, share resources and information, conduct joint training sessions, or train central office staff to serve the entire system as peer mediation trainers.
- When schools pool their resources, there may be more options for funding. Some foundations and federal agencies are attracted by the economy of scale and prefer to fund larger projects.
- Schools that will pilot the program can be selected on a competitive basis from within the system or district. This leads to better school-based commitment and therefore to better programs.
- Each individual school that implements a peer mediation program has more support when its district or the school system is committed to its success.
- In-house trainers serving an entire system have the opportunity to conduct numerous trainings in a relatively short period of time. This enables them to become proficient trainers more quickly than coordinators in a single school who only train once a year.

Peer mediation programs can be implemented in school systems vertically, horizontally, or using some combination of the two. In the *vertical* approach, the program is implemented in schools that "feed" into one another. This might mean that five elementary schools that feed into two middle schools that feed into one high school would all implement a program. The *horizontal* approach, on the other hand, means that only schools at the same level implement the program: all the high schools, all the middle schools, or all the elementary schools within a designated system.

The horizontal approach is easier to implement for a number of reasons. Everything learned in one school is clearly transferable to the others. (You can repeat and continually refine your training program, for example.) In addition, working with only one school level means only having to interact with a single level of the educational bureaucracy. Disadvantages of the horizontal approach include that students are not able to apply their mediation skills formally when they graduate,[46] and it can give students and educators the false impression that peer mediation is only suited for one level.

---

[46] Some systems get around this by expanding the program as students progress. Peer mediation programs might be implemented in middle schools at first. Then, when those students graduate and attend high school, the program is initiated at the high school level.

The strength of the vertical approach is that it enables students to continue to develop their skills and take advantage of the mediation process as they graduate from school to school. It is more challenging from a training and programmatic point of view, however, because the training and the implementation process are different at each level. Regardless of the approach you take to implementing peer mediation programs in numerous schools simultaneously, bear the following cautions in mind:

- **Beware of the top-down approach.** A top-down, districtwide implementation model often forces schools to implement peer mediation programs. Just because the program works well in one school, however, does not guarantee that it will be effective in other schools even within the same system. Mandating programs for schools that do not want them is counter to the spirit in which this program operates and only wastes time and resources. Start with schools that want the program, and the others will follow if and when they are ready.

- **Beware of expanding too rapidly.** It is common for systems to implement peer mediation programs in many schools at once and end up with only a very few healthy programs. Rather than spread your resources too thin, it is better to create a handful of strong programs and expand gradually from there. Success in a few schools will lead to success in the others.

- **Beware of the politics of large systems.** As implementation plans become bigger and more ambitious, the politics become more complex. Individual schools lobby to be selected as pilot sites, and administrators are pressured to select schools for reasons other than that they are the best candidates. Try to build in safeguards against this whenever possible. One such safeguard might be a heterogeneous (students, teachers, administrators) administrative committee empowered to oversee all aspects of implementing the peer mediation effort.

APPENDIX E

Organizing Conferences for Student Mediators

As the peer mediation concept expands, increasing numbers of conferences are being organized for the benefit of student mediators. At these conferences, mediators from many different schools spend time learning from each other, sharpening their skills, and having fun. Conferences help mediators grow personally as well as "professionally." Some of the objectives of peer mediator conferences are

- to improve mediators' skills;
- to strengthen participating mediation programs by sharing resources and renewing the enthusiasm of students and staff;
- to build students' pride in their work and in themselves, honoring them for the contribution they make to their schools;
- to give students a greater understanding of the range of applications of the mediation process (family mediation, court mediation, landlord-tenant mediation, labor mediation);
- to show students and staff that they are part of a larger movement by bringing them together with others involved in similar work;
- to provide students and staff with the opportunity to share common interests and build relationships with peers from different racial, ethnic, religious, cultural, and socioeconomic backgrounds;
- to educate the wider community about school-based peer mediation both as an end in itself and to generate support for the programs. (The local press is usually invited for this purpose.)

PLANNING CONFERENCES

Although conducting a conference for mediators requires a great deal of planning, the intense effort invested in advance is the only way to ensure that the event will be a success. Ideally, the burden of this planning should be shared by as many people as possible. In most cases, volunteers from participating schools do a good portion of the work. Student mediators can also be involved in the planning, helping with everything from creating the agenda to designing materials to preparing the conference site.

The first step in planning a conference is to resolve these five fundamental questions:

1. **Who will take the lead role in planning the conference?**
   One person (or small group) should act as the primary organizer of the event and coordinate all aspects of the planning. If the conference will serve students from only one school system, designate someone who works in the central administration to take on this job. There is also some precedent for having a community mediation program staff member serve as conference coordinator.

2. **Which peer mediation programs will participate?**

   Decide how widely you will cast your net for participants. Will the conference be attended by student mediators from the same school system or by students from the same county, region, or state? Do these schools have the interest and the energy to make the conference work?

3. **What is the target age group for the conference?**

   Peer mediator conferences should be designed for mediators from a particular level of schooling (elementary, middle, or high school) or even focused on a specific grade level (fifth, seventh, eleventh). When student conferees are all the same age, activities and ideas resonate among the group in a way that increases the impact of the conference. The age of the conferees will also determine the focus and the format of the event.

4. **How much money is needed to hold the conference, and how can this funding be secured?**

   Expenses include compensation for conference organizers, substitutes for participating teachers, transportation to the conference site, food, office (telephone, copying, postage), site rental, prizes, and awards. Although much of this can be donated by participating school systems and local businesses, sometimes money must be raised through fund-raising events, grants, donations, and conference fees.

5. **Where will the conference be held?**

   There are many possibilities here, although you must ask administrators of potential sites whether they feel comfortable with young people. It is usually necessary to have one large space where all conferees can meet and eat together as well as numerous break-out rooms for smaller groups. Conferences have been held in schools, hotels, on university campuses, and in environmental education centers.

THE PROGRAM FORMAT

Aside from these structural questions, the most crucial element for a successful conference is the quality of the program. Both the substance and the format must be exciting to young people. This means, first and foremost, that it be *age-appropriate*. Remember: sixth-grade mediators are very different from twelfth-grade or even eighth-grade mediators. The amount of structure, the program focus, the length of individual exercises, the size of small groups, the degree of peer facilitation, the activities and games used—all will vary depending upon the age of the students.

Consider these other suggestions for designing an effective program:

■ **Make the event as "student centered" as possible.** This is perhaps the most important guideline, and it recommends that you involve students from the start. Find out early—by inviting them to planning meetings and/or by distributing questionnaires—what interests student mediators and what problems they would like to address at the conference. Design a format that is active and participatory. Lectures should be kept to a minimum in favor of group discussion and interactive exercises. In addition, encourage peer mediators to run as much of the conference as possible. Students can facilitate or cofacilitate workshops, lead discussion groups, welcome people to the conference, emcee the proceedings, serve on panels, deliver the keynote address, and serve as guides for the day.

■ **Use adults wisely.** Students are the focus, but adults provide the structure that holds the event together. This is especially true with conferences for younger students. While every effort should be made to give students the opportunity to take on leadership roles, adults should be right behind them in case they need help. Adults facilitate and cofacilitate workshops, monitor conference logistics, and do any other task that is necessary and that students cannot do. It helps to have as many adults on hand as possible; conference organizers typically require that participating schools plan a minimum adult-to-student ratio (one to five is ideal). When adults are plentiful, they can conduct parallel workshops and problem-solving sessions for program coordinators and teachers. This provides a refreshing and much-needed chance for the usually isolated program coordinators to interact with *their* peers.

■ **Keep the logistics tight and the program flexible.** Your planning should make it easy for students to understand the when, where, and how of the conference. This includes arrangements like what group they are a part of, what workshop they should be attending, when and where that workshop is held, when and where they should eat lunch, and where the bathrooms are located.[47] Once students are where they should be, however, the program design should be flexible enough to follow their interest and enthusiasm. It should not cause problems if the agenda calls for a fifteen-minute discussion of an exercise and the group is still engrossed in it after twenty-five minutes.

■ **Create a program that is diverse and balanced.** The best conferences "mix it up" by offering a dynamic and varied program. You need to balance time spent

- in the large group vs. in small groups,
- in the home school group vs. in groups composed of students from various schools,
- moving vs. sitting still,
- working vs. playing,
- thinking vs. feeling.

There is no simple formula for this besides keeping things moving. A great deal depends upon the other variables of your conference (age of students, focus of conference, conference site, and so on). Consider having students spend a good portion of their time in a group composed of students from other programs or schools. And do not hesitate to do activities just for fun. Successful (and intellectually stimulating) conferences include group cheers, banner making, singing, dancing, relay races, talent shows, prizes and awards, balloons, and related merriment.

---

[47] One effective way to accomplish this is to use color-coded name tags for each student. When students arrive, they are handed a colored name tag, a schedule, and a map so that they know exactly where their "green" group should be at all times. These badges also prevent students from staying with their friends because they are noticed immediately if they are not in the correct group.

SUGGESTIONS FOR WORKSHOP TOPICS

As a final aid to conference planning, the following is a list of workshop topics appropriate for peer mediation conferences. Many of these topics were suggested by students themselves. Do not limit yourself to these, however. Feel free to come up with your own.

- **The Review Session.** A comprehensive and fast-paced review of mediation—active listening, summarizing, finding issues, building agreement, mediator teamwork, writing agreements, confidentiality
- **Forums.** Presentations, exercises, and/or discussions of issues that students feel are important including AIDS, racism, teen pregnancy, sexual harassment and date rape, violence, drugs, counseling, being a school leader, and gangs
- **Diversity and Prejudice I.** An awareness session of games, exercises, and discussion
- **Diversity and Prejudice II.** Discussion and role-plays regarding how to deal with the issue of prejudice in a mediation session
- **Dealing with Difficult Cases.** Observation, practice, and discussion of how to handle difficult situations including parties that won't talk, violence in the session, strong emotions, parties walking out, and losing one's neutrality
- **Conflict Resolution as a Way of Life.** Discussion and role-plays on applying mediation skills outside of mediation sessions with co-workers, family members, friends, and neighbors
- **Facilitating Meetings.** A workshop on how to facilitate effective meetings
- **Ethical Roundtable.** Discussion of ethical dilemmas involving issues like confidentiality, neutrality, and power imbalances
- **Training Others to Mediate.** An introduction to training others to mediate, including a chance to practice facilitating role-plays
- **Strengthening Your Program.** Discussion of ways to make peer mediation programs stronger and more effective
- **Convincing Friends to Try Mediation.** Role-plays and discussion on how to convince other students to try mediation
- **The Panel of "Elders."** Older, experienced mediators answer questions and lead discussion among new trainees
- **Mediation Careers.** Professional mediators who work in a variety of contexts discuss their work and lead role-plays for student mediators
- **Fantasy Mediations.** An opportunity to mediate disputes that have all the dynamics of real mediations, but in which the parties are "fantasy" characters (i.e., two space aliens, two animals, a star athlete or model negotiating a contract, or a conflict from history)
- **Student Mediators as Presenters.** A session in which students develop presentation skills like public speaking and leading group exercises

Bibliography

Axelrod, Robert. *The Evolution of Cooperation.* New York: Basic Books, 1984.

Baker, Falcon. *Saving Our Kids From Delinquency, Drugs, and Despair: Solutions Through Prevention.* New York: HarperCollins, 1991.

Barnes, Pat. "Planning Conferences for Student Mediators." Unpublished paper, 1990.

Baruch Bush, Robert A. "Efficiency and Protection, or Empowerment and Recognition?: The Mediator's Role and Ethical Standards in Mediation." *Florida Law Review* 41, no. 2 (Spring 1989): 253–86.

Bell, Jonathan. Unpublished notes on the oppression of children.

Berry, Wendel. *The Hidden Wound.* San Francisco: North Point Press, 1989.

Brion-Meisels, Steven, and Selman, Robert L. "Fight, Flight or Collaboration: Individual and Institutional Development in the School." Unpublished paper, 1992.

Buena Regional High School Mediation Program, New Jersey. Unpublished materials, 1993.

Cetron, Marvin, and Gayle, Margaret. *Educational Renaissance: Our Schools at the Turn of the Twenty-First Century.* New York: St. Martin's Press, 1991.

Conciliation Quarterly Newsletter. Akron, PA: Mennonite Central Committee, 1987–93.

Crum, Thomas F. *The Magic of Conflict.* New York: Simon and Schuster, 1987.

Curle, Adam. *True Justice: Quaker Peace Makers and Peace Making.* London: Quaker Home Service, 1981.

Davis, Albie. *A Primer on Power.* Unpublished collection of readings. Salem, MA: District Court Dept. of the Trial Court of The Commonwealth of Massachusetts, 1986.

———. *Ten Reasons for Starting a School Mediation Program.* Unpublished, 1984.

DC Mediation Service Training Manual. Unpublished mediation training manual. Washington, DC: Center for Community Justice, 1980.

Domestic Violence: No Longer Behind the Curtains. Wylie, TX: Information Plus, 1991.

Drew, Naomi. *Learning the Skills of Peacemaking: An Activity Guide for Elementary Aged Children on Communicating, Cooperating, Resolving Conflict.* Rolling Hills Estates, CA: Jalmar Press, 1987.

Edelman, Marian Wright. *Families in Peril: An Agenda for Social Change.* Cambridge: Harvard University Press, 1987.

———. *Portrait of Inequality: Black and White Children in America.* Washington, DC: Childrens Defense Fund, 1980.

Einstein, Vivian. *Conflict Resolution.* St. Paul, MN: West Publishing Company, 1985.

Eron, Leonard D. "Aggression through the Ages." *School Safety Magazine* (National School Safety Center) (Fall 1987): 12–17.

Finn, Chester E., Jr. *We Must Take Charge: Our Schools and Our Future.* New York: Macmillan, 1991.

Fisher, Roger, and Ury, William. *Getting to Yes: Negotiating Agreement Without Giving In.* New York: Houghton Mifflin, 1981.

Fiske, Edward B. *Smart Schools, Smart Kids: Why Do Some Schools Work?* New York: Simon and Schuster, 1991.

The Fourth R (Newsletter of NAME). Amherst, MA: The National Assocation For Mediation In Education, 1986–93.

French, Dan. "Opening Comments: Drug Free Schools Conference." Presented at Marlborough, MA, spring 1992.

Fuchs, Lawrence H. *The American Kaleidoscope: Race, Ethnicity, and the Civic Culture.* Hanover, NH: University Press of New England, 1990.

————. *Women's Quest for Economic Equality.* Cambridge: Harvard University Press, 1988.

Fullan, Michael G., and Hargreaves, Andy. *What's Worth Fighting For?: Working Together for Your School.* Ontario, Canada: Ontario Public School Teachers' Federation, 1991.

Gallagher, Nora. "Feeling The Squeeze: In Tough Times, the Fallout from Money Fears Affects Us All." *The Family Therapy Networker* (April 1992). Excerpted in *Utne Reader* (Sept.–Oct. 1993): 54–61.

Garlington, Jocelyn A. *Helping Dreams Survive: The Story of a Project Involving African-American Families in the Education of their Children.* Washington, DC: National Committee for Citizens in Education, 1991.

Gatto, John Taylor. *Dumbing Us Down: The Hidden Curriculum of Compulsory Schooling.* Philadelphia: New Society Publishers, 1992.

Gilligan, Carol. *In a Different Voice: Psychological Theory and Women's Development.* Cambridge: Harvard University Press, 1982.

Girard, Kathryn; Rifkin, Janet; and Townley, Annette. *Peaceful Persuasion: A Guide to Creating Mediation Dispute Resolution Programs on College Campuses.* Amherst, MA: Mediation Project at University of Massachusetts, 1985.

Glickman, Carl D., and Wolfgang, Charles H. *Solving Discipline Problems: Strategies for Classroom Teachers.* Boston: Allyn and Bacon, 1986.

Goble, Frank. *The Third Force: The Psychology of Abraham Maslow.* New York: Grossman Publishers, 1970.

Goetze, Rolf, and Johnson, Mark R. *Boston Population and Housing Profile: US Census STF1, 1990.* (Profile 2).Washington, DC: U.S. Bureau of the Census, 1991.

Goodlad, John I. *Teachers for Our Nations Schools.* San Francisco: Jossey–Bass Publishers, 1990.

Graham, Patricia Albjerg. *S.O.S.: Sustain Our Schools.* New York: Farrar, Straus and Giroux, 1992.

Greenawald, Dale, and Grant, Johnson. *Conflict Resolution in the Schools: Final Evaluation Report.* Boulder, CO: Social Science Education Consortium, 1987.

Hacker, Andrew. *Two Nations: Black and White, Separate, Hostile, Unequal.* New York: Charles Scribner's Sons, 1992.

Hewlitt, Sylvia Ann. *When the Bough Breaks: The Cost of Neglecting Our Children.* New York: HarperCollins, 1991.

Illegal Drugs and Alcohol: America's Anguish. Wylie, TX: Information Plus, 1991.

Jacoby, Tamar. "A Portrait of Black and White." *Wall Street Journal* (European edition), July 7, 1992.

Kaufman, Sandra. *Assessment of the Implementation of Conflict Management Programs in 17 Ohio Schools: First Year Report (School Demonstration Project 1990–1993).* Columbus, OH: Ohio Commission on Dispute Resolution and Conflict Management, 1992.

Kent, George. *The Politics of Children's Survival.* New York: Praeger, 1991.

Kilman, Ralph H., and Thomas, Kenneth W. *Thomas-Kilman Conflict Mode Instrument.* New York: Xicom, Incorporated, 1974.

Kohls, L. Robert. *Developing Intercultural Awareness*. Washington, DC: The Society for Intercultural Education, Training and Research, 1981.

Kotlowitz, Alex. *There Are No Children Here: The Story of Two Boys Growing Up in the Other America*. New York: Doubleday, 1991.

Kreidler, William J. *Creative Conflict Resolution*. Glenview, IL: Scott, Foresman, 1984.

————. *Elementary Perspectives 1: Teaching Concepts of Peace and Conflict*. Cambridge, MA: Educators for Social Responsibility, 1990.

Lakey, Berit. *Meeting Facilitation: The No Magic Method*. Philadelphia: Movement for a New Society, n.d.

Lam, Julie A. *The Impact of Conflict Resolution Programs on Schools: A Review and Synthesis of the Evidence*. 2d ed. Amherst, MA: National Association for Mediation in Education, 1989.

Leimdorfer, Tom. *Once Upon A Conflict: A Fairytale Manual of Conflict Resolution for All Ages*. London: European Network for Conflict Resolution in Education, 1992.

Lickona, Thomas. *Educating for Character: How Our Schools Can Teach Respect and Responsibility*. New York: Bantam Books, 1991.

Lucas, Eileen. *Peace on the Playground: Nonviolent Ways of Problem-Solving*. New York: Franklin Watts, 1991.

Maday, Michael. "The School Mediation River: How Wide and How Deep?" *The Fourth R* 39 (June–July 1992): 9.

Maslow, Abraham. *Towards a Psychology of Being*. New York: Van Nostrand Reinhold Company, 1968.

Maxwell, Jennifer P. "Mediation in the Schools: Self-Regulation, Self-Esteem, and Self-Discipline." *Mediation Quarterly* (Jossey-Bass Inc.) 7, no. 2 (Winter 1989): 149–55.

McCarthy, Peggy. "Analyzing Television's Message: Yale psychologists develop high school curriculum for separating TV's fantasy from fact." *Boston Globe*, August 9, 1992, 37.

McCormack, M. Melissa. *Mediation in the Schools: An Evaluation of the Wakefield Pilot Peer-Mediation Program in Tucson, Arizona*. Dispute Resolution Papers Series No. 5. Washington, DC: American Bar Association, 1988.

Meyer, Dan. *Ongoing Training Activities for Student Mediators*. Tucson, AZ: Our Town Family Center School Mediation Project, 1989.

Miller, Alice. *Banished Knowledge*. New York: Doubleday, 1990.

Miller Wiseman, Janet. *Mediation Therapy: Short-Term Decision Making for Couples and Families in Crisis*. Lexington, MA: Lexington Books, 1990.

National School Safety Center. *Gangs in Schools: Breaking Up Is Hard to Do*. Malibu, CA: Pepperdine University Press, 1988.

Newman, Katherine S. *Falling From Grace: The Experience of Downward Mobility in the American Middle Class*. New York: Collier Macmillan Publishers, 1988.

Oakes, Jeannie. *Keeping Track: How Schools Structure Inequality*. New Haven, CT: Yale University Press, 1985.

Pastorino, Ray. *The Mediation Process—Why It Works: A Model Developed by Students*. Grinnell, IA: The Iowa Peace Institute, 1991.

Pauly, Edward. *The Classroom Crucible*. New York: Basic Books, 1991.

Perry, David G. "How is Aggression Learned?" *School Safety Magazine* (National School Safety Center) (Fall 1987): 23–25.

Persell, Caroline Hodges. "Schools Under Pressure." In *America At Century's End,* edited by Alan Wolfe, 283–98. Berkeley: University of California Press, 1991.

Pollack, Stanley. *Teen Empowerment Program: Implementation Manual.* Boston: Teen Empowerment, 1987.

Project S.M.A.R.T. *Project SMART: A School-Based Mediation Program Sponsored by the Victim Services Agency.* New York: Victim Services Agency, 1987.

Prothrow-Stith, Deborah. *Deadly Consequences: How Violence is Destroying Our Teenage Population and A Plan To Begin Solving the Problem.* New York: HarperCollins, 1991.

Putka, Gary. "'Tracking' of Minority Pupils Takes Toll." *Wall Street Journal,* April 23, 1990.

Rain, Barbara, and Walker, Julie. *Procedure Manual: RAPP (Resolve All Problems Peacefully).* Ferguson, MO: Ferguson-Florissant School District, 1989.

Rossi, Peter H., and Freeman, Howard E. *Evaluation: A Systematic Approach.* 3d ed. Newbury Park, CA: Sage Publications, 1989.

Rubin, Carol and Jeffrey. *When Families Fight: How to Handle Conflict with Those You Love.* New York: William Morrow, 1989.

Sarason, Seymour B. *The Predictable Failure of Educational Reform: Can We Change Course Before It's Too Late?* San Francisco: Jossey-Bass Publishers, 1990.

Seleskovitch, Danica. *Interpreting for International Conferences.* N.p.: Penn and Booth, 1978.

Selman, Robert L., and Glidden, Michelle. "Negotiation Strategies for Youth." *School Safety Magazine* (National School Safety Center) (Fall 1987): 18–21.

Slavin, Robert E. *Achievement Effects of Ability Grouping in Secondary Schools: A Best-Evidence Synthesis.* Madison, WI: National Center on Effective Secondary Schools, 1990.

Smith Melinda. "Thinking Big: Funding and Implementing Multi-District or Statewide Mediation Programs." *The Fourth R* (National Association for Mediation in Education) 31 (Feb–March 1991): 1.

Sorenson, Don L. *Conflict Resolution and Mediation for Peer Helpers.* Minneapolis: Educational Media Corporation, 1992.

Storti, Craig. *The Art of Crossing Cultures.* Yarmouth, ME: Intercultural Press, 1989.

Susskind, Lawrence, and Cruikshank, Jeffrey. *Breaking the Impass: Consensual Approaches to Resolving Public Disputes.* New York: Basic Books, 1987.

Toufaxis, Anastasia. "Our Violent Kids." *Time Magazine,* June 12, 1989, 55.

United States National Commission on Excellence in Education. *A Nation at Risk: The Imperative for Education Reform.* Washington, DC: GPO, 1983.

Ury, William. *Getting Disputes Resolved: Designing Systems to Cut the Costs of Conflict.* San Francisco: Jossey-Bass Publishers, 1988.

The Way Out: Student Exclusion Practices in Boston Middle Schools. Boston: The Mass Advocacy Center, 1986.

West, Cornel. "Learning to Talk of Race." *New York Times Magazine,* August 2, 1992, 24–26

———. *Race Matters.* Boston: Beacon Press, 1993.

Where Your Income Tax Really Goes. New York: War Resisters League, 1992.

Index

A

Academics, impact of peer mediation on, 65–66, 67

Accommodating, 26

Administrative structure, in collaborative conflict resolution, 40

Administrative support, importance of, for long-term viability of peer mediation, 62–65

Administrator in charge of discipline, 64

Adolescence, psychological characteristics of, 7

Adolescent psychology, and peer pressure, 7

Advisory councils, 79–80

Aggression, role of fathers in teaching children to manage, 4n

Agreement, in mediation, 32–33

Arbitration, 27–28, 36
differences between mediation and, 29–30

At-risk student inclusion of, in mediation training, 115–16
peer mediation for, 49

Availability, in selecting trainees, 114

Avoiding, 26

B

Business cards, 125

C

Case analysis and discussion, in mediator meetings, 146–47

Classroom climate, creating positive, 35

Climactic moment in conflict, 14

Co-coordinators in peer mediation, 78

Collaboration
listening in promotion of, 204–5
speaking in promotion of, 199–203

Collaborative conflict resolution, 23–27
integrating, into school, 38–40

Colleges, as source of mediation training, 107

Co-mediators, use of, 109

Commitment, in selecting trainees, 113

Communication skills, need for, in collaborative conflict resolution, 26

Community mediation program, 42
as source of mediation training, 107

Community partnerships, 85

Community press, 125

Community volunteers, 78

Competition, limits of, 21–23

Compromising, 26

Confidentiality, 96–99
in mediation versus arbitration, 30
and school safety, 242–43

Conflict
appropriateness of, for mediation, 134–35
arbitrating, 36
definition of, 12
determining whether mediatable, 91–92
escalation of, 196–98
interpersonal, 12
intrapersonal, 12
mediating, 36
as normal, 175–76
as positive, 178–79
at school, 5–6
and students, 3–5
suppressing, defusing, or ignoring, 35–36
triggers of, 18–19
understanding, 12–13

Staff education, in collaborative conflict resolution, 39–40

Structural violence, 3, 6

Student conflict, increase in as symptom of a larger disease, 8–9

Student mediators, organizing conferences for, 249–52

Students
and conflict, 3–5
determining parties to conflict, 133–34
empowerment of, in training programs, 111
in peer mediation, 68
strategies for convincing to try, 132–33
strengths of, as mediators, 44–45
use of peer mediation in empowering, 48

Supervise, duty to reasonably, 240–41

Surveys, use of, in needs assessment, 68

T

Teacher, 65, 78
concerns about peer mediation, 65–66
needs assessment questionnaire for, 220–21
permission to mediate form, 226
tools for needs assessment and support building, 68
meetings and presentations, 68–69
questionnaires and surveys, 68
workshops and training, 69–70

Temporal orientation, in mediation versus arbitration, 29

Third-party judgments, in mediation versus arbitration, 29

Torts, law of, 238

Tracking
definition of, 6
research on, 6

Trainers, quality evaluation in, 110

Training institute approach, 106

Triggers of conflict, 18–19

U

Universities, as source of mediation training, 107

V

Vertical approach, in implementing peer mediation program, 247

Violence
interpersonal, 3–4
as pressure, 5
structural, 3, 6

Voluntariness
in mediation versus arbitration, 29
and peer mediation, 95–96

W

Winners and losers, in mediation versus arbitration, 29

Win-win solutions, 27, 28, 180–81
finding, 186–87

Workshops
in needs assessment, 69–70
suggestions for topics, 249

Z

Zero sum game, 21
possible outcomes of, 21–23

About The Author

Richard Cohen cofounded School Mediation Associates to promote the use of mediation and collaborative conflict resolution in schools. Since 1984 he has worked with thousands of educators and students around the world. Mr. Cohen is a music enthusiast and lives with his wife, Rachel, in Massachusetts.

About School Mediation Associates

Founded in 1984, School Mediation Associates (SMA) became the first organization devoted to the application and promotion of mediation in the schools. SMA offers a range of awareness and skill-building training programs on mediation, conflict resolution, negotiation, communication, violence prevention, and prejudice reduction/racial justice. SMA also issues a newsletter called *The School Mediator* and plans to publish *Resolving the Tough Cases: Advanced Issues in Peer Mediation Case Work*. Schools that work with SMA receive

- training programs designed to meet their specific needs;
- dynamic, experiential training sessions that engage students and staff;
- high trainer-to-trainee ratios that enable trainees to receive the individual feedback necessary for mastering mediation and conflict resolution skills;
- a committed and enthusiastic conflict resolution team that results from SMA's attention to group building;
- comprehensive, field-tested materials for both training and implementation.

Goals of SMA Programs:

- To teach students and educators the skills necessary to resolve conflict nonviolently and collaboratively
- To help students and educators see conflict as an opportunity for personal and institutional growth
- To provide trainees with the skills and the confidence to begin to mediate the disputes of their peers
- To teach an approach to problem solving that welcomes diversity and respects difference of opinion
- To provide educators with the knowledge, the experience, and the materials necessary to conduct their own mediation and conflict resolution trainings and integrate conflict resolution into their professional practices and curricula
- To transform schools into safer, more caring, and more effective institutions

For more information about School Mediation Associates, contact:

School Mediation Associates
134 Standish Road
Watertown, MA 02172
617-876-6074

2675